ANGEL
OF ARMAGEDDON

ANGEL
OF ARMAGEDDON

A NOVEL BY
ROBERT MARCUM

Bookcraft
Salt Lake City, Utah

Library of Congress Catalog Card Number: 92-85094
ISBN 0-88494-854-4

First Printing, 1992

Printed in the United States of America

To my parents
Laverne and Ruth Marcum
who taught me the value of reading good books
at a young age
and evoked in me the desire to emulate
their good lives

EXPLANATION OF TERMS

Abu Hassan (Mustafa Hassan). Not to be confused with Ali Hassan Salameh, former leader in the ranks of Black September, the secret PLO-controlled terrorist organization that carried out the attack against Israeli athletes at the 1972 Munich Olympics and other outrages; and in Force 17, Yasser Arafat's covert Praetorian Guard.

Mustafa Hassan is a fictional character who was to become the direct leader of the House of Hassan (also fictional) until his death while performing terrorist attacks on Israel.

Abu Ibrahim Ibn Allah. A fictional terrorist working with ANGEL for the overthrow of Israel. A formidable terrorist with his own dedicated butchers and assassins who wants nothing more than to kill for power and money. One-time leader in the PLO who was ousted because of his extreme methods.

Abu Jihad (Khalil Ibrahim Machmud Al-Wazir). A real person. Former number two man in the PLO and overall military commander of the organization. He was killed by Israeli commandos on April 16, 1988.

Al Aqsa Mosque. A real mosque. The secret entrance used by Jerisha and her brother is fictional, as is the stable master's room, although the stables did exist in that location at one time.

Aman. Israeli Army Intelligence.

Armageddon. The last great battle between Israel and her enemies, in which Israel is laid waste. It is the Christian belief that this is the battle which ushers in the second coming of Christ to the Jews.

Basilica of St. James at Mt. Dothan. A fictional church.

Golan Heights. An area in northern Israel taken from Syria in 1967, when Syria attacked Israel. It is presently being settled by Israelis and has been annexed by that country. Syria refuses to pursue peace without its return to them.

Greenline. The (border) barrier between Israel and the West Bank.

House of Hassan. A fictional Arab tribal organization which represents fanatic-organized efforts to destroy Israel and begin a new society and government in that land.

IDF. Israeli Defense Forces.

Intifada. Uprising by Palestinians living in the West Bank and the Gaza Strip that began in December 1987.

Likud. A political party in Israel.

LION. A fictional helicopter based on fact, present capability, and scientific development. The chopper of tomorrow.

Mossad. The Israeli Secret Service.

PFLP (Popular Front for the Liberation of Palestine). Headed by George Habash, the PFLP was formed in 1967 and is part of the PLO, although Habash and Yasser Arafat are often at odds as to method and purpose.

PLA (Palestinian Liberation Army). With a total strength of between twelve and fourteen thousand men, the PLA serves as the PLO's military arm. Its name was officially changed to the National Palestinian Army in 1983.

PLO (Palestinian Liberation Organization). Umbrella organization dedicated to achieving an independent Palestinian state. Headed by Yasser Arafat. In early days the PLO was well financed by Arab nations and personal friends of their cause. Now it is financially independent and uses its funds to finance other terrorist groups, the Intifada, and the suppression of those who oppose both its methods and its success, particularly on the West Bank.

PNF (Palestinian National Fund). Fund established to finance all PLO activities.

SCUD. A Russian-developed ground-to-ground missile that Saddam Hussein used in Iraq. Under the guidance system he had, it was very ineffective when fired more than a certain distance. However, intelligence has revealed scientific work on developing both a better guidance system and a warhead that can carry either chemical or nuclear payloads.

Sword of Megiddo. A fictional myth used to enhance the story.

x

TERROR1. A fictional terrorist operation designed to overthrow the economy of the United States and keep it out of the Middle East, allowing Saddam Hussein to carry out his plans there. Developed in book one in this series, *Dominions of the Gadiantons.*

West Bank. Israeli-occupied territory taken from Jordan in the Six-Day War of 1967. Up to that time Jordan ruled the West Bank and the Palestinian people were subject to that government.

Zionism. A political movement created in 1897 by Theodor Herzl in Europe establishing the idea in world politics of a homeland for the dispersed Jews. After that came the Balfour Declaration of 1917, which favored the establishment of a Jewish national home, even though there were less than six thousand Jews in all of Palestine. Zionism received a tremendous boost after World War II when the Holocaust was fully discovered and the world felt a need to atone.

Thus came the partitioning of Palestine and the war of 1948. Since that time the politics of Zionism have brought millions of Jews to the new state of Israel, while displacing millions of Arab Palestinians and creating the Middle East's greatest strife, over which numerous wars have been fought and thousands of lives taken.

*In that day shall there be a great mourning in
Jerusalem, as the mourning of Hadadrimmon in
the valley of Megiddon.*

*The first angel sounded, and there followed
hail and fire mingled with blood, and they
were cast upon the earth: and the third part
of trees was burnt up, and all green grass
was burnt up.*

*As a leader of the House of Hassan I prophesy
the destruction of Israel as seen in their own
scriptures. We who are the true royalty of
Palestine, we who are destined to begin a new
order, we shall surely destroy their land. And
upon its ashes we will build a new kingdom,
with a new glory, and the House of Hassan will
rule forevermore.*
> *—The Angel of Armageddon, 1982, at the
> time TERROR1 was instituted.*

PROLOGUE

In the southeast corner of the temple mount in the Old City of Jerusalem, underneath what is known as Al Aqsa Mosque, are caves that once housed King Solomon's horses and chariots. A gate and stairs in front of the main entrance to the mosque allow a person to enter. But this entrance is seldom used, and only with special permission from authorities.

At least one other little-known entrance can be found in what is known as the Prayer Hall for Women of Al Aqsa Mosque. The door is hidden behind a panel of fine olive wood and opens to reveal a set of winding stairs leading to a small room hewn out of solid stone. This room was once the quarters for the stable master responsible for King Solomon's several hundred well-bred horses housed in the adjoining caverns.

It is through this entrance that two people had come to meet a dozen times over the last twenty-three years, and to which they now came for the last time.

The younger of the two arrived first. She had only been in Israel a matter of hours, coming by way of the West Bank after being smuggled through Egypt and the Sinai, a common route for expatriate Palestinians who were considered enemies of the state of Israel.

She was dressed in typical Arab garb, a long, black silk gown, embroidered with flowers and other designs in blue and gold thread. She wore a veil over her dark hair; a Bedouin veil of the same color and embroidered design as the gown. It covered her hair and face except for her dark, penetrating eyes. She wore expensive gold rings with diamonds and rubies on each of her manicured fingers and a set of thin gold bracelets around each wrist. The clothing of an Arabian woman, who was beautiful and considered by some to be of royal lineage.

She was born an Arab, but her family was forced to emigrate to the United States while she was a young girl, when, after the Israeli occupation of 1948, many Arabs fled for their lives at the point of Jewish guns.

She and her entire family became American citizens, while never forgetting their true heritage. Her father saw to that, schooling her and her only brother in the history, culture, and destiny of the Palestinian people, and of the role they would some day play in freeing their country from Israeli rule.

Her father, Khalid Salamhani, married well when he took as his wife a daughter of Jabib Hassan in 1942. The House of Hassan, a royal house among the Arab Palestinians and ruled by Jabib Hassan, had been cursed, giving no sons to the aging Jabib to act as heir to the sheik of Palestine's leading tribe. By marrying one of Jabib's daughters—a marriage which had taken a good deal of Khalid's inherited and hard-sought wealth—Salamhani had secured his and his children's future. Only his wife's eldest sister's offspring would be Sheik of the House of Hassan before his own.

As Allah would have it, the partitioning of Israel came before either family would take power from the ailing Jabib.

Khalid Salamhani, wealthy merchant, highly educated statesman of his people (a rarity in Palestine at that time), found himself running for his life, the Israelis sweating to destroy every show of Arab authority in their newly acquired country.

Being driven from Palestine by the Israelis was the ultimate humiliation for Khalid and his young family, and he swore he would return for revenge. This task he began planning and working for the moment he crossed the border into Jordan, a penniless man, stripped of his money and his future.

Khalid had a son, then a daughter. From the time they were old enough to understand he taught them of their heritage, and of the land, stolen from them and inhabited by men and women they must never think of as anything but their enemies. He taught them to hate—and to plan. He scraped together money, sacrificing every personal convenience to have them educated in the finest schools.

And he taught them. Taught them about their eventual return to Israel, their reestablishment of the House of Hassan, and the destruction of the Jewish state.

Khalid Salamhani had become seriously ill in 1956, his purpose for living unfulfilled. On his deathbed, with his last words, he had extracted from his two children a promise, sworn before Allah, that they would finish the task. Then he died, a smile creasing his chalk-white lips.

It was for the furtherance of this purpose that the woman had come to the chambers of Solomon's stables. It was for this that she had lived every day of her life. For it she had married a man she never loved, and had used his millions to bring about her purposes, only to have her plans dashed at the last moment as a result of her husband's own greed and stupidity, and because of a single American.

She smiled. The bumbling husband, Fillmore Duquesne, was dead now, out of the way. The American would soon follow.

Her light laughter filled the empty chamber. What had happened in Wyoming was done. It would not stop her—could not.

TERROR1 was only *one* way to Armageddon.

She heard feet hitting each stone of the rock steps leading from the prayer hall above and turned to face the entrance, a dark hole in the cave's solid rock walls. The small lamp's light bounced around her, giving shadow to the corners of the room and an unearthly red light to her dark eyes.

He stepped lightly from the last stone, his tall frame filling the entry. He saw her; she knelt and bowed her head. "I honor you, my brother, future king of our people."

He reached for her hand and lifted her to him. The embrace was in the traditional Arab fashion; then he looked into her eyes. "And you, their queen."

Removing her veil, she revealed an olive-tone complexion, smooth except for the forty-two years of worry lines developing around her large eyes. Jerisha reached out and touched his curly dark hair. "My brother is well?"

"Yes, and you?"

She nodded, smiling. "Fully recovered from the untimely death of my husband."

"It has been some time since we last met in this place," he said.

"Nearly five years."

"It falls quickly behind our meeting in Washington. Is something wrong?"

She shook her head. "No, just last-minute details I did not want to take chances with. We're too close for even the smallest mistake."

"Then we are ready?" he smiled.

"Yes, Mahmoud! We are ready. The American will arrive in a few days. We will have our revenge, while removing his country's influence from this region.

"And the sword?" she asked.

"I am close. If things go as planned . . ." He smiled, watching her for a reaction. After receiving her broad smile, he finished. "It will be ours."

She hugged him tightly, then looked up into his eyes. "Mahmoud, my brother, you have suffered much. I know in these twenty-five years it must have pained you to keep quiet when you knew secrets that could have killed many of our Jewish enemies. But it will all be worth it! We will rule again, Mahmoud! The House of Hassan will rule again! Not Iraq's Hussein! Not the murderous Assad! But you, and I! Palestine will be ours! We have planned and worked for this day!" She raised a clenched fist and shook it. "Now we must seize it!!"

He pulled her to him, hugging her with excitement. She had always been the one who kept him going! Always! She had seen that he was properly trained in Jewish ways, making him learn Hebrew with a German accent, building him a background that had become such a part of him that he talked about it in his sleep! Driving him, reminding him about the promise to their father! Now, because of her they were about to succeed!

"There were times, little sister . . . times when I thought it was over. When TERROR1—"

She put a finger to his mouth. "Shhh . . . do not think of the past. Think only of the future. Soon we will have the Sword of Megiddo; soon Israel will be forced to its knees; soon we will have our revenge on those who tried to stop us!" She paused, her eyes turning hard as stone. "Soon our father's dream will be a dream no more, but reality!" She seemed to shake lightly, then the darkness that draped her face—much like the veil she now held in her hand—lifted. She smiled. "I have come to give you last instructions."

She began to pace, outlining the details, carefully repeating those things he must remember, telling him how he would escape. Dates, times, places, names he must remember. An hour passed.

"I understand," he said. "Sabrila will be my contact. A good choice. She is not known in this country."

"And dedicated to me. I have had her under my care for a long time. Her hate is strong. And, as a member of the House of Hassan, our aunt's daughter, she will serve us well."

Jerisha pulled up the sleeve of her gown, revealing a gold-banded watch. "It is time." She took both his hands. "Allah be with you, my brother."

"And you, Jerisha, must be careful. You are the one who will make this dream reality. The Duma plant is ready?"

"We have the chemical warheads. The other one is very near completion. By the time we finish with the American, it will be finished as well."

She dropped his hands and moved toward the stairs leading to the mosque above. As she disappeared, Mahmoud Salamhani's smile waned into a frowning and wrinkled brow. He was tired. Twenty-five years as a spy in the Israeli Army had worn his nerves to a frazzle, every day spent wondering if it would be his last. The destruction of TERROR1 had nearly destroyed him, and if Jerisha hadn't sent word, he . . . he had only been inches from taking his own life when the message came.

Mahmoud ran his fingers through a full head of curly black hair. It was a miracle he had survived so long, but he had done nothing against Israel, not yet, anyway. Except to infiltrate the very highest ranks of her army and political machinery. Waiting for the right moment . . . the moment when he and his dear little sister had what they needed to destroy the Jews. That time had come.

He walked to the small table, bent over, and blew out the lamp. The absolute darkness enveloped him like death, sending a chill up his spine, leaving him feeling cold and afraid. He pulled out a cigarette and a Bic lighter, illuminating the room while calming his frayed nerves. He kept the lighter on, moving toward the stairs.

In reality he had little to fear. He had always been removed from the action. No one knew of his existence. No one except Jerisha. Fillmore Duquesne, his sister's husband, whom Mahmoud had never met, surely had never been told, nor had anyone else. Soon the whole world would know.

Mahmoud wrapped the kafeyeh around his head and

across his face, then slipped through the door, closing the panel and sealing off the darkness from the room below. In less than ten minutes he had passed the temple mount guards of Arabian descent and moved into the streets of the Old City. Mahmoud knew exactly the position of the Israeli patrols and used side streets and alleys to avoid them, eventually wending his way to a nondescript door just inside Stephen's Gate. Letting himself in, he checked his watch. Right on schedule. Quickly he removed the Arab garb and donned his official uniform, that of a general in the Aman, Israeli Army intelligence.

Moments later he strode toward the gate itself, his heart pounding. He had come through the checkpoint earlier, his pass and papers in order, but one never knew . . .

The guard faced him, saluting. "Good evening, sir. Your meeting was a success?" He took the papers, stamped them, and immediately returned them.

"Yes, thank you. Have a good night." He smiled as he passed through the gate, saluting the other guards, giving them the same salutation.

"Yessir," each of them returned.

Mahmoud smiled, crossing the street to his waiting car and driver. They would never question the movements of a general, especially if he was the assistant minister of defense. Never.

Day One

CHAPTER 1

2:00 P.M., Israeli time, above the Mediterranean sea

Colonel Thomas Macklin, United States Marine Corps, was now Dov Giladi, Israeli businessman returning home from Rome after a successful business venture. It had been a long, tiring transition. From Thomas Macklin, marine, to Swedish industrialist Gerhardt Bitton for a two-day stay in Rio de Janeiro, Brazil—two days cooped up in a hotel room. Then the flight to Rome under the same name, where he stayed at the Hotel De La Roma, finally becoming Giladi for the flight aboard El Al to Tel Aviv.

Dov. He wondered what on earth it meant in English.

He looked around at the plane's occupants. Some were definitely Israeli but most were Russian. Immigrants under perestroika escaping one battlefield for another! They probably knew less about their "promised land" and what they were in for than he did.

Israel. The last place on earth Thomas Macklin wanted to be. Especially undercover. He didn't like sneaking around under assumed names, faked passports, and lies, so many lies. It stunk like the CIA or Mossad, the Israeli Secret Service. Both had cost him pain and misery with their slipshod game-playing. Their last little bit of intelligence work had cost him good men, and had put him in the hospital with a bullet hole the size of a donut in his shoulder.

To divert his mind from that unpleasant thought he slipped the small leather book from the inside pocket of his sports jacket. It had been packed inside a special delivery box that was handed to him in recovery at the field hospital in Riyadh, Saudi Arabia.

He touched the soft leather with his fingertips. The slip-cover carried his name and the words *Survival Manual* engraved in gold across its center. When he had first opened it some eight months ago, he discovered a worn copy of the Book of Mormon with a note scribbled on a loose piece of paper stuck in the flyleaf. It read:

Colonel:

Hope you're not offended. This book is one of my most prized possessions. I give it to you as a gift because I sense your need is greater than mine right now.

The book has been to hell and back. Three pages are stained with blood, my own and that of two dear friends. Its words and teachings will save all three of us eventually.

I marked passages I like the most when I read them. You'll probably find a few passages you like better. Feel free to mark them and read them often.

God bless you and keep you safe.

Jeremiah Daniels

With decent reading material hard to come by in the hospital, he had started it, found the story intriguing . . . then confusing . . . but quite often compelling. He had related to the man called Captain Moroni and his battle to save his people even though it cost precious blood.

By the time Macklin was battle-ready again he had read it twice. The second time he saw beyond the wars and the infighting, the Gadianton robbers and nonbelieving peoples. He saw Christ.

He patted the outside of his jacket where the book slid to rest in the inside pocket. Somehow it was comforting.

"Mr. Giladi?" asked a stewardess in English.

"Yes," he answered, surprised that she knew his name and didn't speak the Hebrew or French his passport indicated were his normal languages.

"This is for you," she said, smiling, handing him an envelope, then turning and going back to her station.

"Uh, thank you," he said to her back. "I think."

He undid the clasp, reached in, and pulled out a letter and a photograph. The photograph got his immediate attention. It was of a nice-looking woman in military uniform, colonel insignia on the shoulder boards. Curly brown hair, dark eyes, dark tanned skin. Age? He guessed about thirty. Figure? Streamlined but definitely feminine, even in the military attire. Height maybe five foot seven and weight about 110.

He read the letter.

Mr. Giladi:

Welcome to Israel. I will meet you at the airport wearing a white dress, sandals, and a wedding ring you recently gave me.

Please return this to the stewardess.

Colonel Ruth Levona

So this was his counterpart, the one in charge of the operation to which he had been assigned. Not bad! In fact, very nice. He perused the picture again, smiling. Easy to control. Probably very little experience, especially in field operations. He should have things his way.

He looked back at the letter. Wedding ring? A very nice cover. Husband, wife . . . He looked once more at the picture and smiled.

The stewardess was back. "Mr. Giladi? Are you finished?" He was still smiling when he handed her the envelope. Israel could prove to be most interesting.

––––––––––

Colonel Ruth Levona wheeled the Mercedes into a public parking lot near the terminal exit. The Mercedes was often used in Israel. Jews had helped develop it before the word *Holocaust* was part of their vocabulary. This one was not the usual bare-minimum version and was hers for the next two weeks, a part of the package when you were working with foreign operatives.

She turned off the key and glanced at her watch. The flight would arrive in ten minutes.

She checked her makeup in the rearview mirror. She didn't use much, just a little around the eyes and lips, enhancing her natural beauty. As an Israeli Army intelligence operative she had played roles before. Shopkeepers, secretaries, a saleslady in Tunis—but never a wife. She hadn't liked the idea much but knew it was simply a matter of getting the American into the country incognito. After that, except for times when they were in the public eye, the role would be over. She slipped on the gold band and gave it a moment's scrutiny. Nice!

Checking her watch she got out of the car, aware of those around her, always alert to possible trouble. In her business, caution was life. She locked the Mercedes, arming the alarm with the device attached to the key ring, and moved quickly across the lot and into the terminal. Gate 12 was already spewing forth passengers, mostly Russian immigrants, who were immediately taken to an area where they would be processed. It was a long, grueling time ahead for them. If they had known how it might end, they might have thought twice before leaving their beleaguered Russia. They came expecting homes and jobs. Both were in short supply in Israel right now, and the government was still scrambling around trying to decide what to do. It would be a while before these Jews saw anything but crowded homes and apartments, and they'd get only just enough food to get by. But then, from all that she had heard, it was worse in Russia.

She saw him. The photograph had been of an impressive marine in full dress uniform. The square jaw hadn't changed much, nor the piercing blue eyes. Only the slightly receding hairline, sports jacket, slacks, polo shirt, and sunglasses were new. Weight? Maybe 170. Height? Nearly six feet. Handsome.

She wondered how he had reacted to her picture. He was probably expecting a man. A tough Marine Corps officer in the famed Red Five Special Operations group being led about by a woman. It had to hurt!

When he cleared the gate she took a deep breath, waiting for him to see her. When he did she waved and moved quickly to him. The uncomfortable part. Hugging a stranger, appearing to be his wife was not an easy thing to do. Especially for a Jewish girl raised in a home where any contact with the opposite sex had been frowned upon until relationships were fixed by parents or matchmakers. But that life was behind her.

She put her arm around him, kissed him gently on the

cheek, speaking lightly in Hebrew, slowly, knowing he had only a little knowledge of the language.

She saw the surprise turn to acceptance, then to . . . what? Mischievousness? He grabbed her around the waist and pulled her to him, kissing her. She was confused, forcing herself to play along, knowing someone might be watching. When he released her Ruth's blood was boiling, but she kept a pleasant smile painted across her face, using only her eyes to convey her dislike for what he had done. His eyes danced with laughter as he pulled her toward the door.

He halted outside, a satisfied grin on his face, waiting. "Very nice cover, Colonel," he said. "Where to?"

She couldn't speak, but only pointed.

"Come along, then. We have much to catch up on." He put his arm around her waist and they walked quickly to the crowded lot and the Mercedes. She wanted to punch him, rip his eyes out, the anger and embarrassment of his intended intimidation hot in her breast.

When they got to the car no one was within listening range. "You so much as touch me again and I'll break every bone in your body!" she said through a phony smile and with a pat to his cheek.

He smiled. "Give me the keys. I'll drive."

"Over my dead body!" she said, pushing him aside and unlocking his door for him. "Put your luggage in the back! Get in." She went around to the driver's side and unlocked the door.

After starting the engine, she turned half in the seat to face him. "You are now safely in Israel, Colonel," she said, tight control stiffening the muscles in her face. "The charade stops until I determine it is needed again. Understood?"

Macklin forced a smile. She put the car in gear and exited the parking lot, then spoke again.

"Furthermore, Colonel, while you are in *my* country I am the ranking officer and will receive the respect that rank affords me! Is that understood?"

He pulled himself together. "Don't try rank on me, Colonel, it doesn't sell. My orders show equal authority in this operation. And," he said, smiling again, "the kiss I gave you *was* a show of respect, and admiration. You're a beautiful lady."

His answer, intended to fluster, missed its mark. "And a colonel in the Israeli Army. Do you kiss all the colonels you work with?"

He laughed lightly. "Only the ones who tell me they're married to me."

It was Ruth's turn to force a smile. Colonel Macklin was very smooth, but she recognized his ploy. In a man's army like Israel's a woman dealt with two kinds of men: those who tried to intimidate by authority and force, and the Macklins, those who resorted to flattery and smooth talk. Ruth had learned to play both games. What Macklin didn't know was how well.

"Well said, Colonel." She smiled pleasantly. She always liked to give the Macklins of the world a feeling of control before she ripped the rug out from under them.

She signaled and pulled the car off the side of the road, jamming it into park before it came to a complete standstill. She faced him in the seat again, her small frame suddenly looming in his direction, a smile on her face.

"Don't talk down to me, Colonel!" she said, bouncing her finger off his chest. "And get something straight. I am in charge of this operation. You and your men are to carry it out, when I say, how I say." She took a file from an attaché case between them. "If your superiors left you in the dark about that, I'm sorry, but it's all written in there. You'd better read it."

Macklin took the file, his mind empty of a comeback.

"I am responsible for this operation, Colonel Macklin, because I have the expertise and ten years' experience in such things. I am good, Colonel, and you'd better believe it! Your life may depend on it in the very near future." She turned and faced the front, jamming the gearshift into first drive and stepping on the gas. The Mercedes catapulted onto the highway, the tires depositing large amounts of rubber on the pavement.

Macklin sat red-faced, unable to speak. How had he lost control so quickly?

Levona went on, her voice steady. "We have a very important job to do, Colonel. One on which the lives of thousands of people might depend. You're good at what you do, probably the best. I won't interfere with your operations in the field because I know that. I hope you will allow me and my team that same authority." She smiled.

She was done. Set, match, game, she thought. Macklin was—

"Colonel Levona, I am going to share a piece of classified

information with you, because I think it will help you understand why I won't give you the carte blanche you are trying to establish. And why you *and* your team are going to have to prove yourselves to me *before* my team follows even one order you might have an inclination to give.

"A few months ago my men and I carried out an operation in Kuwait City based on the supposed indisputable word of the Israeli intelligence organization. They told us that there would be no opposition to me and my men, citing evidence from their sayanim, I think was the word, their local spies. Not only was there opposition, but we nearly lost everyone, including the emir's son and grandson whom we were to rescue."

He paused. "I found out later that Israeli intelligence knew what was going to happen, but the emir had papers they wanted. They lied to us to get them."

"I know of this operation, Colonel Macklin. Those papers were very important. They helped us find the factory you are here about."

"You—Israel—lied, Colonel. We still would have done the job—it needed doing—but with less risk and casualty if you hadn't lied. You seem to find it easier to lie to accomplish your purposes. That's why I won't trust you until I see how you operate."

His hard glare bore a hole in the side of Levona's head. "You're right, Colonel," he went on. "I am the best, even though you said it only to flatter. What makes me the best is that I don't let rank, even if the shoulder boards belong to a woman, tell me when, where, and how to run an operation in which I and my men put our lives on the line."

It was silent for a long time.

The climb was fairly steep but an easy one for the Mercedes. The scenery was of tall pines bordering the modern, four-lane freeway.

"I didn't know you had pine trees," Macklin said, trying to ease the tension.

"Planted after we started coming to Israel in 1948," she said.

He saw the empty shell of a red, vintage armored vehicle by the side of the road. Then another. "What are those?"

"Monuments to those who died trying to get supplies from Tel Aviv to Jerusalem during the war for independence in 1948. Many men died in this canyon."

"Will we have any free time?" he asked.

"A little. And after we are finished you will have as much as you want. The rich businessman Dov Giladi can afford a vacation," she said, smiling. "He has a nice bank account to prove it."

"Then Giladi does exist?"

"Very much so. He has been a person for nearly ten years. Created by us, of course, for just such needs."

As Jerusalem came into view Macklin let his eyes scan it. The sprawling metropolis spread like vines over hills in every direction. He didn't expect it to be so large.

"Will you teach me about your land and your people?" Macklin asked, in a stumbling attempt to start their relationship over.

"I would be honored," she said, accepting the attempt.

Macklin took a deep breath. "You're right about the lives. A lot depends on our success."

Ruth glanced over at him, contented to begin on even ground.

"Nice place," Macklin said after they had moved through each furnished room. "Any chance of a bug?" he asked, tongue in cheek.

She smiled patiently, moving to the far patio door and opening the curtains to display an early evening view of the temple mount.

He whistled. "Beautiful!"

"You are in the Jewish section of the Old City. This is what you Americans call a safe house. It is not bugged, but it is watched, very closely, by our own people." She went to the phone. "This phone has a scrambler attached. We can call anywhere in the world from here and will only be discovered if the phone at the other end is not protected in a similar way."

She moved into one of the bedrooms and opened a closet, sliding back a panel to reveal a small door. She opened it, displaying several weapons, a night scope, a camera with a zoom lens, gas masks, and a number of other items.

She handed him a 9mm Makarov pistol. "Are you familiar with the weapon?" she asked nonchalantly.

It was his turn to smile patiently.

"Good. I assume you have fired the Uzi as well," she said, pointing at the well-known machine gun on the shelf. "Do you want a shoulder holster for that pistol or do you prefer—"

"This is fine." He lifted his sports coat and placed the gun at the small of his back.

"Not easy to get at," she said.

"Not easy to see, either. I prefer it that way."

She closed the panel, flipped off the light, and led him into the kitchen. "Are you hungry?"

He nodded. "Starved. What do you have?"

"Anything you want. I can fix you a filafala or a steak, take your pick."

"Had a filafala once. Good."

"Coming up." She busied herself and he went back to the patio door, letting himself onto its four-by-six-foot space, taking in the view as the setting sun exploded off the top of the golden dome on the temple mount. The feeling was one of splendid awe. He watched as people prayed at what he knew was the Wailing Wall. Some moved with their prayer, using every bone in their body in order for their petition to reach their God.

After removing his jacket he took two chairs and a small table from the living room and placed them on the patio, then sat down and watched the sun's rays from behind his building slowly creep up and disappear on the far hill behind the gold dome of the mosque. If he remembered his Sunday lessons right, that would be the Mount of Olives. The place to which scripture said Jesus would return.

Ruth joined him, setting several plates of vegetables and meats on the table, then a bottle of wine and two glasses.

"Mind if I just have water?" he asked, trying not to offend.

"Not at all," she said, surprised. "The wine is good. Made in Israel."

"I don't drink. Muddies the brain, the reflexes, sorry."

She waved it aside, inwardly impressed, then sat down and showed him how to fill the pita bread with the delicious items she had prepared. As the shadows deepened she lit a candle and placed it in the middle of the table.

"This is wonderful, Colonel. It has been sometime since . . ." He hesitated.

"Since?"

"The last part of my life I have been sitting in a tent in the middle of the desert. Armor, tanks, jets everywhere. The sounds of war."

"Umm. I have heard those sounds."

"Here in Jerusalem?"

"Yes, here, but mostly in the area where I grew up. And in times of war."

He waited.

"My parents arrived here in 1954 from Poland, young, idealistic, hopeful, penniless. The nation was new, still reeling from the war of independence in 1948, but they and many others were willing, ready to turn the desert land into a beautiful place.

"They were sent north beyond the Galilee to a moshav, a cooperative village called Nahariyya near the Lebanon border and on one of the most beautiful beaches of the Mediterranean. It is mostly a resort town now where people go to vacation.

"My parents worked hard, bringing two boys and then me into the world while fighting the Arabs from Lebanon who tried to drive them from the land with raids. They survived, may God be praised, until I was sixteen. Father even came through the Six-Day War in 1967 without so much as a wound.

"By 1974 my oldest brother was in the IDF, the Israeli Defense Forces, and the other, two years older than me and nearly old enough to join, was away at school in Jerusalem."

Her face clouded as the memory returned.

"They came in large numbers, encircling our homes, attacking in the night. Because of our position near the border we were well-armed and trained. Even I knew how to use the weapons. I had practiced in the nearby hills with my brothers. It was not a place to be without such knowledge.

"They overran our part of the town. My father moved us to a house easier to protect. He left me with one of the rifles; mother had a pistol. Our men finally drove them back into the hills when reinforcements from another section of town came to help us. But we did not know it, and we waited, afraid, my fingers cemented to the trigger guard of the rifle I held.

"Then a noise was at the door. I lifted the rifle, shaking, but ready to kill if I had to. A voice spoke through the wooden door. It was the leader of our community. He had

Father in his arms with a bullet hole in his chest. He died in our home that night."

She rubbed her arms as if chilled. "I have been hearing the sounds of war ever since," she said stiffly.

She paused, taking a deep breath. "Both my brothers were killed in an attack on another village in 1978. The night before her sons were called to help expel some of the Arabs, Mother knew it was coming, felt it, and began even then to mourn for her sons, who refused to stay in Nahariyya and be cowards.

"She never recovered. I took care of her for a year, then she died and I buried her next to my father and brothers in the graveyard of Nahariyya. I have been in the army since then."

The cloud hung over her, dark, frightening, then with a wave of her hand she dispelled it. "Enough. It's late. We have a lot to do tomorrow." She took the dishes and headed for the kitchen. Macklin stood and took a last deep breath of Jerusalem air. The smells, the difference, filled his lungs. Ruth Levona was unlike any of the women he had known in his life. Different than his former wife, who whined when there wasn't enough hot water. But something deep inside Colonel Levona frightened him a little. Something unknown, maybe dangerous.

He shrugged his shoulders. In time he would know her better, when she wished it. For now she was right—they had a job to do.

CHAPTER 2

9:00 P.M., Duma, Syria

Colonel Fami Badannah sat at his desk studying the scientists' progress report. He did not understand all of the numbers and the words, but he could see that they were only days away from having the warhead ready to mount on the new SCUD missiles he knew would be arriving within days. Important people would think highly of his progress. He laid the papers down, pleased with himself, but still harboring a pain of worry deep in the pit of his stomach.

The phone message had been short. Israel knew something of what was going on at Duma and had sent an agent to gather information. ANGEL wanted no chance of that agent fulfilling his responsibility. Badannah was to eliminate the possibility.

Badannah stood and went to the small window of his office. The factory was stark against the setting sun, the building's huge size looking small in contrast to the large sky that framed it.

Badannah had never met ANGEL. Twice a courier, a young woman calling herself Sabrila, had delivered cash, letters full of instructions, and code books. More times than he could count, messages had come by radio. Short bursts of Morse Code, curt and to the point, always from ANGEL.

Because Badannah didn't like loose ends he had finally settled his mind by deciding that his faceless boss was, in fact, Abu Ibrahim, the feared rebel terrorist who had openly denounced peace talks with Israel and had sworn vengeance on the heads of all those who participated. Duma was Ibrahim's city, bought and paid for with seemingly endless stacks of American dollars. And, he had the connections necessary inside the Syrian military and government, probably even paying Syrian President Assad for his help, or at least his silence. How else could one explain an entire garrison— Badannah's garrison—being deployed without question to protect the factory and its warhead project? Badannah had made a few subtle inquiries, discovering that Ibrahim was responsible for bringing the German scientists, now under Badannah's care, to Syria. A connection too solid to ignore. His mind was satisfied. ANGEL and Ibrahim were one and the same. If the man wanted to use a code name for security purposes, Badannah would play along. If Ibrahim had the money to buy off Assad, the entire Syrian Army, and still leave a hefty sum for a lowly colonel . . .

He shrugged. It did not matter who ANGEL was. It was apparent he had very powerful friends. His orders had come through and had never been challenged by anyone. It took lots of money and power to do that, even in Syria, and he wasn't about to question where that money came from or how high up the Syrian military ladder it went. Such questions got people killed.

He smiled to himself. Besides, his half million dollars was safely placed in a foreign bank account.

Badannah's mind returned to the present. He still had to earn the half million.

He went back to his desk, wondering how even ANGEL was able to get such detailed information about Israel's knowledge of the Duma project. But ANGEL had done it, and that was all that mattered. Now it was Badannah's responsibility to act on that knowledge. He picked up the phone.

"Sergeant, this is Colonel Badannah. Come to my office, please. We need to discuss your security arrangements. When I came in this morning I noticed only a few guards on the west fence." He put down the phone. The sergeant would be shaking in his boots when he arrived, making it easier to manipulate him and get things done.

The knock came at the door and Badannah stood to accept the salute. "Sergeant, be seated," he said, his eyes cold. The sergeant was already afraid. That was good. "This project is very important, Sergeant. I want no mistakes here, do you understand?"

"Yes, Colonel Badannah!"

"Things have been prepared at the west fence?"

"Yessir, by your orders. The area is prepared. If our enemies come that way . . ."

Badannah smiled. "They will, if they come at all. We have made every other place visibly formidable. The west fence will look most appealing."

Khalis began to sweat. At first he had agreed with Badannah's ploy, even thrown himself into the project, giving it his full support. Now, he wasn't sure. Badannah seemed too obvious, too inviting. And Khalis knew that if it didn't work, if anything went wrong, he would receive the blame.

He calmed himself. He had done everything he could, and with the seemingly unlimited support of General Command had protected the factory in every way possible, letting Badannah think his west fence project was a brilliant ploy while stiffening defenses around the rest of the factory.

"The men are doing duty in the bunkers, then? They are prepared to surprise the Israelis?" Badannah asked.

"Yessir, they are ready."

"Good. The rest of the defenses?"

"Solid, sir. A great deal of antiaircraft capability . . . and the radar. We can have fighters from Damascus in the air before they can hit us."

"Is the radar protected? Could it be knocked out?"

"There is always that chance. But it is not near the site. As you instructed, it is in the residential area a few blocks away. And, sir, it is well camouflaged."

"A weakness. We cannot rely on the air force or the radar. Not enough against Israeli pilots. Notify Famuna at General Command that we want a ground-to-air missile unit sent here. SAMs. Are you using only Famuna for purchasing as I told you to?"

"Yessir. We have had no problem."

"Good. And who built your tunnels at the west fence?"

"Contractors from the town."

Badannah faced Khalis, his countenance passive. "I have it on good authority, Sergeant, that an Israeli agent is working Duma trying to find out what is going on at this factory. We take no chances. See that the contractors are taken care of."

Khalis's mouth dropped open; he felt sick. He knew what that meant. He knew that if he did not do it, someone else would and he would be shot along with the innocent workers. He saluted. "Sir."

Turning on his heel he left the room, ready to throw up. He had killed, but never civilians. Never his own people. Never family.

He braced himself against the outside wall of the administrative building, his arms on his knees and his head lowered. He had hated this project ever since Badannah had shown him the orders from Damascus. He did not like military operations done in such a manner, and he did not like the way Badannah handled the men, his constant questioning of their methods and motives. Two had been shot because of minor infractions of Badannah's "rules of conduct," in which they could not even mention their current responsibility to family or other members of the military.

He retched, his dinner splattering over his boots. He had encouraged his cousin to bid for the contract for digging the bunkers, trying to give him an economic lift he needed. The cousin had been successful, had done the job well, priding himself in his work.

Now, he was to die. Khalis's stomach churned and the rest of his dinner found its way onto the street.

Day Two

CHAPTER 3

6:00 A.M., Jerusalem

The ride through Jerusalem in the early morning hours had been interesting for Macklin. For a city that was often portrayed as old, dilapidated, and wracked with violence, he found it clean, beautiful, and peaceful.

They left the Old City and headed west into New Jerusalem, then into an area of office buildings and apartments. Colonel Levona parked the car on a side street and they walked a short distance to an apartment complex. They proceeded through a garden court, entered one of the buildings, and descended a stairwell.

"Where are we?" he asked.

"What we do is not to be known by any other government agency, so we cannot meet in regular places such as Aman headquarters in Tel Aviv. We have chosen this place as a base of operations."

She passed a door and pointed. "Our security people operate from there. We occupy the rooms at the end of the hall. All the others are sealed off, unoccupied."

As they approached the door she removed a small device from her pocket and punched several keys. Macklin heard the lock of the door click open and turned the knob.

As the door swung inward four men standing near a desk and a map snapped to attention. The one sprawled on the sofa against the far wall intensely reading a white paper was caught momentarily off guard but quickly joined the others. Only one man, dressed in civilian clothes and sitting at a desk against the far wall, didn't get up.

"As you were," she smiled. "This is the American, Colonel Thomas Macklin." She introduced the five men standing in front of him, then turned to the civilian. "Colonel Macklin, Manlik Hoshen, minister of defense and a general in our army."

"Minister." Macklin shook the outstretched hand.

"Glad to have you here, Colonel," Hoshen said, a broad grin across his firm jaw. "Your General Biggs speaks highly of you."

"Thank you, sir. He said you'd fill me in on details."

"Colonel Levona will do that. She's very qualified. My only purpose in being here to greet you is to make sure everyone is clear on responsibility."

Macklin and Levona looked at each other. Levona responded. "We have discussed it, Minister. It's clear."

"Good." He focused on Macklin. "Your men will be flown here for any actual infiltration into Syrian territory and you will lead that operation—is that how you understand it, Colonel?" Hoshen's best politician's smile showed a clean set of perfectly formed white teeth.

"Yessir. What is the target?"

"A factory in Duma, Syria. We believe chemical, and possibly nuclear, warheads are being built and tested there, but we are not sure of their progress. Colonel Levona has developed a plan by which you will go to that plant and find out exactly what they are up to. Make copies of their plans, get photos, anything that will help us understand what is going on. Then we will decide what to do about it."

"Whether or not to blow up the factory?"

"Yes. We must be sure of our position before we invite an international incident, don't you think?"

"It won't be easy to get in and out undetected."

"Can you do it?"

Macklin smiled. "You have weapons for our use?"

"You will use equipment of a neutral nature that any mercenary might use, except for one item, a helicopter. We will introduce you to it later. I think you will find it both interesting and valuable. No one outside of a select few in the Israeli government knows of its existence, but it has been fully developed and is prepared for operations such as this. We have given much of the technology to your country in exchange for other things. In fact, it is my understanding that you have an attack helicopter very much like it, used for special operations of a very secret nature. However, there are things on this one that are not on yours, unless you stole something from us without our knowledge." He smiled. "We will use the LION, if you give your word that things you see will not turn up in your arsenal in the near future."

"In other words, keep my mouth shut about it."

"And we expect any of your men used in this operation to do the same. Eventually we will give your country the rest of the technology anyway, in exchange for something we need, but for now we have an advantage that, should you say the wrong thing to the wrong people, we may lose. Can I trust you?"

"Loose lips sink ships. Yes, Minister Hoshen, you have my word for myself and my men. We understand better than most the importance of such an edge. But if it goes down . . ."

"It won't." The minister took a step toward the door, then faced Macklin again. "You're probably wondering why we aren't using one of our own commando units. It's politics, Colonel. Don't bother yourself with it. Besides, they say you're the best. We in Israel want only the best."

He started to close the door again, then turned back. "We think Abu Ibrahim is running this operation. He is very dangerous. He will not hesitate to use the new improved SCUDs our intelligence organizations tell us have been shipped to Duma."

"You know they have them?" Macklin asked.

Hoshen nodded. "Yes, and two German scientists who worked for Hussein before your American coalition took some of the sting out of his bite." He smiled again. "We only wish you had finished the snake off. Anyway, the Germans know how to make the warheads and the SCUDs can reach anywhere in Israel from Syria. Do not be fooled. Those behind this have sworn vengeance against others who seek peace. Those missiles will also reach as far away as Riyadh, Teheran, and far into Turkey. Thousands of innocent people would be under threat of death. With your help that will not happen."

Hoshen paused for effect. Everyone noticed and glanced up. "Good luck. Israel depends on you." He closed the door behind him.

Macklin knew men like Hoshen. A true politician.

A young woman came from an adjoining room. "Sergeant Merriame," said Levona, "This is Colonel Macklin. Have you received any more information from Duma?"

"No, Colonel. Tonight."

Levona looked at one of the soldiers. "Mori, Colonel Macklin will need to be completely briefed on the factory and what we have planned so far." Glancing at Macklin, she continued. "He has some doubts concerning this operation. Let's see if we can put him at ease."

Mori moved to the wall of maps and began pointing to a large blowup of a rusted metal building. "Antiaircraft weapons on the roof. Heavy patrols around the perimeter, some two hundred soldiers in the vicinity, half inside. The radar is in a residential area nearby."

"Half inside?" Macklin asked.

"Yes, Colonel."

Another man stepped forward with some photographs.

"Colonel, these are the most recent photographs. You can only get to the roof from inside, but we can only account for fifty of the men reported entering the building arriving on the roof."

The one introduced as a Lieutenant Gad pointed to a display on a table. "This is the layout to scale. Completely surrounded with high electrified wire, razor wire attached to the top. The radar is here in this residential area, the fifty men we can account for are located here, here, here, and there. As you can see in that photograph, compliments of your most recent satellite placed over the region, they operate heavily armed antiaircraft batteries.

"The guns are radar operated and have the capability to hone in on aircraft traveling at Mach 1, possibly Mach 2. Of course, Syria has a defense system that would alert them to our regular aircraft the moment we crossed the border. They can intercept within three minutes." He paused, picking up a paper from the desk. "One of our listening posts picked up this traffic from Duma this morning. It was going to Syria's central storage facility in Damascus. They ordered another dozen missiles. SAMs, we believe."

Macklin looked carefully at the pictures, moving under the fluorescent desk lamp. The new satellite photos were very good. The best he had ever seen. He could almost tell the rank emblem on the shoulder boards of a man standing on the roof.

"There don't seem to be many soldiers around this west fence. How come?" Macklin asked.

"We're not sure," said a third officer, the one who had been lounging on the couch when they came in. "But we suspect it is well-mined on both sides of the fence. There may be several large-caliber weapons trained on it from inside the factory." He pulled out an architect's rendering of the floor plan. "The building was put up by a French firm. They were kind enough to share the plans with us. You will notice that on the second level there is a catwalk overlooking the west fence. The entire area could be watched and defended from there. Our intelligence network in France also tells us they are using French-made motion sensing devices that can pick up a man's footsteps within a hundred yards of the factory perimeter, pinpoint them, then, through a computer controlled system, explode mines at or near the spot of detection."

Macklin didn't like it. "Impregnable," he said softly.

"Sir?" the young man asked.

"Okay. What do we know about the interior? Where are the Germans working on the warheads? Which area is storage? Do we have any idea of guardposts?"

"We don't know very much, but our agent in Duma says the Germans are working within a laboratory built inside. A very sophisticated one. He thinks they have everything needed for producing both chemical and nuclear weapons."

Mori went on, and Macklin began to formulate a plan while listening. It would take deception this time. A fortress like this wouldn't allow direct entry.

"What's the size of this place?" Macklin asked, in awe.

"Half a million square feet, sir. One of the largest buildings in Syria. The doors are large enough for a 747 to get in with room to spare. It was an aircraft manufacturing plant in the early seventies. Since then most of the airstrip has been removed or other buildings have been built on top of it."

"Enough left to land a transport?"

"No, sir."

"All right, how many men are on factory premises at any given time?"

They each looked at one another. Levona spoke. "Three to four hundred."

"You can't narrow it down?" Macklin asked.

"As we've stated, sir," Gad said, "we are not sure where they all are. Fifty on the roof, possibly a hundred and fifty in the building. The rest are in guardposts, maintenance buildings, the administrative complex, and the laboratory itself."

"I need better information on numbers, and that west fence! Any way you can get it . . ."

"We hope tonight," Mizrah said. "Our agent inside."

"Then we wait," Macklin said. Going in by parachute

would be suicide, of course; so would trying to cut through the fence along the perimeter. Unless the west fence really was a weakness. Could they be that lucky? He didn't think so.

Levona spoke to the others. "Do we have the weapons ready? The helicopter? Clothing? Lieutenant Gad, how quickly can we have documents prepared?"

"Four hours."

Lieutenant Gad was a big, burly, hard-muscled man with the face of a nineteen-year-old still using his first razor. His size made Macklin wonder how quick he would be if he was ever needed in a pinch. He shrugged it off. He'd never know.

"Lieutenant Mizrah. Have all the contacts been made to get Colonel Macklin's group out through the underground if necessary?"

"Yes, Colonel. And the uniforms and weapons are ready at the training site."

"Colonel Levona," said one soldier with a somewhat flushed face. "I must still protest the use of the LION. If it is shot down . . . If we lose it to the Syrians . . ."

"I understand your reluctance, Captain Irbev, but the helicopter is needed, you know that. No other system can evade their radar and still help with a battle at close quarters if the colonel and his men must fight their way out. With it we have the advantage." She looked away from him in the general direction of the others. "Anything else?"

There was no answer. "Good," she smiled. "Colonel Macklin and I will go to the training site. I want him to see the mockup. There is nothing to be done until we hear from Duma. Sergeant Merriame, I have my beeper. When you hear from Imad, inform me immediately.

"All of you, I do not wish to get to the next phase of this operation and discover someone has left a task undone or overlooked. Go over everything again. Make certain!"

Macklin was awed.

5:00 P.M., *Northern Israel*

Colonel Levona pulled the car back onto the main road and drove south toward Tel Aviv.

"I'm impressed, Colonel," Macklin said, half turning in his seat.

"The base is not much different than an American special operations base, is it?" she asked.

"Not just the base. The way you have control of this entire operation. I see why you Israelis have the reputation for military organization you do."

"Have we put your mind at ease?"

He smiled. "Mostly."

"Our thoroughness is just a matter of necessity."

"How do you mean?" Macklin asked.

"We live with fear in this land. Preparation brings sleep." She shifted the Mercedes into high gear.

Macklin was thinking. Ruth Levona had been even more impressive throughout the day. Authoritative, in control, well respected by those under her command. No wonder she was the highest-ranking woman in the Israeli Army, a man's army.

But he had noticed something else.

"Your people at the safe house this morning. They're quite young."

She smiled. "Yes. Minister Hoshen and General Ativa were able to get me the assignment, but others refused to give me anyone with experience."

He stiffened. "You mean . . ."

"Yes, Colonel. They have no experience in planning such operations, only schooling. There are those in high places who know how critical this operation is, and they have been convinced I am the one to see that it happens. I have helped plan several like it. They know it cannot be planned by the regular ministry of defense; there might be a leak. They gave it to me because I am least likely to be discovered, while still having the skills to accomplish it. When I first requested experienced people for assistants, they told me that there was too much risk of discovery!" She hit the brakes hard as they approached a curve.

He felt the nervousness return to his stomach. He did not like a plan run by amateurs. Especially one of this magnitude. One little mistake could mean life or death.

She continued. "Others agreed with my assignment, but for a different reason."

"What reason?"

"If I fail, everything the Israeli system says about women in the military will be true. They're not good enough to do the really important things. Let them clerk, fetch coffee, sweep the floors, but don't let them be in charge!" She hit the brakes again, then punched the gas. Macklin tightened his seat belt.

"Nothing personal, Colonel," he said, "but this is no time to fight the male versus female wars. I—"

"We fight it every day in Israel, Colonel, but it won't get in the way of my ability to carry out this job."

Macklin smiled. "After yesterday, I'm a believer. But I am a little nervous about people with no experience planning something like this."

"My people are some of the future leaders of this country. They are motivated, determined, and very intelligent. When I was told I could not have those I wanted, I began a search. People in high places made several suggestions. Everyone had a fair-haired boy to keep an eye on Colonel Levona and her operation! I went outside the circle to find the ones who could make it work, and whom I could trust to stay clear of the politics. It took me two weeks of interviews, eighteen hours a day. Those six people are the chosen ones."

"You say that almost reverently," he said.

"I mean it so."

They rode in silence for several miles, past groves of citrus trees and olive orchards.

"One of my men is on probation. He may be court-martialed."

Macklin sat straight up, looking at Levona's concerned face.

"You, lady, are just full of surprises. You spend the whole day building my confidence in your organization, then in a matter of minutes you blow that confidence to kingdom come."

"Lieutenant Gad. Desertion of his post." She smiled, continuing. "I think the way to your heart is in telling you the truth."

He halfheartedly returned the smile.

"He won't be going into combat, remember," she smiled. "I asked for him personally."

Macklin waited, unsure of how to respond.

"He and two others were traveling back to their posts in the north, near Lebanon. The jeep gave them trouble, and they were forced to stop and work on the motor. A group of terrorists had somehow eluded our people and were hiding in a stand of bushes only a hundred yards away. They decided the soldiers were easy prey. When Gad and the others saw them come out of nowhere they grabbed their weapons and ran down a ravine to find cover. Then they ran—left the area without engaging the enemy."

"And?" asked Macklin.

"The army called it desertion. I call it wisdom. They were outnumbered five to one. The terrorists had large-caliber weapons, explosives, everything. I think our men were right to go to the nearest village and sound the warning. The terrorists were confronted and those who gave up were taken prisoner; the others were killed."

Macklin thought it through. He had been petrified on every mission he had ever gone on. Sometimes he had withdrawn his men, not always sure he wasn't playing the coward.

"He should have gotten a medal," he said softly.

She smiled. "I gave him another chance instead. The system still hasn't cleared him. They wait to see if he will embarrass me."

They drove on, quietly enjoying the late afternoon sun and the fresh air coming off the Mediterranean sea. At places Macklin could see the waves breaking against sandy shores.

"Colonel Levona. Stop."

"What?"

"Stop. Up there at the turnout. I want to see the Mediterranean up close. Are we in a hurry?"

"We have nothing pressing until we hear from Sergeant Merriame." She downshifted, a delighted look on her face. It had been some time since she had let the waves soothe her tired feet.

After removing an Uzi from the trunk she locked the car and they worked their way onto the beach. Although it had rained earlier in the day, cooling off the air, the sun was shining and warmed them as they walked south, pant legs rolled up to their knees and their shoes in hand.

"You carry that everywhere?" he asked, nodding at the Uzi.

"It is habit." She pointed toward the sea. "Terrorists come from there, often. They have killed a number of people along these beaches. Some of them tourists, like you." She smiled. "I do know how to use it, Colonel, trust me."

He decided to go on with what he had to say. "I'm trying, Colonel Levona. You're good. I've seen that, but I'm not sure I trust your people. As a military man I have seen what lack of experience can do to an operation like this."

"I understand your concern, but how can you trust me

and not them? They are mine. They do as I command, and they do it very well. If something is neglected it will be because I have left it undone, or unmentioned."

"Experienced people can solve that, can't they?" he returned. "Because of experience they remember and they bring to our attention what we might be missing."

"Ah, I see what you mean. Battlefield experience gives perspective. I meant only that my people have had no experience in planning the battle, not in fighting it. Only Sergeant Merriame has not been on a battlefield, Colonel."

"Uh, excuse me, Colonel, but could we use first names and dispense with the colonel stuff?" Macklin asked with a smile.

She stopped, thinking. "Yes, except when we are in front of other military personnel. You may call me Ruth, I will call you Dov!" She grinned.

He rolled his eyes. "Dov! What does that mean, anyway? I can't say I like it much!"

She frowned. "You shouldn't feel that way. It means bear, and is considered a name of great power in this country." She looked in the direction of the sea. "You should treat it with respect."

"Umm, sorry. I'll try to like it in public, but I prefer you calling me Tom in private, okay?"

She sighed. "Americans. Yes, okay. Now where was I? Oh, yes, Colonel . . . Tom. Those five soldiers average an age of twenty-eight. All of them have at least ten years' experience in the military, in war games, serious war games. All of them have served on the West Bank, a most difficult assignment, but a military one that takes a great deal of finesse and good judgment. Three of them belong to Sayaret Matkal, the most elite commando unit in the Israeli forces."

She stopped and looked at him. "How many combat missions have you planned and led?"

"A fair question. Fifteen as commander and leader. Four in the Middle East you may have been told about, several in various other places, one in the United States eight months ago."

"And your men?"

"Touché, Ruth. Most of them . . . just the four missions in Kuwait. Three men have also been in two other missions in which they saw action."

"The rest of their experience is in war games, then?" she asked.

"Yes, I see your point. You win. I trust you all! Uncle, uncle!" he turned and put his hands in the air, faking surrender.

"Uncle? Oh, you surrender. Good." She laughed, then sobered. "We will not fail you, Colonel," she said firmly. "You can depend on us!"

"I am, Colonel Levona. With my life and the lives of my men."

They walked again, silent. Macklin saw a pink and tan shell the size of a dollar. He stopped to pick it up. Ruth bent down to look at it.

"Beautiful," he said, noticing the darkness of her brown eyes.

"But so defenseless."

"Hardly!"

"They cannot fight back, only hide. They are subject to the strength of the waves, and those that seek to capture them. I call that defenseless."

"Umm." He realized what she was talking about. "You're right." He stuck the shell in his pocket and they headed back toward the car, the sun falling behind dark clouds again.

"What have you planned for this evening?" she asked.

"Free as a bird," he said lightly.

"Do you have a tie that goes with that jacket, and a white shirt?"

"No, but I've got a black suit with a red power tie. The kind you see on the front cover of *G.Q.* magazine."

"It sounds like what would be expected. We must hurry, then," she said. "We can't be late." She took his hand and headed for the car.

His arm still tingled when they pulled onto the highway.

CHAPTER 4

8:45 P.M., Jerusalem

Shuli Merriame was lying on the couch half asleep when the radio came to life. She jumped immediately, knowing she would have only seconds to respond before her contact would cut away for fear of being pinpointed, discovered, and killed.

She sent the coded words, then waited. The message came, again in code, then the machine was silent. She had written each word down carefully, her heart beating faster with each one that came. Imad had found a contractor who had worked at the plant recently and who knew about the construction; a man who would cooperate because he had discovered that the military had orders to kill him, his men, and their families. Imad would bring him out.

Shuli dropped her pencil. "Come out!" she said aloud. How? When? She looked at the radio. Could she take the chance? Was he waiting for a reply? Was the enemy waiting for her to transmit? Listening?

She flipped it on, giving the code words quickly. How? When? Time? Where?

She waited. The seconds seemed like hours. Then came the coded words that she deciphered as:

Tonight. Midnight. Exit point three.

Shuli picked up the phone and dialed Colonel Levona's beeper. Nine o'clock. At least she would not be sleeping.

By Macklin's watch it was 8:00 P.M. "Where are we going?" he asked as they walked down the narrow street from their parking place.

"To a wedding."

"Yours?" he said, only half joking. In the white dress she could pass for a bride.

She laughed. "No, but some of those you will meet are wishing it was so!"

"Why is that?" he asked curiously.

"I am a blight upon my family because I am so old and so unmarried! In Israel, especially among the faithful, the religious, for a girl to be unmarried later than eighteen is a thing for worry. By then we are supposed to be settled down with a husband, usually somewhat older than ourselves, and a home with neighbors among whom we can gossip and raise children."

"So, you not only are bucking the odds in the military but also in the culture. Quite a little troublemaker, aren't you!"

"Umm. Here we are." She stopped. "I should warn you. This will not be like anything you have ever done before! Are you sure you want—"

He took her arm. "Possibly the highlight of my stay in Israel! By the way . . . you're beautiful, do you know that?"

He had never seen her blush before. It added another dimension. He liked it and decided he would cause it more often.

She knocked and the door was immediately opened. The greeting was warm, but in Hebrew. Ruth quickly explained the language barrier and the rotund little lady immediately switched to English.

"Mr. Giladi. Shalom! Shalom! Welcome! Welcome! We are glad you have come to celebrate the happy day with us. We only wish it was the day for our Ruth!" She rolled her eyes. "But, never mind, come." She motioned them inside. "The family and friends are in the backyard, the ceremony will be soon."

Ruth leaned close. "I told you! The black sheep!" She was smiling.

The yard was not a big one and looked even smaller packed with people, tables, and chairs. At the far end was a canopy where the ceremony would take place. Against the high yard wall stood several tables laden with good foods, where small children and even adults were sneaking a taste. He and Ruth hadn't had lunch or dinner, and his mouth began to water.

"Mr. Giladi! Welcome to my home!" said a heavyset man with a voice like waves beating against the beach.

"Dov, this is my uncle, David Levona. It is his last child that is being married here tonight."

"Yes, and at a respectable age, too," he said, looking at Ruth, his eyebrows raising. "I still have one more child to see married, you know."

"Uncle David, you promised," she said, scolding a little.

"I remember! And you shan't hear another word from me on the subject, except that I have been approached by several prominent men about—"

"Uncle!"

"Ah, well, let your father turn over in his grave, then!" He turned to Macklin. "Mr. Giladi, do us all a favor and marry this child so she will no longer—"

"Uncle!" She was more serious now.

"All right, all right! Come along, then. The rabbi has arrived and we must begin."

They went down the stairs and into the yard. Ruth's color gradually turned from scarlet to her normal tanned brown. Macklin couldn't stifle the laugh until she elbowed him in the ribs.

The bride sat in a white chair, her mother and the mother of the groom on each side. She was a pretty girl, probably just out of high school. Very much like Ruth in build and complexion.

"She is so young!" Ruth said. "But at least she is marrying someone she likes."

"What do you mean?" Macklin asked.

"Even though Israel is a modern country, many still hang onto the old ways. This marriage was made by a matchmaker. But, unlike some, Uncle David does not think money and tradition are everything. Mattas, that's the bride, was allowed to decide if she would accept the proposal. The groom happens to be a man of a good family from just down the street. The bride and groom have known and liked each other for many years."

"If your father were still alive would you be married by now?" asked Macklin, seriously wanting to know.

"If my father were still alive I would still be living on the moshav in northern Israel, and, yes, I would be married. But my family's death changed all that." She stiffened. Macklin felt the chill wind again.

He saw the groom coming from the back of the yard, approaching the bride, both families close beside them.

"This is the bedeken, ceremony of the veil. It used to be separate from the marriage and was the sign of betrothal. Sometimes it was done while they were still children."

The groom stood before the bride, taking her veil and placing it over her face. The rabbi was saying something in Hebrew.

The couple moved to the wedding canopy, the tears of Ruth's aunt were flowing freely, and Macklin noticed that most of the other women were crying as well.

The rabbi began to speak. "The wedding blessing," Ruth said quietly, then began to translate. "Blessed are you, O

Lord our God, Ruler of the Universe, Creator of the fruit of the vine. Blessed are you, O Lord our God, Ruler of the Universe, who has sanctified us by your commandments and commanded concerning forbidden relationships, who has forbidden unto us those to whom we are merely betrothed, but has permitted us to those who are married to us by means of the wedding canopy and the sacred rites of marriage. Blessed are you, O Lord our God, who sanctifies his people Israel by means of the wedding canopy and the sacred rites of marriage."

Macklin was silenced by the beauty of the words and the reverent way Ruth said them. His attention was diverted momentarily from her face by the groom's giving a ring to the bride and saying something in Hebrew that made Ruth flinch.

"What?"

"Shh! Later." Others looked at them. The rabbi began to read from something.

"What is that?" asked Macklin quietly.

"The ketubbah, a marriage contract."

The groom picked up a cup of wine and drank as the rabbi began to speak again. Macklin decided he would have to learn Hebrew. "Now what?"

"He recites the sheva'berakhot, the seven wedding blessings, hoping for God's blessing on their marriage, that it will be fruitful and happy. At the end the rabbi will give his last words of counsel."

Macklin waited, then jumped a little as the groom threw a glass to the floor, shattering it in a million pieces and causing an outburst from the audience.

Ruth laughed. "It is over."

"Why the glass?"

"A sign to remember, symbolic of Israel and its fragile condition. We have been broken and scattered before. It could happen again."

Everyone was congratulating everyone else while heading for the tables. Macklin noticed something else he had not paid attention to earlier.

"Why all the beards?" he asked as they moved through the crowd toward the bride and groom.

"Uncle David is very orthodox. Beards are prominent among the Orthodox Jews because our tradition says men should not shave. Some carry it to the extreme, never shaving."

"Why did you flinch during the ceremony?"

"In Israel, when a woman marries she becomes the man's property!" she said tightly. "Just another piece of furniture!"

They had reached the new couple. When the bride saw Ruth she threw her arms around her, hugging and thanking her for coming. The love between them was evident. Ruth introduced Macklin to the couple, then took his arm, moving into the crowd and toward the tables.

"Hungry?" she asked.

"Starved! Any limit to how much you can tank up on here?" he asked.

She laughed as several went by with overflowing plates. "Need you ask?"

They filled plates with cold cuts, salads, the ever-present olive, and a dozen other delicacies, some of which he could identify, some of which simply looked good, and were.

"I think I could fall in love with Israeli food!" he said, devouring a cold cut stuffed with some sort of creamed cheese.

Suddenly the beeper went off, hardly audible above the crowd. Ruth took it from her purse and looked at the brief message.

"C'mon! It is Sergeant Merriame! Her contact wants out! Tonight!"

They dropped their still-full plates in the wastebasket and hurried up the steps. His appetite had suddenly gone.

Colonel Levona's entire staff had already arrived when she and Macklin entered the apartment command center. The appraisal in the men's eyes for Ruth in her dress was evident, but so was their concern. All of them forgot to salute.

"What has happened?"

Sergeant Merriame seemed pale to Macklin, her lips dry and tight across her mouth. "My contact . . . Imad wants out."

"And?" Levona asked, a little impatient.

"And, Colonel, he has someone coming with him," Merriame said, trying to regain her composure. "A man who helped with the recent construction at the factory."

"Imad cannot give us that information through usual channels?"

Merriame smiled. "He does not have it yet. The one who does will not give it to him until he is safely out of Syria. Badannah has begun a purge of the workers. He must be afraid they will talk."

Macklin saw the concern on Levona's face. "Family. The man must have a family. He . . . he won't leave them behind. They would be killed for his treason."

"Did Imad mention a family?" Macklin asked Merriame.

"No, but the colonel is right. He wouldn't leave his family behind. Not to sure death."

"When do they want to come out?" Levona asked.

"Midnight."

Levona's head came up with a jerk. "Tonight!"

"Yes, exit point three, an out-of-use military airport, Sahles Sahra. They will be in the old administrative building. Imad and I set it up before he ever went in. He must be desperate, Colonel. He sent two messages, and to come out so quickly . . ."

"He has to wait longer," one of the other aides stated. "We can't get government clearance for such an operation in that amount of time!"

Shuli Merriame turned on the young lieutenant. "His life is in danger, Mori! They cannot wait longer! If they find them . . ." Macklin sensed something in Merriame's voice. Tension. More than that of one agent for another.

The lieutenant raised his hand, giving a slight smile. "I apologize! I understand!"

They all looked at Colonel Levona, who had gone to the map. Macklin was watching the lithe figure with more than professional interest as she stretched to see the spot mentioned by Merriame, and was surprised that the interest of the other men in the room ticked him off.

"Sergeant, get Minister Hoshen on the phone," Colonel Levona said. "We'll need top clearance, immediately. I must tell him what we intend to do."

Merriame had already picked up the phone when Macklin realized he was going to Syria with an untried team.

CHAPTER 5

10:00 P.M., Sahles Sahra, Syria

Imad strained to see through the darkness, watching, listening. Nothing. But he knew someone was out there, waiting. Waiting for reinforcements so they could tear the ruins of Sahles apart looking for him and those with him.

He took a deep breath. It had been a nightmare getting the informant and his family safely to the abandoned airfield.

He looked at them, dark figures huddled together in an even darker corner, afraid for their lives. They were being hunted now. Those who were old enough to think of such things knew that if found they would be tortured, then brutalized until they stopped breathing. Their fear was surely justified.

As was his own, and not just for himself. He knew now that the factory was for more than testing. A half-drunk German scientist out for an evening with some Arabic friends had boasted too loudly. They would have to move much quicker than even he had thought or Israel would be annihilated.

He took a deep breath, wiping the sweat from his brow, then onto his soiled shirt. His own stink was almost unbearable. But soon . . . soon he would be back in Israel to a hot shower, his family, his country.

He forced his mind back to reality and the smallest child's momentary crying. Four children! When the informant had told him of his family Imad had almost called it all off, then knew he couldn't. They were already hunted by Badannah's soldiers. Without his help their fate was assured. He could have left them behind. He had enough to prove the need for an immediate strike on the plant. But . . .

He smiled. How could one plan for such things? He looked at the frail child in his father's lap. Crippled from birth, the little boy was in constant pain and had no qualms about letting it be known. He had nearly given them all away twice while leaving the city under protection of darkness. Imad finally had been forced to give the child something to put him to sleep, before the boy's mother suffocated him as a result of her own fear. He thanked God for such medicine.

He looked around him. The room was dirty and smelled of human and animal excrement that cluttered and stained the floor. Fortunate, he thought, that none of it was fresh. He knew bedouin wanderers and their animals used all of the old buildings to escape the elements on occasion, but during this season most were camped near the Bekaa Valley, where water was in greater supply for their animals and families.

He saw the movement of a dark form against a lighter background near the old flight tower. He slowly moved into deeper darkness, knowing quick movement would give away his position as it had theirs. As he approached where the family sat he put his finger to his lips and spoke in muffled Arabic.

"Come. There is someone out there."

"Is it Badannah?" asked the woman, alarmed.

"Maybe. They have not shown themselves, but we cannot take chances."

Imad mustered strength and lifted one of the children into his arms. Every muscle in his body ached from exhaustion. He thought the strong winds had covered their tracks. Unless Badannah's men had some other way of knowing where they had come, the presence of men in the compound outside indicated the wind hadn't been thorough enough.

"Come. We must hide," he said, forcing his legs to move toward the place he had prepared for himself a few weeks ago, feeling grateful he had made it bigger than he had first intended.

"What . . . ?" the informant began to ask as they approached the plank wall.

Imad put his finger to his lips, then reached out and pushed a section of the plank wall. Four feet of wall slipped toward them, then to one side as it rolled quietly on acrylic casters, allowing them room to enter the three-by-twenty-foot space behind the false wall.

He beckoned them to enter. "You must be quiet. It is a thin wall and they can hear from both outside and inside the building. Is the boy asleep?" The informant gave a hesitant nod. "Good. Will he need more of the sleeping medicine?"

The informant shook his head as Imad checked the room behind them, watching, listening. He heard the distant movement of feet on gritty dirt.

He slipped in next to the father and child and pushed the section back in place, bringing total darkness. He heard one of the children start to whimper, then the muffled command of a frightened parent trying to console a more frightened child. The evening seemed stifling. Sweat trickled down his neck and back. He heard footsteps on the warped floorboards in the room beyond the thin wall, then voices. His breath caught in his throat and he prayed, prayed that the children would be still, and that help would come—soon.

11:00 P.M., Duma, Syria

Colonel Badannah sat rigid in his chair, his eyes and face impassive, cold. Sergeant Khalis stood at attention near the desk, sweat trickling down his neck and onto his collar.

Badannah spoke through lips drawn tight across his teeth. "When did you discover they were gone, Sergeant?"

"Five hours ago, sir."

"All of them? Have any been found?"

"Yes, sir, some, involved in the construction. Somehow they found out we were looking for them. Somehow . . ."

Badannah's eyes flared violently at the sergeant. "Somehow?" he yelled in Arabic. "Somehow! You, Sergeant, will not only find out how they discovered our plans, but you will find them. All of them! Do you understand?!"

"Yes, Colonel. We are already searching for—"

"Good! At least you have assigned the best man I have given you! Has he found any of them yet?"

Two had been found. Two had been shot. Khalis could only take solace in the knowledge that he had given them a fair chance to save themselves. "Yessir. Two have been found. They have been dealt with, sir."

"Good! Any clue about the rest? And what about the man who contracted this job?"

Khalis's mouth felt dry and he had to force himself to speak. "He . . . his family . . . they escaped into the wilderness west of Damascus. He hasn't been found."

The sergeant felt the twitch in his cheek and only hoped the colonel would not see it. If it was ever discovered that the contractor foreman was his own cousin . . .

Badannah leaned back in his chair, a smile on his face. "The others I do not know about, but you will find him and his family at the deserted Sahles Sahra air base, Sergeant. I have sent trusted men there already. Maymuna is leading them. They are waiting for you to bring help. So far they have not discovered where the foreman hides."

"How did you—"

The colonel's smile was crooked. "Never mind. Just bring them here. Do you understand that, Sergeant?"

"Yessir." The sergeant saluted, turned on his heel, and went into the small outer office. His stomach was a bundle of knots and his muscles ached all over. Something wasn't right. Maymuna could not have discovered his cousin this soon. Where could the information have come from? What contacts did Badannah have? Did he know about Khalis's relationship with the foreman?

He was suddenly very frightened. If his cousin should be captured he would be forced to tell about Khalis's warning. But if Khalis didn't follow Badannah's orders he would be shot as a traitor, some trumped-up charge written tersely across his file in military archives.

He found himself outside the building, walking toward his office in darkness. He must get to Sahles, try to save his cousin. How, he did not know, but if he didn't they would both die before Badannah's firing squad.

CHAPTER 6

11:30 P.M., High above Syria's eastern border

Macklin had that empty feeling in the pit of his stomach that he always got just before jumping from an airplane at thirty thousand feet with nothing but hard ground waiting for him. The picture in his mind was always the same: his chute failing to open, his body falling helplessly toward bone-crushing rock.

He shook his head. No time for bad memories. He had been saved that time when his chute finally ripped free and caught air at two thousand feet. He had suffered only a broken ankle . . . and an extreme fear of heights he kept tucked inside his intestines.

"Colonel, time to go," said the jump master. Macklin put the high-altitude oxygen mask in place while the young soldier checked his chute one last time. Then he checked Lieutenant Gad's. The young Israeli's brow was wet with moisture, and Macklin could see the fear in his eyes. Maybe allowing him to come along wasn't such a good idea; he had never jumped from thirty thousand feet. But, better to have him where Macklin could keep an eye on him. It was a two-man operation anyway, and on paper the young lieutenant had all the qualifications. He just prayed Gad would be the needed man.

Macklin pulled on the insulated gloves. It was below zero at this altitude, and the long johns and insulated jumpsuit were not luxuries. Without proper protection a man could freeze to death before he could pull his cord.

On the radarscope their plane was designated as a French turboprop carrying a group of archaeologists into sites in southern Syria. The plane would go on to a small airport near those sites, drop off said equipment, then return to Rome, Italy. It had been no small feat to find such a flight over Syria. He knew Israel must have pulled some pretty long strings to get him this ride, but he still wasn't grateful. Not at this height.

"Go!" the jump master said. Macklin took four steps and leaped out of the back door, the icy air gripping the edges of his mask. Gad was right behind him.

Levona looked at her watch, then finished fastening on her gear. Macklin and Gad should be in place. She hadn't liked Gad going with Macklin. If he froze or ran he could ruin everything. The Arabs would be the victors, with an international incident to beat her country over the head with, Imad would be imprisoned, and she would be out of a job.

She shook her head, trying to rid herself of the thought and the lack of faith it revealed. She had selected Gad because she believed in him. This was no time to waver in that belief even though she had never intended that Gad see action in which other lives were at risk . . . especially that of an American colonel.

"All right, let's move it." She stood and walked to the door, the four young soldiers at her heels and unhappy about her presence. Macklin had agreed to lead the infiltration as long as he was given full charge. They saw her decision to go aboard the LION as a breach of her promise to him that she wouldn't interfere. She saw her role as minor and one that would not infringe on Macklin's leadership. She had no intention of interfering. Not when she knew how Macklin felt about such things.

Their plan, her brainchild, was a good one, well-orchestrated down to the smallest detail. And it would work. She relished the memory of Macklin agreeing.

It hadn't been easy to pull everything together, and Minister Hoshen had been reluctant until Macklin had pointed out that his job might be a whole lot easier if they got their hands on someone with inside information. After a time-wasting discussion with David Stein, Hoshen's aide, and General Ativa, both of whom were opposed to the operation, Hoshen called the prime minister. Ruth had held her breath until she realized Hoshen was getting the go-ahead from Israel's top leader. Now it was up to her group to make everyone look smart. She wanted no mistakes. The prime minister wasn't about to take the fall, nor was Hoshen. Ativa was against the operation and so was Stein; that cleared them. Only one person would shoulder the burden of failure and she wasn't about to take any chances of a career-ending episode.

Before getting into the LION Levona turned back and spoke to Merriame. "Sergeant, we'll get him out. I promise."

Merriame's smile was weak, but she nodded lightly as Levona jumped aboard. The colonel knew her worry. Imad was really Eytan Merriame, Shuli's brother, and a man who hadn't wanted to return to Syria because of a dream he had had, a premonition of death he had called it. Even gentle pressure from General Ativa hadn't changed his mind. Only Manlik Hoshen had finally convinced Eytan to return one last time. For the good of Israel.

Levona shook her head. He shouldn't have gone.

She felt the sudden lift of the powerful chopper and grabbed for a handhold.

The LION. Israel's newest and best troop attack helicopter. Patterned in some ways after the American Sikorsky Eagle, the LION went several steps beyond. Two 1500-KW turboshaft engines gave her a fighting speed of over 200 miles per hour, nearly twenty better than the Eagle. Her reserve power could move the LION beyond 220 miles per hour if needed.

But her beauty was in her maneuverability. Handling more like a small helicopter, the LION was a breakthrough in combat air-to-ground battle worthiness. She could literally dodge incoming missiles at a high rate of speed, turn on a dime, and do high-powered loops at low altitudes without a sputter.

The LION was completely armored with Kevlar nearly three inches thick, which could stop a .50-caliber bullet at close range. The chopper's avionics allowed her nap-of-the-earth navigation, literally following the earth's contour only a few feet above ground. At better than 200 miles per hour it took a strong stomach to stay with her. She was protected from heat-seeking missiles by Black Hole IR suppression systems. Offensively, her capabilities far surpassed even the Americans' Apache two-passenger attack chopper, well known from its active role in the Gulf War. She had the added capability of being able to identify her own soldiers, who each wore a device that emitted signals read by the LION's radar. In the heat of battle the LION's computer automatically directed her fire away from the signals, honing in on "unfriendly" targets not wearing the device and destroying them within seconds.

Levona got chills up her spine as the chopper sped into the darkness, the LION's missile pods, 50mm chain guns, and six Stinger missiles attached under her fully extended fuselage wings, giving her an ominous, futuristic appearance.

Even though other choppers had many of her talents, one other weighed the balances for the LION. She could not be seen on radar.

Levona placed a set of headphones over her ears, her method of keeping track of the entire operation.

"Captain Ariel, Colonel Levona," she said to the pilot in Hebrew. "How long to KaShil sector one?"

KaShil was Hebrew for sledgehammer, the name selected for the mission. Sector one was the Syrian border.

"Five minutes, Colonel."

Levona looked at the four men, now securely fastened into seats lining the fuselage. That left seven empty seats and hopefully enough room to bring Imad and his informant's family to safety, along with Macklin and Gad.

"Colonel?"

"Yes, Captain?" Levona responded in the mike.

44

"General Ativa sends you his love."

She smiled. Ativa knew she would go along on the operation. In feelings about Israel and its Arab enemies they were two peas in a pod.

"Are you fully armed, Captain?"

"Yes, ma'am, but this baby has never been tried in real combat before. Thought we might get the chance a few months ago in Iraq but—"

"No time like the present." She looked at her watch while clicking on her microphone so all could hear through similar headphones. "Everybody okay?" she asked generally.

Lieutenant Mori responded. "Fine, Colonel. Just a little motion sickness."

She leaned her head against the fuselage, feeling a bit woozy herself as the LION jumped almost violently, following the contour of the earth only a matter of feet below them. She closed her eyes, concentrating, going over the plan one more time.

"Colonel Levona. Sergeant Merriame. Do you read me?"

"Go ahead, Sergeant."

"Imad . . . Imad called . . . he was cut off. He wouldn't have called . . . he had no choice!" she sounded desolate.

"Calm down, Sergeant. Is he in place for the pickup?"

"No, he remains in building three. He has a small hiding place, prepared months ago. You will have to get him from there."

Levona looked at her men, who were deep in their own thoughts, oblivious to the decision that now needed to be made.

"Colonel?" Merriame asked.

Ruth was silent, sweat beginning to roll off her forehead. Imad was her man. Hers. A part of the team. His life must be saved.

And the informant. Didn't Macklin say it would be easier for her group to get to the factory if he had the informant? Didn't the Duma project hinge on getting him out? Wasn't it crucial to defeating Badannah? A hundred things rushed through her mind. She knew most were rationalizations, but she didn't have time to pick through each one. Only one thing mattered.

"Colonel?" Merriame said again.

"We'll get them, Sergeant. Just pray Macklin can adjust to a new set of rules." She switched the mike on again.

"Gentlemen, a change in plans. The Syrians are searching for Imad. We have to go into the compound. We can't allow Imad to be taken by Badannah." She saw them come to full alert, eyes pinned on her, waiting for orders. Now their lives depended on her.

It was quiet now, but Imad could taste the fear in the small, tight enclosure. The enemy had come into the building while he was in the open room using the radio. Luckily, they had entered the hallway at the far end, and he had enough time to slither back into the small, stinking hole and slide the false wall into place. He had nearly fainted when he realized that the gunnysack in which he had packed the radio had been left behind. Long minutes had passed as Badannah's death squad searched the outer room. If they had found the raggedy sack they had made no sense of it. He breathed easier and tried to pass his relief on to the family.

"Your prayers to your Allah have been answered, again," he told them. And my prayers to the one God, he thought. But those prayers would have to be answered many times over. Badannah's soldiers were all over the place, coming within inches of discovering them half a dozen times, leaving their nerves frazzled and near breaking. The children had been angels, sleeping some of the time, always quiet. Imad had thanked God that he had cut a hole in the floor leading to the crawl space underneath, which they could use for toilet facilities.

God had kept them safe thus far. Now, if Colonel Levona could only become his hands and pluck them from sure death!

He tried to get more comfortable, thinking how she might come. By land or air? Maybe both. He would be ready. He reached into a small space between two boards of the floor and took out the Kalishnikov and several curved metal clips, each holding thirty rounds of ammunition. He would help them all he could.

He put his ear to the outer wall and listened. Nothing. Maybe . . . He looked up at a hole in the ceiling, then whispered to the father. "You and your family are to stay here until I return. Do not move or open the false wall until I return through the ceiling." He pointed at the hole. "I will not come through the wall." He said this in perfect Arabic. "Do you understand?"

The man answered in a quavering whisper.

Imad slipped a clip into the rifle and put the other into his deep pants pocket, then he slung the rifle over his shoulder by its strap. It was uncomfortable but it left his hands free for use. He jumped and grabbed hold of one of the rafters, pulling himself into the attic space. The light of a full moon peeked through several cracks and holes in the rotting roof, accounting for the light they had in their hiding place. He moved carefully to a hole that seemed large enough and as quietly as possible widened it by picking away rotted wood. Finally the hole was big enough that he knew his slim body could go through.

Then he waited. When Levona came . . . when he heard the first sounds of choppers or track vehicles . . . he would be ready.

Macklin didn't like it. Soldiers were all over the place. So far he had counted nearly fifty, with another truckload just arriving. They were definitely doing a full-scale search. He let the night vision scope on his rifle fall on the building farthest away and full of the most activity. He could hear the place literally being torn apart as the soldiers looked for Imad and his group under floors and in ceilings. He let the scope drift to the administration building, the one in which Imad was supposed to be waiting. It wouldn't be long until the searchers arrived there.

He adjusted the earphones and small microphone, then made sure Gad had his in place as well. Two, maybe three minutes and the chopper would be within range and he could talk to them, tell them to back off. The odds were definitely against them.

The moon was no help either. It was a miracle they hadn't been seen trying to get as close as they were. Macklin wondered why such a concentrated effort? Did they really know Imad was here? How? He didn't like that thought. It meant his own presence might also be known. He shook it off. No, only the team itself knew when they had actually left for Sahles, and none of them were traitors; at least, he didn't think so.

He bit his lip, his stomach in full uproar at not being able to help the seven people now relegated to sure death, but he wouldn't send more to join them by trying the impossible.

He let the scope wander through the complex, looking for a way. There was nothing except a direct assault. For that they didn't have enough men. It would be suicide to go further.

"KaShil One, this is KaShil leader, do you read?" he said into his mike.

"Leader, this is one, we hear you."

Good. The LION was in range. "This is leader. Abort. No go. I repeat, no go. Troops everywhere."

"Uh . . . leader, we have a change of plans, sir," said Captain Ariel. "We—"

"What? KaShil One, this is leader! Do you understand that word? Do—"

"Leader, this is Ruth, do you read me?"

His anger pushed steam through dusty pores. "Levona, what the—"

"No time for that! Listen!"

"I hear you! Go ahead!" He said hotly.

"They were nearly discovered just minutes ago. They couldn't get to the pickup point. They are in building three. It is either now or never. The Syrians—"

"I know about the Syrians, Colonel, there are better than seventy-five soldiers down here now, not to mention a number of armored vehicles. They are well prepared to stop the seven . . . excuse me, the eight of us! But there are other considerations. Your country—"

"Colonel, Imad is part of my country. The people he has with him may be able to save my country. The Syrians are preventing us from freeing them. They are in our way. We must move them."

Macklin wiped the sweat from his face. They didn't have time to argue all the finer points, and Levona wasn't about to give in. He'd straighten that all out later. "Where are you?"

"Five minutes away."

Another twenty seconds passed while he thought.

"All right. Does that overrated piece of scrap metal have

the capacity to place a missile wherever I want it, without being seen?"

A male voice answered. "Captain Ariel. Yes, Colonel. Unlike the Apache—"

"I know what the Apache can do, Captain. All right. How many are you carrying?"

"Twelve Stingers, sir."

"Okay. Here's what you do."

Imad did not hear anything until the whiz of missiles passing very close overhead and the explosions that followed. He went up through the roof, placing himself against the still-warm wood and slowly moved toward the peak. Four explosions had lit the sky with fire and had sent men dashing and screaming in all directions, wondering where the enemy was. Another explosion and a vehicle disappeared in a ball of flame, lighting up the terrain and revealing a scene that frightened Imad. Soldiers were everywhere!

Imad clicked off the safety and fired, working to lessen their numbers. Suddenly he heard the sound of something unworldly behind him. He rolled over and saw the monster's belly as it flew over him, spitting fire from its huge black mouth before swooping into the darkness. He quickly gazed into the chaos below and smiled. They had more than seen the monster from hell, they had felt the fire of its fury.

He belly-crawled to the hole and slithered through, returning to the frightened family. He flung open the false wall, his gun ready. Finding the room deserted, he took a small child in his arms and told the others to follow him.

The woman, her eyes wide as silver dollars, hesitated, then ran for the opening, apparently deciding anything was better than dying in the dark hole of the wall.

They slunk across the room, the eerie darkness broken by the explosions of light coming through the windows as the LION exploded its arsenal on their enemies. Imad stopped in front of a window, where he motioned the family to keep their heads down. Cautiously he checked the compound, sizing up the situation and deciding how best and when to flee from the building. As he watched, frantic for some sign of help, the monster burst from the darkness beyond the fence and flung a fiery missile at the dilapidated tower where a machine gunner was trying desperately to bring the flying serpent to the ground. The tower exploded into a mass of flames, the top half obliterated, its occupants instantly placed in the next world.

Imad smiled. The LION had driven the enemy clear of the compound, giving them a chance of escape. Setting the child down, he broke out the few remaining panes of window glass, clearing their exit, knowing that in seconds help would arrive. They would be ready.

Macklin and the five Israelis watched the first missiles explode on target, then prepared to move as the LION swept the area with its cannons while flying at more than 190 miles an hour. Macklin was momentarily awed as the old guard-post at the gate exploded into oblivion, but was quickly awakened by the explosion of the hand-held TOW missile Lieutenant Gad had fired at the fence. Macklin ran for the smoldering hole, his rifle barrel sending bullets at anything that moved. The four men from the chopper joined him and Gad and they quickly fanned out in the compound, moving straight toward building three. Macklin saw Gad to his left, no hesitation in his approach. If he had ever been the coward, that part of him had been repaired or overcome.

Macklin heard the breaking of window glass and at the same time saw the Syrian soldiers bolt from behind the building. The Israeli to his right fired, forcing them back.

"KaShil One! Get in here! Small arms opposition on the south end of building three! Now!"

He fired along with the others while Imad lowered the children into Lieutenant Gad's arms. Then came the woman, the informant, and finally Imad. Gad slapped a small sticky strap to each as he helped them get clear of the window. The patch emitted a signal so that the LION could identify them as friendly.

All of them ran for the north end of the building, away from the fighting. There Mori had taken up a defensive position to keep them from being surrounded. As the LION came out of the darkness again and used her .50-caliber cannons to pin down the enemy soldiers, Macklin signaled the others to begin moving across the open tarmac to the now-smoldering hole in the fence.

"All right. Time for the coup de grace, Captain," he said into the mike. "We'll meet you at the rendezvous!"

The LION swung away as Macklin ran through the hole, the last to leave the compound. He looked up in time to see the chopper deliver another Stinger at a distant dune, a track vehicle and truck unitedly exploding into flames as they attempted to breach the perimeter of space the LION had set up to protect them. Then he saw a tongue of flame in the distant darkness of another hillock. A missile! Hand-fired at the chopper, it was moving at a thousand feet per second toward the seemingly soft underbelly of the LION. Macklin hesitated, his stomach caught in his throat.

The LION's computer read the incoming death blow and sent out strips of metal and small exploding bombs as a diversion while changing its direction in midair, streaking straight up into the heavens. The missile flew by harmless and sped into the darkness, exploding in a distant desert spot as the chopper completed a full circle, guns firing at the missile's spot of origination, annihilating any enemy left there.

Macklin was awed. Lying on his belly near the fence, he took a deep breath and gave an order through his mike headset. "Evasive withdrawal."

Gad and Akitsa took defensive positions behind small mounds of earth, aiming their guns past Macklin and into the compound, which was now alive with frightened soldiers moving in their direction as a commanding officer yelled and pointed toward their escape route. Macklin and the others began a running retreat toward the ravine as Gad and Akitsa opened fire on their pursuers, creating fresh havoc and fear, scattering them. After a hundred yards Mori and Irbev dropped to the ground and covered while Akitsa and Gad ran to catch up. Macklin grabbed the arm and wrist of one of the children as he entered the ravine, hurrying the child along. Another hundred yards and the LION would pick them up.

He heard the engine before he actually saw the cat track, but his experience in the Saudi desert had trained his ear to the sound of the Russian-made vehicle.

"KaShil One, we have company! Probably more to follow. Delay rendezvous!

"Gad! Need a TOW! Now!"

He saw Gad stop fifty feet away and prepare the light, hand-held TOW for firing, moving it to his shoulder as the vehicle careened over a small ridge of sand, its lights cutting a path in the darkness, seeking them with its tongue of fire, ready to devour anyone in its path.

Fear suddenly leapt into Macklin's chest. The child had left his side and now stood several yards away, riveted by the lights. Macklin knew he was too far away but leapt up the bank of sand toward the boy, yelling.

"Fire that missile, Gad! Fire!"

The TOW leaped from its chute and headed for the relentless lights, but to Macklin it seemed to move in slow motion and would never get to its target before the cat track's .30-caliber bullets drank the blood of the helpless child standing frozen in the sand. Macklin gritted his teeth, punishing his body to move through the slipping, sliding stuff beneath him. The bullets honed in, seeking a target.

Then from nowhere came the man, grabbing the child and flinging him out of the path of the deadly fire. Macklin watched with horror as the speeding balls of metal ripped into the adult savior's body. The scream stuck in Macklin's throat as the TOW struck home, exploding the vehicle into flames a second too late.

Macklin dived for the injured man, grabbing him as another vehicle plummeted over the embankment toward them. He shouldered the body, feeling the wet, sticky blood flowing down his shirt as he ran for cover, the others filling the air behind him with bullets. He heard the thump of a TOW being fired, then the explosion as another enemy vehicle blew into the air. He was running, pulling the child, stumbling toward the rendezvous point, his wind gone, muscles aching with the added burden over his shoulder.

Two more vehicles appeared out of the night. They had no more TOW missiles. Everyone dived for cover.

"All right, KaShil One!" Macklin screamed into the mike. "Move it! We need help. Now! Two tracks! One on the right of us, one on the left."

Captain Ariel was already on the move. Levona had waited, watched on the radar, then ordered the pilot into the fray. The computer was already delivering the Stinger at the armored vehicle farthest away, while filling the near one with armor-piercing shells from its .50-caliber cannon. Ariel used the computer-controlled .30-caliber machine guns to throw chaos into Syrian foot soldiers trying to get to the fight from the compound, watching as the computer screen showed its avoidance of friendlies wearing the high-tech signal devices.

Macklin saw the family just ahead. He felt their panic and fear but knew there was nothing he could do now but hurry them faster to the pickup point. He couldn't see the other team members but only heard the small arms fire to his right, left, and rear. He was conscious of the blood flowing much too freely down the back of his shirt, but he forced himself to run faster as he encouraged the children and parents to do the same.

He heard the weapon and saw the woman stumble, moan, and hit the ground. Instinctively he went down, sensing the hot lead zipping through the air around him. He yelled, and the children fell to the ground by their mother, shaking with fear, two of them crying loudly. Macklin tried desperately to find the flash of light, the telltale sign of enemy fire. He saw it! His own weapon jumped as he automatically fired at the spot, instantly stopping the sound of the gun and the life behind it.

The LION was hovering, then touched the ground only a few feet away, her small cannons firing into the unknown darkness. Macklin struggled to his feet, lifting the body, forcing his legs to go on! Past the man kneeling by his wife, past the children staring with wide eyes at their parents, to the chopper. As he reached the door Levona stopped firing the .30-caliber weapon and jumped down to his aid.

"The woman . . . ," he gasped, ". . . has been hit! One child—can't walk—needs help." He placed the unconscious body on the chopper's floor. Levona grabbed Macklin's automatic and rushed into the darkness.

Ruth saw the enemy soldier, aimed, and fired, cutting his legs out from under him. She fired again, forcing two others to run for their lives, her automatic kicking up sand all around them. She saw one go down and the other dive for cover behind a low bank of sand. The sweat poured from her forehead as the clip ran out and she became cognizant of her surroundings. Two children stood shaking a few feet away, the crippled child paralyzed by fear. She threw the gun down and grabbed him with one hand and the other child with the other, carrying and pulling them toward the chopper. As she passed the father she spoke to him in Arabic, motioning toward his wife with a nod of her head. "Pick her up! *Now!*" But he didn't move.

"Pick—" she started to yell, but stopped when she saw her men coming out of the darkness, running toward the chopper. Gad fired his last rounds, tossed the gun aside, and picked up the woman. He half stumbled, half ran toward the LION. Levona shoved the man after Gad, trying to jar him loose of the fear that atrophied his muscles. She pulled the one near-hysterical child with her, Mori herded another. The others, frozen by fear, refused—unable to move. "Come on," she said in fluent Arabic, as calmly as the adrenaline would allow. "We're almost free. Come on." The children responded and they were soon running in the direction she wanted them to go.

The chopper's cannons seemed to roar in Ruth's ears as they searched for the enemy that must only be a short distance away. She heard the thud and plink of bullets as they careened off the chopper's metallic body or bored in the Kevlar armor, creating a fear that made the hair on the back of her neck stand on end. She tried to focus only on getting the children into the chopper and to safety, trying not to think about one of those small metal projectiles snuffing out her life in less time than it took to cough.

Macklin was firing with the .30-caliber weapon hanging from the door mounting while the others jumped and rolled into the relative safety of the fuselage. Gad put the woman down as gently as he could, then helped the informant as he struggled into the chopper. He lifted the children and finally Ruth to safety. As he climbed in himself the LION leaped from the ground. He lost his grip and slipped earthward. His fingers grasped the edge of the chopper floor, his body dangling free, an easy target. Fear leapt into his heart as he felt his sweaty fingers begin to slide free of the metal. He looked at the ground now hundreds of feet below and knew he was about to plummet back into enemy hands at best, death at worst! Then he felt Macklin's firm hold around his wrist hoisting him to safety as the LION roared into the darkness and toward the distant border.

"Buckle up," Macklin said to him as they stood in the safety of the LION's belly. "The life you save may be your own." Gad looked at him curiously as he collapsed in one of the seats.

Levona was bending over the woman, whose head was lying in her husband's lap. The wound was serious, but if they could get her help quickly she would live. Ruth turned to the wounded man, trying to keep her balance as the chopper turned on its computer and began its nap-of-the-earth return to Israel.

She rolled the body over, her heart filling with a deep ache. Eytan Merriame, alias Imad Basrah, was dead.

Day Three

CHAPTER 7

3:00 A.M., Jerusalem

The room was small and sterile, smelling of rubbing alcohol and Lysol. There was no bed, just a few odd-shaped, brightly colored padded chairs. Macklin sat in one, his eyes shut against the fluorescent light. He had tried to get his brain to shut down, but the adrenaline continued to pump through his system, refusing to give him the much-needed sleep.

The door opened and Lieutenant Gad slipped in.

"We can go if you're ready, Colonel," he said, his language slurred by exhaustion.

Macklin sat up, motioning to the chair. "Sit."

Gad moved to the spot nervously.

"You knew she was going along in the chopper and yet—"

"No, sir, but I knew she might. That's the way she is, sir."

Macklin frowned, but let it go.

"What's going on? Why am I isolated?"

"Security, sir. Remember, no one is supposed to know you're in our country."

"All right, how is Sergeant Merriame?" Macklin asked. He hadn't found out about Eytan Merriame until their return to

Israel. Mori had informed him when Shuli Merriame had fainted on seeing her brother's half-faceless body.

Gad looked at the floor, fiddling with the rip in his blood-stained sleeve. "She'll make it."

"Will she?" Macklin responded through his teeth.

"Yes, sir. All of us do."

"All of you?"

"There isn't one of us that hasn't been through it before. I lost a brother. You can't live in Israel and not be touched by death from war. We are a small nation whose enemies refuse to leave us alone."

Macklin looked at him. "You did well, Lieutenant. If I were your commanding officer I'd see that you were commended for your action under fire."

"Thank you, sir. I . . . I appreciate your faith, sir . . . and Colonel Levona, she . . ."

"Tell her, Lieutenant," Macklin smiled. Gad would find it easier to sleep now, knowing, not just believing, that he was not a coward.

"The informant? His wife is all right?" Macklin asked.

"Conscious, sir. But they will all have some sleepless nights for a while."

"Is he still going to help you?" Macklin asked.

"Yessir! More than ever. But the Syrians know we have him now, so his information may not be helpful. They could set traps, change things."

"Umm. Everyone else okay?"

"Yessir."

"Good." He paused. "I'm not leaving until I talk to Colonel Levona, Lieutenant. Understood?"

Gad fidgeted again. "She said—"

"Doesn't matter what she said. Get her, please."

Gad stood. "Yessir." He went out.

Macklin stood and went to the small window. The moon was high above the city now. How long had it been since their return?

He thought about the LION and its pilot. The chopper was better than anything he knew of, and Captain Ariel was as good as any American pilot he had ever seen! Under constant warlike conditions the Israelis must be sharp, but he had never seen such ability.

He smiled. Sometimes being a soldier, working with such people . . . saving lives . . .

The smile left. Losing lives . . .

The door swung open and he turned to see Colonel Levona, pale and drawn, tired. She was moving to the nearest chair. He sat next to her.

"You okay?" he asked.

"Yes, thank you. Why did you want to see me?" she asked, all business.

He stood and went back to the window. If that was the way she wanted it . . . "Colonel, you were out of line. You broke our agreement and jeopardized the entire mission. Why?"

"In Israel, Colonel, things don't always go according to plan. I felt I needed to be along with my people. They hadn't—"

"That's not a reason, Colonel. You agreed to let me run the operation once it started. You broke your word."

Her voice went cold. "I did not interfere with your running the operation."

"You did. Your very presence interfered, Colonel Levona. You were not to see combat." He paused. "When I contacted you, I fully intended to call everything off, regroup at the very least. But you had already made a decision to the contrary, forcing me to jeopardize all of our lives. And, Colonel, now it will be next to impossible to make an attempt on that factory. If they didn't know we were interested in their little operation before, they know now!"

"The family . . . they would have died if—"

"Does the colonel see into the future as well?" Macklin interrupted, returning the coldness.

"No, Colonel, I don't, only a gut feeling. We often have to rely—"

"Sorry, Colonel. Not good enough. Your gut feeling cost a man's life and put the rest of this operation in serious question."

She suddenly stood, angry. "Imad was one of my men, and don't you forget it!"

"I haven't, Colonel. But at the time he was under my command, and your changing the plan in mid-stride forced me to make a hasty decision that may have caused his death."

"There wasn't any choice." The anger cooled a little.

"Explain, please."

"Imad said it was only a matter of minutes before Badannah's men found them. It was then or never. I felt . . . I felt his life was more important than . . . "

"Than thousands of Israelis who might now have to face those missiles?"

He bit his tongue, wishing the words back.

"Colonel Macklin, I'm tired, confused, and angry. At myself mostly, but this is not the time to go over this. You may do as you like. Report what you feel to General Ativa; tell the press. I don't care." She moved to the door and opened it. "I did what I thought was best at the time. Whether I was in the chopper or back in safe territory is not the issue. The decision would have been the same."

"The decision wasn't yours, Colonel. It was mine. I was in charge of the operation, you were in charge of the planning, remember. You should not have been in a position to make the decision, period!"

She looked at him with icy eyes, then turned and walked out, the door swinging closed behind her.

He watched the shadow through the cut glass disappear. He had said too much. He wanted to go after her, but couldn't; his pride was getting in the way. He was right. She had stepped out of line. He shouldn't have let her, that was his fault.

But would he have acted any differently?

No. He would have done the same thing. People's lives were at stake. You save the life and figure out what to do about the factory later.

Then why was he being so rough on her? Because she scared him. He had never seen a woman use weapons like Ruth had. It was as if . . . as if she shut off the world, cold, calculated. He was afraid for her.

He turned and looked out of the window again. And, if she had been hurt . . .

Tom Macklin had to face it. To him Ruth Levona was more than his counterpart in the military. That was the biggest reason. He had seen her stumbling through the dark toward the chopper, children in hand, bullets kicking up dust all around, and he had nearly panicked. Instead, he used the .30-caliber, trying to protect her, afraid she'd never make it.

He was in love with her.

Question was, what to do about it.

3:00 A.M., Duma, Syria

Sergeant Khalis stood in front of Colonel Badannah knowing full well he was only inches away from a firing squad. When they had first arrived at Sahles Sahra he had commanded Maymuna to begin a search, sweating every minute of it. After several hours of finding nothing in the darkness he was beginning to relax a little. Suddenly all Hades had broken loose. He became just another soldier fighting to stay clear of flying bullets and exploding missiles. He still couldn't forget the picture of the beast from heaven raining death and destruction upon all of them. He had never seen anything quite like it. In fact, he knew there *was* nothing like it.

The sergeant could tell Badannah was measuring his words, trying to decide what to do next. He could only hope other heads would topple before his own.

"Sergeant Maymuna was in charge of the search?" Badannah asked.

"Yessir."

"And you feel he is responsible for the loss of the contractor and his family?"

"Sir, no one . . . The enemy—"

"Yes, yes! But was he in charge?" Badannah's voice was two octaves higher and the sergeant knew he was looking for only one thing—someone on whom to fix the blame. Khalis knew he should thank Allah it was Maymuna, but wished it were the man in front of him.

"Yessir. He was."

"Have him arrested. I will prepare the necessary letters of explanation, but do not send him to Damascus until I give you the order. Understood?"

"Yessir," Khalis said, feeling a mixture of relief and disgust.

"And what of this 'beast from the skies' all of the men are ranting about? What do you make of it, Sergeant?"

"I saw it, sir. An attack helicopter. At first I thought it was an American Apache, but it moved too fast, had too much maneuverability. I think it . . . well, sir, I think the Israelis have a new and very effective fighting machine."

"Indeed. Can you identify anything about it? The weaponry? Anything?"

"It was very dark, sir, but possibly between all of us who survived . . ."

"Yes, possibly. Get reports from all of the men. Put together a profile, Sergeant." He paused. "Now, what do you intend to do about the protection of our factory? The Israelis took that man for only one reason. They intend to pay us a visit."

"We will be ready, Colonel, I assure you."

"Maybe. Bring me a plan of your preparations by noon tomorrow. I will discuss it with those in Damascus. Possibly they will want to move things to a different location." He paused again, seemingly in deep thought. "Umm. That is all, Sergeant."

The sergeant saluted, "Thank you, sir," and turned and went to the door.

"Oh, and Sergeant. This time others were in a position to take the heat, so to speak, for both of us. *You* may not be so lucky next time. Do not fail me!" His voice was calm and calculated, sending chills down the sergeant's back as he closed the door behind him.

Noon, Jerusalem

Colonel Ruth Levona lay on her bed, cold and shaking. She had left the hospital only after Merriame and her parents had gone home and the informant and his family were safely in the hands of authorities who could protect them.

She wiped the tears from her eyes and tried to lift herself from the bed. The memory of Imad's family was clearly etched in her mind. The mourning of Imad's mother, coupled with Shuli Merriame's cold, distant reception . . . She shuddered.

It was such an easy operation. In and out! No one hurt! Everyone home to celebrate how they had made the Syrians look like fools!

How had the murdering Badannah known where Imad was? Had she made a mistake? Was there a leak in her organization? Were they able to decipher Merriame's code?

Or was it just bad luck?

She put her head in her hands. The fate of Israel had rested with her. Israel! When were the few to be sacrificed for the many? Had she done the right thing?

Fear and confusion made her stomach nauseated again. If Ibrahim or whoever was responsible, ran, if he moved his factory, made them hunt for him all over again . . . they would never find him in time. He would complete his warheads and it would be her fault! Her decision would doom thousands to die. Why hadn't she thought of that? Why hadn't she taken the time?

She leaned forward and began untying the boots, the lace slipping from one metal eye after the other.

Her stomach retched and she ran to the bathroom, but nothing was left. Most of it had come up at the hospital when Imad's body was taken from the chopper, his face half missing from the .30-caliber shell that had killed him as he flung the child out of death's way.

She moaned, the nauseating, empty pain deep in the pit of her stomach. She propped her head against the cool seat of the toilet, trying to hold back the tears, but couldn't. They turned to gut-wrenching sobs as the sudden emotional release overwhelmed her control system.

Tom had hit a nerve in his condemnation of her actions, pulling at deep-seated feelings. He had made her realize there was another reason for her decision. The same reason she was in the military, had accepted difficult missions among the Arabs, and used weapons like the one she used last night.

She wanted revenge for her family's deaths. She wanted Badannah humiliated, then dead.

She had always wanted it, from the first day her father had been brought to them with a hole bigger than her fist draining his life away. She had wanted it more when her brothers' bodies were put under burial clothes and dumped into graves next to her father. She had declared it her life's work when her mother died of a broken heart after losing so many of those she loved most.

Her desire for revenge had never gone away. And the hate had become stronger.

She had always controlled the hate. As long as she controlled it . . .

After long moments she lifted herself onto her feet, and began slipping out of her fatigues, the fear of her self-discovery tugging at her stomach.

She wiped the last of the tears with the back of her hand. She needed a hot bath.

She finished disrobing and put on a housecoat, then turned on the water and waited while it filled the large tub, one of the luxuries for whose installation in her small but comfortable apartment she had paid heavily.

As the steaming water poured into the ivory white porcelain, Ruth thumbed through the pages of a magazine, trying to keep her mind from looking further inside her own soul.

She slipped from her housecoat, magazine still in hand, and let her aching body slide into the hot, wonderful fluid. It had never felt so good.

Control. She had been doing it since she was a child. Each crisis was the same. When the demon inside tried to escape, when fear or doubt threatened to overwhelm, she had learned control. It was all a matter of disassociation, a mental game played with rationalization, denunciation, and denial. Her mind played it well.

CHAPTER 8

6:00 P.M., Tel Aviv

The Sinai Hotel in Tel Aviv was comfortable but not ostentatious. Jeremiah had selected it because he knew it was a short walk from the Mediterranean and, on a sunny day, provided a beautiful view up and down the coast.

But today the sea was gray-green and the wind was moving a storm quickly inland. It made him shiver and he left the patio and slid the door closed behind him. He had hoped for better weather on their first afternoon in Israel.

Mike exited the walk-in closet where she had been hanging up their wardrobe and went to the window.

"The beach is deserted," she said, a tint of disappointment in her voice. "I guess we'll have to put off a swim until we see the sun again."

He looked at his watch. "It's getting late anyway. Let's take a look at the itinerary, then grab a bite to eat. After that, your choice." He took her in his arms and they kissed gently.

They had been married three months now and life was good for Jeremiah Daniels again. TERROR1 was a thing of the past, a bad memory, and an occasional nightmare, matching those of his years of hell as a chopper pilot in Vietnam. After Mike's recuperation from a near fatal bullet wound in the chest they had tied the knot in the Idaho Falls Temple and returned to Jackson Hole to live, renting a place in town while their new home was being built. It would be finished in late fall.

In reality Jerry wasn't sure how he had gotten here. He knew that Senator Freeman, his father-in-law now, wanted him in politics, was preening him to be the next senator from Wyoming. He also knew that the president felt much indebted to him and Mike for what had happened to their lives because of TERROR1—and gratitude for those same efforts. Put the two together . . .

Jerry inwardly shrugged. His degrees in economics and his military record had helped, he supposed, and Washington's elite were always impressed by "kills" and congressional medals of honor. After all, *they* gave them out.

As he pushed the suitcase onto the closet shelf he shoved that debate aside as well. It didn't matter whose idea it was, or how much lobbying by the good senator and the president it had taken. He was here for his own reasons more than any others. That's all that mattered.

"When do you meet with the others from the peace commission?" Mike asked.

He would have liked to forget that their trip was business along with pleasure. The president had asked him to serve as a member of a fact-finding peace commission, working along with several others to smooth the way for talks that were to begin in Spain. Other members of the team were working in the Arab countries involved. In fact, he first had been assigned to Saudi Arabia but the assignment had been changed. It had been a pleasant surprise for both him and Mike. Jerry had been to the Holy Land before, with his first wife, who died a year or so later. Mike had wanted to come since she was a kid.

"Four days," he said. "That gives me four days of leisure time with you. How would you like to spend it?"

"Here," she said, kissing him gently.

"In the hotel room?" he smiled. "Naughty lady."

She grinned. "Maybe we can see a little of Israel as well.

When does the Israeli representative come to welcome you to his fine land?"

"Tonight." He looked at his watch as he rubbed the socket that encased his artificial eye. "In an hour and a half. Which gives us enough time to eat."

Mike touched his cheek below the eye. "The new plastic bothering you?"

He shrugged. "A little irritation after all these years with glass." The eye had been the easiest thing to leave behind in the jungles of the Delta. It was the people he missed. "Come on," he said, shoving old haunts behind him. "There's a restaurant downstairs." He opened the door and waved her through.

The elevator was only thirty steps down the hall. As they passed the first door to their left a man stepped out on Jerry's blind side, and they lightly collided.

"Oh, so sorry," said the man, stepping to one side. "Nearly knocked you down, I—"

"No problem," Jerry said, noticing the man's British accent.

They all continued and boarded the elevator.

"I'm Alistair Benson. From Britain." The man extended his hand.

"Stuart. William Stuart. This is my wife, Allyson. Glad to meet you." Jerry remembered to use the aliases. "What brings you to Israel?"

"Business. Import, export. Shreeve and Sons, in Hampstead. You?"

"Vacation, to see the Holy Land," Mike answered.

The door opened. "Well, then, enjoy yourselves," said Benson as he headed for the main desk.

Jerry stood watching him.

"What's the matter, honey?"

Jerry shook off the feeling. "Oh, nothing."

The paranoia was the reason he had decided to come. He had to overcome his fear. Fear of a dead and buried Fillmore Duquesne. A fear that somewhere someone was waiting for him. Waiting to pay him back for what he had done to TERROR1.

He shook his head. He knew it was probably just his overactive mind. The feeling that they were being watched in Jackson, the extra clicks on the phone that made him wonder if it was tapped—it had made him reclusive and he had to overcome it. He couldn't spend the rest of his life hiding, looking over his shoulder, wondering. In reality the trip was a test. They had decided they needed to make sure the past was really the past, that they were free to live their lives without fear.

"Come on," she said, pulling him toward the restaurant. "I'm starved. And that food smells wonderful!"

He smiled, glanced once more after the man from England, then followed Mike toward the pungent smells of the kosher restaurant.

Alistair Pike, alias Alistair Benson, climbed in the Mercedes and turned to his companion. "That's him."

The young woman answered. "You did very well, Alistair. Keeping tabs on them must not have been easy."

"All a matter of connections, my dear, and a lot of cash changing hands. I appreciate your generous expense account. They are traveling with false passports under the name of Stuart. A good English name, don't you think?" He smiled wryly.

She ignored his attempt at humor.

"What now, love?" he asked. "I assume you have plans for the Stuarts."

"In due time. For now they can wait. Take us to Jerusalem. I have people who will get us across the greenline, the border between Israel and the West Bank. We have a meeting there tonight. You have done well, Alistair. I will have the additional fifty thousand put in your account tomorrow."

She placed her hand gently on his arm. "I need your continued help."

"Maybe. Catching up with the Danielses wasn't easy, he said stiffly. "My people have earned that hundred thousand. You know, it's always a matter of money, Sabrila."

She pulled away. He shrugged, keeping his eyes glued to the highway.

Her eyes focused on a distant space out of the window, ice in her voice. "You will be properly paid, Alistair. You always have been."

"Just as long as we understand one another, love."

He shifted down as they approached the old wall of Jerusalem near Damascus Gate, the lights playing on the limestone creating eerie shadows. He smiled to himself. Sabrila Hassan, or whatever her name was, had a heart not unlike the wall. He had seen such hate before. Seen what it did not only to the person feeling it but to those around them. One of his people—curiously enough, a Jew—had cost him three good men because of such hate. Yes, he would need to watch her carefully. Sabrila would kill for her purposes and to protect those for whom she worked. He would watch Sabrila Hassan. Somehow he knew his life might depend on it.

CHAPTER 9

7:30 P.M., Sinai Hotel, Tel Aviv

Jerry and Mike sat on the couch in the outer room of their suite, the Israeli minister of defense in a chair opposite them. Jerry was surprised that such a high-ranking government official had been sent.

"We in the Israeli Defense Ministry appreciate your coming to our country as part of the advance body of the American-sponsored international peace commission." Minister Hoshen smiled.

Jerry returned it. "Mr. Hoshen, when we're finished with all of this I can only hope you will be as happy with the results. Negotiations will cost both sides something more than they presently want to give."

Hoshen crossed his legs nervously. "The politics are a topic for a later discussion," he said. "My only concern is your safety. Your request to come early and see some of our country while you are here makes that more difficult. I have come to ask you to reconsider."

"Minister," Jerry said firmly, "our experience with terrorism has changed our lives in a lot of ways, but we refuse to let it make us prisoners in a hotel room or our own home. We trust that the precautions about our identity have brought us here without the knowledge of those who might want revenge."

"We don't want secret service people all around us," Mike said. "Give us one man, your best man. If he senses *any* danger, we'll do as he asks."

The minister uncrossed and crossed his legs again, an unbelieving smile creasing his full lips. "One? Surely you don't understand that if . . ."

Jerry leaned forward. "One, Mr. Minister. All we want is one."

Hoshen looked at them, measuring. "Very well. One. If you wish to be foolish with your lives, it is your business. But there are some places we will not allow you to travel."

"The West Bank?" Jerry asked, an edge in his voice.

"Yes. As you know from the news, the Palestinians on the West Bank are escalating the violence. There are many, Mr. Daniels, who do not wish to see you and your peace conference successful. If you have enemies, it will be in the volatile West Bank that they come after you. Your presence would endanger others as well as yourself, and it would be unfair to place our man, and your beautiful wife, in such a position." He smiled a politician's smile.

Mike responded. "Don't use me as a bargaining chip, Minister," she smiled. "It won't work. Coming here was my idea as much as Jerry's. We feel no more danger here than we would anywhere else, and we refuse to succumb to fear of the past." She glanced at Jerry. They had discussed all this before. Both of them knew they needed this trip, needed to know that they were safe even in Israel.

Jerry leaned back in the chair, doing a little measuring of his own. "You don't like outsiders going to the West Bank, do you?"

"The West Bank is not safe," the minister said tightly. "Since the war with Iraq it has not gotten better."

"I have seen it on television," Jerry replied a little coldly. "And, I have talked to several Arab friends, former clients of mine, who used to live in Nabulus, one of your major West Bank cities. They agree with you. It wasn't safe for them, either."

Jerry leaned forward again. "I am going, Minister, to hear

the people and see what I consider to be holy places. I have your government's promise you will not interfere. I expect you to abide by that promise."

Mike took Jerry's hand, calming his emotions. The minister showed no signs of anger but the room was completely silent as he decided how to respond.

Hoshen leaned forward. "Like so many outside this country, you, Mr. Daniels, do not have the slightest idea of what we think or feel here. You do not understand the real intent of the militants in the Arab world, including many on the West Bank. You don't understand that many of them don't want a free Palestinian government. Nor do they want a Palestinian state. They want the destruction of Israel and the death of its peoples. Less than that would be unacceptable to them and would bring great shame upon their heads. Arab leadership can deal with many things but shame is not one of them."

Jerry stood and walked to the window. "I'm not sure I believe that, Minister, but regardless, I want to see them, and the West Bank. I expect you will have someone here to accompany us by morning."

Hoshen stood to leave. "Very well. My man will be here tomorrow. I will allow your trip to the West Bank. You can talk to anyone you like, but it will not change anything. We are a conquering nation like any other. The Arabs have been given laws to live by. They break the peace; we use our weapons to keep the peace. They portray themselves as the oppressed to get advantage; we have learned from them and act accordingly. They can be given nothing. When we do, they consider us weak and unworthy of respect. Only by remaining strong can we keep them from destroying us."

He turned to Mike. "Mrs. Daniels." Then he shook Jerry's hand. "Mr. Daniels. Israel will be either a land of peace or a land of war. We wish it to be one of peace, but not at the risk of losing it. Good day." He closed the door behind him.

Jerry walked to the window; Mike followed, putting her arms around him, resting her head between his shoulder blades.

"You, my darling husband, have a very difficult task ahead of you," she said.

Jerry looked longingly out of the window. "This isn't the Israel I visited in 1984, as a tourist. Men like Hoshen didn't come around and wreck my day with their version of how things are and how they are going to be. Tour guides took us to all the right places and said all the right things and we went away thinking this was a beautiful, peaceful land full of kind and loving people." He paused. "Two bull-headed, strong-willed people duking it out over a piece of rocky real estate no bigger than Yellowstone Park. That's what it really is. Who knows how many lives will be lost before they get tired of being so . . . so . . ."

"Stubborn."

"Yeah, stubborn." He turned into her arms, putting his around her.

She looked up at him with a sly smile on her face. "Kinda like us, aren't they?"

He laughed lightly. "Yeah, I guess they are. The difference is our stubbornness doesn't endanger any lives." Jerry knew Hoshen had a point about the safety of his man, but if someone was after them, wasn't it better that only one life besides theirs be at risk? "We are taking a chance."

The room seemed to grow cold to Mike and she suddenly wanted to go back to the airport and take a plane to anywhere but Israel. But they couldn't run, not now, not ever.

She held Jerry closer, remembering Wyoming. The bullet, the pain. Dying.

Then living again. She didn't want to lose this new life with Jeremiah Daniels, but she knew he couldn't continue hiding. They had known all along that there was a chance someone would come after them. Duquesne had promised them. They couldn't just sit around waiting their lives away, having the threat constantly hanging over their heads. They had to test the water. If they got burned it would be together.

―――――

Hoshen gave orders to his driver while sliding into the back seat of his car, then leaned back in the seat, taking a cigar from a small case in his coat pocket.

"Minister, how did it go?" asked David Stein.

"I wonder if Mr. Daniels will be a thorn in the side of Israeli interests," Hoshen said as he lit the cigar.

The assistant minister of defense laughed lightly. "One man can change nothing. Especially one with little political experience and no idea of how to play the games we play."

"Sometimes, David, men like Daniels are the most dangerous. They owe no one any allegiance and they have no career to lose if they state their mind. If we can't pressure or manipulate them the press tends to think they have a story to tell." Although he didn't inhale the cigar smoke deeply, its presence in his nostrils seemed to calm his nerves.

"Actually, David, as unsettling as men like Daniels are, I don't worry about *them* as much as I do the Arabs themselves. Just between you and me, their lies are working. They are successfully convincing the world that they want peace, even though it goes contrary to everything they have ever done. If they keep it up the political pressure will be so great that *we* will start to believe it. Then they will have us by the throat, and by the time the world sees that it has all been a deadly lie, Israel will be no more."

Stein's brow was wrinkled, his mind somewhere else.

"Well, to other business," Hoshen continued. "Have we stopped any fallout from that disastrous business in Syria last night?"

"There doesn't seem to be any, Minister. At least Syria hasn't said anything."

"Probably won't. They know we'd insist on an inspection of that factory in Duma if they started pointing fingers. That would be an embarrassment to Assad and his government."

Stein didn't respond.

"What is Ativa planning to do? Surely Badannah will be watching for us now."

Stein shrugged. "I talked to the general this morning. He thinks the enemy controlling the factory has the ability to manipulate Assad into putting his air force on full alert. He has eliminated the possibility of using our fighters." He paused for effect. "I made a suggestion to General Ativa."

"I'm listening," said Hoshen, somewhat annoyed.

"There are bound to be political repercussions. Your opponents in the Knesset, particularly from the Likud party, will try to have your job. I suggested that he relieve Levona of leadership on this project, and that Daliyat replace her."

"And Ativa's response?"

"You know Ativa likes Levona. He considers her the daughter he never had."

Hoshen laughed. "Did he kick you out of his office, David?"

"Practically," Stein said, red-faced. "But, I still think . . . Levona thinks a lot of you as well. She wouldn't expect you to take the fall. You're too important to the outcome of the Duma project. Without your getting her the approvals necessary . . ."

Hoshen's eyes hardened. "Not yet. I'll take the heat for now. Levona is good, and replacing her team at this late date would endanger Israel." He hesitated. "How long will it take to get a new team ready?"

"Two, maybe three weeks."

Hoshen shook his head adamantly. "Then, definitely not yet. So far I can handle the fallout. It's all internal and the prime minister remains supportive. Leave Levona on it for now."

Stein's eyes reflected a moment's panic. "But . . ."

Hoshen fixed a hard gaze on his assistant. "No buts, David. She is to remain in place, understood?"

"Yessir, just trying to protect your—"

"I'll take care of that," Hoshen said firmly, then smiled. "Besides, I still have sufficient padding. Before I go, there is Ativa . . . and you."

Stein frowned, glancing out of the window. "Daniels. Will he be a danger to us?"

Hoshen knocked the ash off the cigar in the recessed ashtray. "Compared to the Palestinian uprisings, world public opinion, and faltering politicals in our own land, Daniels is a mosquito, a nuisance at best. But I worry about his travel to the West Bank. He would damage an already struggling Israeli image in the United States if he were taken hostage or killed. Why they ever sent him I'll never know," he sighed. "Put our best man with him, Raffi Ben Shami."

The car pulled in front of the prime minister's home and Hoshen took a deep breath. He and the prime minister did not agree on many things, but the one thing they were solidly aligned on was Israel's right to claim the West Bank. Possibly that was what the meeting was all about. He stepped from the car, mentally going over his own agenda for discussion.

Stein broke his concentration. "I suggest Daliyat's team as a backup. He and I go back a long way. I know his talents. He has never failed us."

Hoshen didn't like Daliyat. He was a political climber. But right now . . . "Tell Ativa. But he is not to replace Levona until I say so. Get it done, David. You know how to reach me." He waved with his hand, a sign of dismissal that David Stein had never liked. He bit his tongue. Now was not the time to lose patience. In days, Mr. Hoshen would be out of his way, a bad memory.

He leaned back in the seat and gave instructions to the driver, a concerned furrow in his brow. Although he had tried to prevent it by getting word to Duma through ANGEL, the informant was in Israeli hands, putting the factory in extreme jeopardy. Luckily, Jerisha had been in Syria. She would take care of things there as she always had, even if it meant moving the factory. He must trust that.

The turmoil in his stomach eased a bit, then began churning again when he thought about Ruth Levona. She was good, and with Colonel Macklin . . . He shook his head. Unbeatable. They had pulled off an impossible rescue he was forced to admire, but he must turn it into a negative, and quickly. They were dangerous.

He had hoped to convince Hoshen of a need for change, appealing to the minister's desire for self-preservation. It hadn't worked. But soon Stein would be in a better position to push them both aside. For now, he would watch them. Carefully.

His mind moved to Daniels. At least that was going well. The foolish American was playing into their hands nicely. Although Stein questioned Jerisha's overpowering desire for revenge, her plans for the fool from the United States had promise. He shrugged the thought away. Sabrila would see to Daniels. He must concentrate on accessing the sword.

Thoughts of his own plan made him smile. Only two men stood in his way. He was in position to replace one, an event he had planned for two and a half days from now when he would present evidence showing General Chaim Ativa as traitor. After that, Minister Hoshen would meet with an untimely death at the hands of West Bank Palestinian leadership, leaving as the new head of army intelligence the honorable David Stein, with sole authority for protection of the sword.

As the car door opened and he put his feet to the pavement, Stein had a grin stuck on his lips. His end of things was going well. Sahles was just a moment's bad dream; ANGEL would handle it.

And Armageddon was still coming for the Jews.

Day Four

CHAPTER 10

2:00 A.M., West Bank, Palestine

Mohammad Faisal waited in the dark near the window, the night air blowing against his body cooling him and the room behind him. He pushed the button on his watch, lighting the display. Nearly 2:00 A.M. He didn't like waiting. Too many things could go wrong when contacts didn't show up on time. He nearly had been taken by the Israelis once because of waiting a short five minutes.

He leaned back in the chair, resting his neck muscles, trying to rid himself of the constant ache that always seemed to course through the back of his shoulders, neck, and skull. His forty-two-year-old body was tired, physically and mentally. Tired of the hiding, the running, the constant fear and pressure.

He kept his eyes on the moonlit narrow street below his second-story window. Another ten minutes. That was all he could safely afford to wait.

He rubbed his irritated stomach. The only reward that twenty-four years of resistance to the Israelis had gotten him was a big ulcer, constant headaches, and his name near the top of the Israelis' most-wanted list.

Years ago he would have thrived on the excitement of such a clandestine meeting. Then, he lived for it, wanted it, was addicted to it. With each act in which his life could have been the ultimate sacrifice Mohammad had felt cleansed, the weight of years of humiliation under Jewish rule lifted from his family name.

Then, he had been an idealistic child, relying on the leadership of men he trusted, men like Yasser Arafat and Abu Jihad. Mohammad's dedication, and the death of so many others, had moved him quickly up the ladder of leadership until he was basking directly in the light of such men. Only to find that it wasn't light at all, but deepest darkness.

Mohammad had seen the PLO change from a form of representation for his people to one he now saw as their worst enemy. It had become a thugocracy made up of greedy and violent factions held together by conspiracy, lying, cheating, and murder. Each wanted to speak for the Palestinian people, crushing any others they could in power play after power play. Arafat had maintained control, but not without sacrifice and loss of the organization's highest goals. Mohammad saw Arafat, in order to keep peace within it, turn the PLO into just another Arab organization, oppressing Palestinians instead of fighting Israelis and trying to free Palestine. He allowed them to be taxed, and he winked at extortion and at assassination of those who opposed his decrees and those of others such as George Habash, faction leader of the PFLP, and the violent leaders of Black September.

During that time Mohammad had become Arafat's lackey with a gun, killing Arab Palestinians who refused to do as Arafat dictated. At first, much to his shame, Mohammad had obeyed, hoping what was happening was only temporary. It wasn't. The PLO with its fourteen factions had become a battleground, the infighting leading to more murder and mayhem than Mohammad liked to remember; and no longer were most of the casualties Jews.

Mohammad supposed that Arafat believed his handling of the situation was the only way it could be done, and possibly it was, under the existing conditions, but Mohammad couldn't handle it. He would rather die an ignominious death at the hand of the Jews than kill another Palestinian who supposedly opposed the PLO's strongest leader, Yasser Arafat.

He rubbed his arms against the cold chill of memory. He had become such an integral part of it all until it was nearly too late. Because he had done everything he was told to like some mindless machine, he had become a part of the inner circle, helping make decisions that kept the balance of power in Arafat's favor. This inner circle met often in private conclaves, secreted out of assassins' reach. They discussed and conspired, deciding which other groups needed weakening or strengthening for PLO advantage, and whether present rivals were better dead, neutralized, or courted. They debated which targets to hit and which to leave alone, which buildings should be blown up by car bombs to create maximum loss of life, and whom they might kidnap and use for negotiation or outright sale.

The conclave made the decisions, the orders were given, and down the chain of command a man in a stocking mask would ram a truckload of explosives down an enemy's throat, giving his life for "the cause," believing he was pleasing Allah by strengthening PLO power.

In reality, they were shaming everyone of Arab nationality and Islamic faith in the eyes of the world.

He sighed deeply. The PLO had lost its military authenticity. They envisioned no concrete plan for war with Israel in which the West Bank could be freed, and yet most factions refused to negotiate for peace. All that most were worried about was getting more money from the Arab nations and watching their investments in the world markets, so that they could buy power among the Palestinian people, controlling them and their allegiance.

In his mind the PLO, and he as part of it, had become the Palestinian people's greatest nemesis. And their greatest shame.

Now he saw a shadow of black move across the background of the lighter stone house across the street. Then another, close behind. At last. He picked up the silenced Makarov 9mm pistol from the lamp table, stood, and turned the chair to face the door. Better prepared than dead. His true self was still very much unknown to PLO leadership and the other factions who were trying to control the West Bank, one of which he was meeting with tonight. With the ever-changing tides of deceit and murder in which he must swim, he had to be careful he didn't drown.

He felt the cold grip of the Makarov pistol he had come to loathe for its destruction. It had been a personal gift from Abu Jihad, the PLO's former number two man, for Mohammad's dedication to the cause in Lebanon. The Israelis found Jihad in Tunis and killed him in 1987. Dying violently was a fate Mohammad knew awaited most terrorists, including himself. He only hoped he could save his sons from a similar fate.

He heard the slight creak where he had loosened the floorboards in the hall and he smiled. They were good, these two. They had evaded his subtle noisemakers on the stairs and had even quieted the creak in the rusty hinges of the front door. That was good. He only worked with professionals; amateurs got people killed.

The knock came. Two, then two again.

"Come," he said quietly, aiming the Makarov at the two dark forms sliding through the door. "Welcome. Please keep your arms extended from your sides." He spoke in Arabic. He heard a woman's voice translate as he reached for the curtain pull and covered the window. "Switch on the lamp on the table next to the door." After she translated, the taller of the two responded, the dim light of the 25-watt bulb pushing back the darkness in a small area around the lamp but leaving Mohammad in shadows, as he liked it.

The woman was taking off her black mask. Very pretty, even in shadow, but very young. Definitely Arab. The coal-black hair, dark eyes, and olive skin reminded him of his own wife, now sleeping soundly at home while her husband carried on a business she knew little about.

The woman moved toward him.

"Better to keep your distance," Mohammad said coldly. "Have your friend remove his mask, please." She gave the order in English.

"Now, your weapons. Please place them in your left hands and give them to me, handle first." This time the English was perfect. They did as they were told and he laid them on the table beside him. "Sit." He pointed at the two chairs he had placed near the door. "I have received word that you need my cooperation. What is it you want?"

Sabrila tried to look at him through the darkness, to put a face with the name. Few ever met with Mohammad Faisal in person. Contact was usually made through intermediaries. Even Ibrahim's leadership in Duma were unsure of where Faisal was. Since coming to the West Bank he had become a very mysterious man. But then, one who played terrorist games in the Israeli camp could do nothing less.

Sabrila had looked forward to meeting Faisal for another reason. He had served with her uncle Abu Hassan, one of the three leaders of the House of Hassan, now dead, and buried by the Israelis. Because his birth would give him the right to help rule Palestine when it was yanked from the grip of the Jews, her uncle had been the man she had always looked up to and respected, and one of those for whom she sought revenge.

"I wish to appeal to the friend of Abu Jihad," she said.

She sensed both men suddenly tense. The name of the former PLO second-in-command was not one to use lightly, but she also knew what she wanted and how to get it. Jihad was a fallen son of the PLO. PLO membership demanded that Mohammad consider her words, based on his allegiance to Jihad's ultimate sacrifice.

Mohammad spoke in Arabic, leaning forward, the metal of the gun glistening as it entered the shroud of light. "Allah's martyr. What is it you want?"

"You are a powerful man here, feared by everyone. We need your help to disrupt Israel's economy, escalate the violence in Israel and the West Bank, and give the Israelis something more than the American peace plan to think about."

Faisal was quiet. Sabrila went on.

"We need you to organize the violence to mean something more than isolated bits of unruly conduct. It must look and smell like total anarchy to our people, and require a strong Israeli military response, draining their resources."

It was not an unusual request. Mohammad had heard it dozens of times, but he knew there was more.

"What you really want is to stop the peace talks."

"Delay them at least," Sabrila responded. "The pompous Americans are feeling very good about their victory in Iraq and their renewed influence among Arab nations of the Middle East. Their peace conference cannot be allowed. The Palestinian people must decisively show the Americans we are not behind these talks."

She sat back in her chair, catching her breath, waiting, and measuring the effect of what she had said. Faisal was quiet, impassive for a long moment. Then he spoke.

"What you ask is contrary to the recent decisions of the Palestinian National Council and the newly stated goals of my own PLO. Has this changed?"

"Not officially, but Arafat has given his sanction privately. He gave us permission to contact you."

"How do I know this?"

"You can call the usual numbers, ask him."

Mohammad rose to his feet and went to the window, trying to calm his fears, keep his face emotionless. He must think clearly. Someone was forcing Arafat to take a new position. Someone very powerful. That did not bode well for his own plans.

Faisal broke the silence. "You ask a great deal. I need more information."

Sabrila squirmed. "I cannot—

Faisal turned and faced her. "Then my organization will not help you."

"But . . . but . . . you are—"

"A cautious man. You are not the first to come to me with such stories, pleading for my help. Why should I trust you? How do I know you tell the truth about PLO involvement? My intelligence sources tell me you come fresh from the lair of Abu Ibrahim. It has been a long time since Abu Ibrahim was even on speaking terms with Arafat. How do I know you are not working for Ibrahim himself, a fanatic who wishes only to fire the lagging war on the West Bank in order to keep his own checkbook bulging, but is too much of a coward to enter Israel and do the dirty work himself? How do I know this story of yours is true?"

"As I said, ask Arafat, he—"

"I intend to," Mohammad said, his eyes cold. "I will meet with him personally and discover what this is all about. It will take me two days, then we will meet again."

"But that will take too long. We . . ." Sabrila caught herself.

"Yes?" Mohammad said.

"Nothing. We have something that needs to be done before that time. We will take care of it."

"You intended that I do it, then tell me what it is," Mohammad said forcefully. "Possibly I will reconsider my time frame."

Sabrila took a breath. She had him now, she could feel it. "An American diplomat is to be kidnapped."

Mohammad stifled a short laugh. "In Israel? Why?"

"To send the Americans a message that we want nothing of their interference, and to avenge some of our people the American was responsible for killing and imprisoning."

"Who is to be blamed for this kidnapping?" Mohammad asked.

"West Bank leadership."

Mohammad's face remained impassive only because of years of experience and training, but his stomach churned violently.

He shrugged. "It is foolish. Israel is no place to attempt such a thing, but I wish you Allah's blessing," he lied. "It will be an event upon which I can build a violent movement if I find you are telling the truth. Give me a number at which I can contact you on my return."

Sabrila handed him a piece of paper. "This number is in Italy. It will route you safely through a number of nations and into Israeli territory, to a safe house in Jerusalem with a protected phone. We will wait for your call."

"I will watch the papers to see if your kidnapping is successful . . . and the obituaries to see if you failed."

He stood and went to the door. "I will leave first. In fifteen minutes you follow." He hesitated, then turned to Sabrila. "You have few connections in Israel, your kidnapping attempt may not be successful. Possibly you should wait until my return."

She smiled. "If we have your word you will help us . . ."

"If I find that you are telling the truth you have my word."

"Then we wait."

Mohammad checked the hallway, then disappeared into the darkness.

Pike waited until he knew Mohammad had had enough time to be out of the building. "You're playing games with him, Sabrila. Why do you really need him?" he asked.

"We don't. We only want him out of the way."

Pike smiled. "You intend to carry out a few operations on his turf, I take it."

She returned the smile. "Mohammad has been discovered disobeying orders from the PLO, protecting West Bank militants who want to guide their own destiny instead of following instructions from Arafat and others. We have notified Arafat of Mohammad's betrayal, and when he returns to Tunis he will be shot. We can go ahead with our own plans at our own pace."

"Then you took quite a chance telling him to call Arafat," Pike said.

"Not really. Mohammad has never communicated with Tunis except by courier or in person. He believes telephones and radio transmissions leave an operative vulnerable to capture. I knew he would insist on going personally, and even if he hadn't, Arafat was prepared to request a meeting. By the time Mohammad realizes he has been fooled he will be in Allah's arms."

"Why do you want him out of the way?"

"When my people make their move against Israel it will cause the sacrifice of many Palestinian lives. They want no interference from wishy-washy West Bank leadership. With Faisal gone, we will be rid of Saad Khourani and his West Bank leadership, effectively eliminating opposition to our plan."

"What about Arafat and the PLO?" Pike asked.

Sabrila smiled. "Arafat is old and barely hangs onto control by his fingernails. The people follow him only because he is the only promise of possible freedom. When *we* give them that freedom his control will be gone. They will follow us."

Sabrila walked across the room to the door. ANGEL's information was one hundred percent reliable. Everything was going according to plan.

"Who is going to kidnap the American?" Pike asked as he slipped the black stocking mask over his face.

"I have you, Pike," she smiled.

"Sorry, love, at present rates of pay I'm not interested."

Her eyes lost the glow from the small lamp and she hesitated in the middle of pulling on her own mask.

"I'm not one of your fanatics who do things because they've been conned into thinking a martyr's death sends them flying into the arms of Allah. I have a price and so do the professionals I work with." He looked at her wryly. "And try to remember, Sabrila, kidnapping an American as important as Daniels in a country with the security reputation Israel has is not something you can do over tea. It takes the very best. That's me and my people, dear heart, and we don't work cheap."

She stared, her eyes turning dull and hard in the dim light. "I will see that you are paid."

"Ah, well now, that's a different story. Two and a half million would be a fair figure for the only man who could do better than Mohammad, don't you think?"

"Inflation?"

"Battle pay. What you have in mind will take a good deal of work and money. In Israel, people can't be worked into a frenzy to get them to do a violent act, as they can in Arab nations."

She looked hard at him. "One of these days, Pike, your tongue is going to be snatched from your mouth for such words."

She walked to the lamp and turned it off, then moved to

the window to check the street. "All right, but I will have to clear the amount with my people." She turned and pointed her gun in his direction, getting his immediate attention. "Remember this, Pike, if you quit me . . ." She pulled the trigger twice, the puff-puff sound of the silenced .22 delivering two bullets into the woodwork of the door near Pike's left arm. "I'll kill you."

He smiled. "I am appalled! Alistair Pike! Quit? When money is at stake? My dear girl . . ."

She smiled tightly as she lowered the pistol. Pike was a true mercenary. Money was everything. "Nevertheless, love," she said, "I will kill you if I sense that you think to take our money without doing the proper work."

She crossed the room to the door, allowing her body to relax a little. They were on schedule.

Sabrila opened the door and looked carefully up and down the hallway. No sign of life. She wondered where Mohammad was but dismissed it from her mind while moving catlike down the hall toward the stairs. She didn't care. There was no more need to worry about Mohammad Faisal.

CHAPTER 11

7:00 A.M., Tel Aviv, Israel

Raffi Ben Shami was five feet ten inches tall and had a modestly broad chest, his curly black hair tinted with gray framing a somewhat square face in the midst of which resided a constant smile. He was dressed in jeans and a blue work shirt rolled up at the sleeves. The word *Guide* was written on the pocket under the name of one of Israel's most prestigious travel companies. He carried a small satchel attached to his belt and an attaché case in his left hand. No one could see the silenced Czech M-52 inside. His weapon of choice.

Raffi had participated in every war Israel had fought since he was able to hold a gun. In a leather case hidden high on a closet shelf were four of Israel's highest medals for valor; honors he would never show his children and which his neighbors would never dream he had bled for. One of the small payments for keeping a good cover.

Raffi shook his head, then began rubbing his temples, something he always did when frustrated or deeply stressed. This was not his typical assignment—protecting Americans. Finding terrorist cells on the West Bank and in several neighboring countries was more to his liking. And for them to request only one man! Idiocy! What was to happen if they ran into twenty terrorists? What then, foolish Americans? What of the danger to the one? And to yourselves?

Agh! he thought. Americans! Coming from the safety of your homes to the dangers of Israel! Your ignorance is obvious when you expect it to be the same as in your country.

He picked up the attaché case and went through some papers. Hoshen's second-in-command, David Stein, had been adamant. The Danielses were going to the West Bank. Raffi must take them to holy sites in Samaria and Galilee, and the Americans were allowed to talk to anyone they liked. The hotel reservations for first-night accommodations were booked in Tiberias.

He roughly stuffed the papers back into their spot, dismissing them from his mind. Minister Hoshen knew Raffi didn't like having his hands bound by a set itinerary, especially on the West Bank. Why was he being so pigheaded this time? He shrugged. It didn't matter. He would establish his own itinerary, and they would stay where he felt it was safe. Hoshen might yell and scream; so be it. Raffi hadn't asked for the assignment anyway.

He saw the Daniels couple cross the lobby toward the restaurant. He waited, eyes in motion, alert to the environment and everyone in it. Were there any others who suddenly took note of the couple? Any quick movements, unnatural appearances?

By the time breakfast was over he had pinpointed only one man. British, he thought. Someone who seemed to know the Danielses and had invited himself to join them for breakfast. They seemed on fair terms, possibly old friends.

Daniels was paying for the meal when Raffi noticed the woman step from the elevator, glance about, then join Daniels, his wife, and the Englishman. She was young and looked Arabic. The hair, the olive-colored skin, the face.

But, possibly not. Many Israelis looked Arabic and vice versa. One could not always tell, unless close enough to feel them. Raffi had a talent for smelling Arab hate.

He filed the beautiful features in his brain, then on the film in his finger-sized camera, held unseen in the palm of one hand.

Finally the foursome broke up and the couples went their separate ways, the Danielses returning to their room via the elevator.

Raffi would beat them by fifteen seconds.

Jerry sensed the presence before seeing the man standing in the shadow of a corner of the hotel suite. While pushing Mike behind him, he reached under his jacket for the gun hidden at the small of his back.

"Not necessary, Mr. Daniels," the shadow said as it stepped into the light coming through the patio door. "I'm here at Minister Hoshen's orders."

Jerry noticed the broad smile and relaxed his hand. "How . . ."

"Pass key."

"No, how do we know you're who you say you are?"

Raffi picked up the phone. "Call the number the minister gave you for emergencies. Give them these numbers." He jotted them on a note pad. "That will verify who I am."

Jerry did.

"Mrs. Daniels, where would you like to go first today? Caesarea, Galilee, or Jerusalem possibly? Although I recommend Jerusalem for last. The frosting on the cake." His obvious confidence immediately put Mike at ease.

Jerry hung up the phone, handing the pad back to Raffi.

"All clear?" smiled Raffi, taking the pad and putting it in his pocket.

"Seems so. Sounds like you're about to guide a couple of novices through Israel." Jerry smiled, warmed by the man's personable way.

"You want to see the tourist Israel or Israel as I know it?"

Mike looked at Jerry, then spoke. "Jerry has been here before and has had the tourist edition. Just be honest with us, Mr. Shami, and show us what is important to you along with what you would perceive as being important to a couple of Christians here to see the Holy Land. That should cover it."

"Your wish is my command." He brushed past them, heading toward the door. "Grab your camera, folks, your lip salve, your passports—just in case—a money belt full of cash, and let's see Israel!" He opened the door and motioned for them to go ahead.

Raffi heard the door shut quietly as he passed it. He took note of the room number and planned to check it later, but somehow he knew who it belonged to. The British man, the Arab woman. Trouble.

They boarded the elevator. "Make any new friends since arriving?" he asked casually.

Mike answered, "A couple from England."

"The ones I saw with you at breakfast?"

"Yes, but they—"

"Not to be alarmed, Mrs. Dan . . . uh . . . Stuart. I do my job. In Israel strangers can either be what they say or . . ." He shrugged.

"Dangerous." Jerry finished, impressed.

"Yes."

"I took a picture of them both when the four of you were in the lobby," Raffi said. "We'll see what we can find out. At least to put your mind at ease. I will only have to make a moment's stop to deliver the film." The elevator door swung open. "Not to worry. If they are up to no good, they will not follow us. I know too much about this country that they don't. Besides, we will not return to this hotel. I will have your things packed and sent ahead to the new one, a special place you will like, I think." He smiled broadly, leading them to the doors and a Volvo sedan parked beyond.

CHAPTER 12

10:00 P.M., Duma, Syria

Badannah's world was unraveling. His radio message to ANGEL had been concise and authoritative, placing the blame directly on the shoulders of Sergeant Maymuna and his men conducting the search. He had pointed out that his move to eliminate the construction workers had forced the Israeli spy's hand, but that another's incompetence had allowed them success, causing the death of a number of Syrian troops. He had waited for the return message but was shocked when he deciphered the code, discovering that Ahmoud Hassan was coming to the factory. Tonight.

He looked at his watch.

Ahmoud Hassan was a terrorist well known for his cruelty. Even Fami Badannah had been sickened by his butchery of innocent people. He was the second cousin of Abu Hassan, the now-dead Palestinian who was purported to be of the House of Hassan, a tribe who claimed royal lineage back to Mohammed and the right to rule Palestine. It was rumored in the Arab world that they had their sights set on much more.

But violent men, even deluded ones, had to be treated with the proper respect. He was a killer, if nothing else. A killer working for an even worse butcher, Abu Ibrahim.

Badannah pushed the button on his intercom and spoke harshly to the guard at the gate. "Call me the moment his car comes. Understood? The moment!"

As he slammed the receiver back in place he went over his explanations again. When Ahmoud asked how he was going to explain the soldiers' bodies, Badannah's prepared response was that he would bury them in the desert near the scene of the battle, something he had already paid several trusted men to do. He could keep their deaths hidden for as long as a month before General Command would need an explanation of their whereabouts.

In response to a question about survivors and wounded, he would say that the wounded had been treated in the field and sent to their homes for recuperation after being told to keep their mouths shut as the alternative to joining their brothers in the desert sand of Sahles Sahra.

He also held one other juicy morsel with which to placate Hassan. The Israelis' new flying toy. No one had ever seen it before, and Ahmoud knew the value of such information in the Arab world. Information that, if verified, would bring a healthy price to those who had it.

The phone rang. He quickly picked it up and listened, then lowered it back in place, standing and straightening his uniform. His mouth was dry and he needed a drink. He reached for the small flask in his desk drawer, then thought better of it. Ahmoud would not like the smell of whiskey on his breath.

His mind was confused, his stomach upset. Why a visit from ANGEL's assassin? Surely they knew the Israelis would not attack now, not with their plans revealed. And if they did, his people were ready, Ahmoud knew that. Badannah had put the entire garrison on full alert, and, by padding the right pockets with American dollars, this very morning they would receive Exocet missiles and men who knew how to fire them.

His brow broke out in a sudden sweat. Had President Assad found out what was going on, and was ANGEL-Ibrahim covering his tracks by eliminating those he felt were a threat to his operation?

He walked to the window and watched the black limousine move slowly toward the headquarters building. If Assad knew of their deception, Ibrahim would need a sacrificial goat. Was that why Ahmoud . . .

No! Assad didn't know. Otherwise Badannah knew he would have been relieved of duty and put in front of a firing squad. Ahmoud would not be dispatched. Assad would pull the trigger himself.

The door swung open and two men entered, AK-47 automatics at the ready. Hassan followed them.

The blue-and-white checked kafeyeh of Abu Ahmoud sat atop a short, five-foot-eight-inch solid frame. Badannah had always been awed in the man's presence but he often wondered why. His physical form was not imposing. Weathered, acne-pocked skin, a scrubby beard, and an unkempt moustache that sat in a round face which gave him a paunchy rather than stern look. The eyes, cold black, disturbed Badannah enough that he seldom looked into them. Possibly that was it, but most likely it was the cold and ruthless mind that sat behind them. The man would kill his own mother if he thought her death would do him good.

Badannah saluted, then gave a quick bow. "Allah be praised for your visit to our humble quarters, Ahmoud Hassan."

Ahmoud looked at the colonel with cold eyes, then gestured to one of his men to close the door as he sat in the padded, straight-backed chair across the desk from Badannah.

"Sit, Colonel," Hassan gestured, then he leaned forward. "I will not waste time hearing your senseless excuses for failure. I know you have already rehearsed them many times. They would only make us both uncomfortable, and we are willing to forget what has happened for now, so quit sweating like an over-worked mule." The smile was with the lips alone, his eyes remained without light, cold and empty.

"Thank you. I will see that those who have failed are properly disciplined."

"Very well, but that is not why I am here. Although you say you are prepared for the Israelis, we will take no chances. Even though we have fed the paranoid President Assad information that the Israelis are planning an attack on his southern border and he has put his forces on full alert, a strike by the Israelis is still a possibility."

Badannah sat straight, the dreams of the riches his success would bring suddenly in jeopardy.

"But I assure you—"

Ahmoud Hassan waved his hand in dismissal. "You are still in charge, Fami." He tossed an envelope across the table. "At this point we have no other choice. But if you fail us again"—his face turned to granite and he spoke through lips drawn tightly across his teeth—"I will personally cut out your heart and feed it to the dogs."

Ahmoud sat back in the chair, letting his words sink in, then leaned forward and spoke again.

"As you have probably figured out by now, we have an agent inside Israel who is keeping us informed of what the enemy of Allah knows about this project. *You*, Fami, can thank Allah that he is where he is, because *he* will save this operation despite the damage you have done, and despite the fact that you have endangered him by forcing us to communicate with him more than we ever intended!"

Badannah took a deep gulp of air, the sweat beginning to push harder through his pores.

"I . . . I praise Allah for his benevolence, Abu Ahmoud, but—"

The hand raised in dismissal again. "Listen, Fami, and be thankful. Because of his diligence we know that the Israelis do not presently know or understand our real intentions. However, they may move their timetable ahead because they are quite concerned that we might move our factory. At present they are waiting to see what we will do. And what *we will* do, Fami, is contained in that envelope, in detail. You must see that it is carried out exactly, do you understand?"

"Yes, I understand! I will do it, exactly," Badannah said with vigor. "Exactly!" He silently thanked Allah for his renewed lease on life—and riches.

"Through our sources in Damascus we have made arrangements for everything you will need and explanations for what you are doing. No one need know the truth, and you are to share only the appropriate orders"—he smiled— "signed by General Command, with those under you, and on whom you must rely. Are they all dedicated to you?"

"Yes, and to Allah."

"Good." He stood, then turned back, came to the desk, and placed his hands upon it, leaning forward. "Fami, the future of the Arab world relies on our success. Do not fail us!"

As Badannah looked into the cold eyes the words were like a slashing sword. His hand slipped to his chest, covering his heart, and he leaned involuntarily back, away from what he knew could be his angel of death.

"I . . . I will not fail!"

Ahmoud let an evil grin cross his face and he patted Badannah's cheek as if he were a child who needed a spanking, but whose parent had decided to be lenient. "ANGEL will be pleased. You are a good soldier, Fami. I know you will keep your word. But if you don't . . ." He reached over and jabbed his stubby finger into Badannah's chest, then turned quickly and left the room, his two bodyguards following and closing the door.

Badannah opened the drawer and took the flask, unscrewed the lid, and guzzled, the hot liquid hitting his stomach like a sledgehammer, then pounding through his frazzled nerves, deadening the anxiety he felt.

He looked at the envelope, realizing that if they had had more time he would be a dead man, replaced by another as if he had never existed. Now everything hinged on how well he did what was contained in a few pages of his "new orders." Ibrahim was a butcher, and if he, Badannah, were ANGEL, he would have Ahmoud kill him without so much as a second thought. Fami Badannah could afford no more mistakes.

After another quick jolt of the whiskey he removed his letter opener from the desk and ran it along the top edge of the envelope. Reaching inside, he removed the pages, laid the several sheets on the desk before him, and began going through them.

First there were the orders from command in Damascus, all probably falsified but with the appropriate signatures. Then another envelope, smaller and sealed. He laid these aside and began reading the detailed instructions.

Half an hour later, after three readings, he laid the instructions aside and picked up the smaller sealed brown envelope, turning it over in his hands. According to the instructions, it contained the final coordinates for delivery of the warheads but wasn't to be opened until ANGEL notified him. Until then he must keep it on his person or in one of his safes.

Badannah felt the adrenaline-induced sweat dampen his flesh. Within forty-eight hours ANGEL would give the order leading to missile deployment. In forty-eight hours the balance of power would change dramatically and Israel would no longer hold the Arab world at bay. The Holy City would be Islamic again. And forever.

He had his instructions, and, although difficult, they were not impossible. He could see the need for the orders, and he and his men would accomplish them without delay. To the smallest detail.

He smiled. The Israelis would never recover in time. And his life—maybe it was worth something again.

His dream lifted from the dust of Ahmoud's indelicate departure. More confident now, he picked up the phone. Much needed to be done before the sun rose. Supplies and trucks must be ordered and on their way from General Command in Damascus. They didn't have much time.

A staff meeting was in order.

Sergeant Khalis sat slumped in his chair, tired and afraid. More and more he didn't like what he was doing.

He leaned forward, placing his forehead on top of his hands on the desk, his mind struggling for options, praying to Allah that what he had seen that morning was not real.

He had no problem with killing the enemy when they threatened the existence of his country and fellow brothers of Islam, but the slaughter of innocent women and children . . .

He now knew that the factory was developing a new

warhead, one which could carry either a chemical or a nuclear payload. An hour earlier he had made up an excuse to go into the factory to review security and had been alone in the two Germans' laboratory and large work area for a brief inspection. He was shocked to find twenty-four chemical warheads completed and prepared for mounting on the new SCUD missile. Five would be mounted on the SCUDs sitting aboard launchers. They already had received two of the trucks and were expecting three more shortly. Nineteen were boxed and crated, prepared for direct delivery to missile sites, where they also would be armed and mounted aboard the Al Abbas SCUD.

Khalis had seen the pictures of the dead Kurds whom Iraq's Hussein had gassed. Bloated, disfigured. Old, young. Chemical gas was an indiscriminate murderer. Aboard the new SCUD, with its improved guidance system, they would land within feet of their intended targets in the population centers of Israel.

In the rear of the large laboratory he found something that took his breath away. A centrifuge. A machine used to enrich uranium by separating gaseous isotopes by passing them through a high-speed rotating cylinder. Did Badannah have enriched uranium already produced, ready to be used in making a nuclear bomb?

After closer inspection of the area he found his answer: a dismantled implosion-type bomb prepared to receive its central sphere of plutonium, neutron initiator, explosive, and tritium deuterium booster. The scientists were only waiting for the centrifuge to provide enough uranium 235 to give them the desired nuclear capability. After that, nothing remained but to put the bomb back together and mount it on the head of another Al Abbas SCUD for a ride across the skies to its bloody end.

Khalis opened his desk and began throwing his belongings into a box, a cold chill shaking him from head to foot. He knew what was happening but was powerless to stop it. If President Assad wanted such weapons, Khalis must follow and do his duty for Syria. But was it Assad?

Since the battle at Sahles, Badannah had taken total charge of every aspect of the factory except defense of its perimeter. He gave frantic orders at first, burying the dead and destroying evidence of the battle—then threatened all of them with imprisonment if they didn't keep quiet, forcefully claiming his orders were directly from Assad. Khalis wondered but was afraid. He knew what Badannah would do if Khalis went over his head or began questioning his authority, and he hesitated, trying to believe his commanding officer. After all, he had seen stranger things instigated at the hands of Syria's president.

Then the visitors had come in their limousine, followed by Badannah's calling a meeting in which he notified staff members of orders from Damascus, even showing them the signed papers. Knowing what was inside the plant, Khalis knew immediately why the orders were given. If the Israelis knew . . .

The orders *were* from Damascus. Khalis must obey.

He flopped himself back in the chair, running his hand through his hair. Never mind! Don't think, just do your duty. Check on your men. Outline everything for them. Go home. Take a hot shower . . . and drink yourself into oblivion.

He caught himself wondering how the Israelis were treating his cousin and family. He had heard that the Jews gave defectors a comfortable monthly wage, land, a home . . . but he had also heard that they imprisoned them, starving them to death. He knew his own government used such tactics; why not the Israelis? The thought was discomforting. Had he pushed his cousin into an even worse existence?

He shook his head, dislodging the thought. No, he preferred to think the other. He picked up the phone and gave his aide orders to bring around his armored vehicle, the one luxury he was given as director of the factory's security.

The light, fast vehicle was patterned after the Americans' Bradley fighting machine but had heavily protected wheels instead of tracks, allowing it a high degree of speed. In the back, where troops were usually housed, this one had a communications system and comfortable chairs for four. It was protected by two missile pods that fired armor-piercing, supersonic missiles similar to the American Hellfire, and by its 25mm cannon, mounted on a turret in its top.

Ordinarily the commander of an operation such as the one at the factory would use the vehicle, but Badannah preferred to ride in the luxury of the chauffeur-driven American Lincoln provided by command. At least, that is who he said had provided it, and he had given the armored vehicle to Khalis.

He went to the window and looked at the factory in the

moonlight. Quiet, gray with dark rust spots streaking down its metal sides, the building hardly looked as if it housed anything of any consequence, let alone instant death for thousands, even millions.

He shuddered. What was in the minds of leaders who wanted only to brutalize and murder innocent people with such weapons? How could they justify such an action to themselves . . . and to their own wives and children? Didn't they realize that Israel, already in control of such nuclear firepower, would shoot back?

He shook his head again, picked up his hat, and went for the door. He *must* get his mind on something else. Check the troops, he told himself. Do your duty.

And prepare to watch thousands die!

Day Five

CHAPTER 13

3:00 A.M., *In the air over Tunis*

At such an early hour Tunis Airport experienced little traffic, and the small private plane was told to land on runway three without delay. The pilot moved the Cessna into position, then shook the man next to him; a passenger whose identity he didn't know and didn't care to know. Trips into the Sinai Desert below Israeli radar detection level were dangerous enough without having to worry about a paranoid terrorist thinking someone as insignificant as a pilot knew his face too well. People had gotten their throats slit for less.

As he taxied the plane toward the tarmac his passenger became tense, watching through the darkness, ready. For what?

The pilot saw the movement out of the corner of one eye

and looked that way. A black limousine was speeding in their direction. Before he could register what was happening, the Arab passenger placed a pistol to his head and spoke.

"Get this plane off the ground within the next thirty seconds or we're both dead."

The pilot hesitated, then saw four other vehicles racing to cut them off from the runway. He throttled the engine and the propeller caught hold, moving them quickly down the pavement, gathering speed. He heard the irate chatter in his earphones and swore while flinging them aside. He had enough problems without some babbling idiot trying to stop them with threatening words. He didn't hear the guns being fired, only the rip of metal as they tore small holes in the plane's skin and plinked against the propeller.

The plane was near speed for liftoff when he saw two problems, a car blocking their way and a large plane just landing. He swerved to miss the car, his small plane's tires bumping across the grass and terrain between runways, then swerved again, bouncing it back onto pavement, more bullets ripping holes in the Cessna's soft skin. As he pulled back on the wheel he felt a burning sensation in his neck, and his vision quickly blurred. He jammed the throttle and yanked hard left on the wheel, his small plane being pummeled by the turbulent air created by the landing thrust of the Egyptian Airlines DC-10. For a moment he thought he would lose control, the plane dancing wildly, trying to keep aloft. Then it leveled out, skipping within feet of a five-story-tall hangar on the edge of the field.

He felt the blood rolling down his back, the sudden loss of strength in his arms warning him of impending unconsciousness. "I'm hit! Take the wheel!"

"What!" Mohammad Faisal looked at the swaying pilot, then dropped his pistol on the floor and grabbed the wheel in front of him as the pilot's head hit the far window. He felt the plane's drop and frantically pulled back on the wheel, bringing up the nose as the Cessna dipped dangerously close to small buildings. The plane came up and headed left, the powerful engine pulling them into the darkness and away from the airport.

Mohammad's arms and muscles were taut with fear, his panicky mind confused by the darkness. He tried to get his bearings by looking down at the city streets, his eyes scanning for the deeper black of the waters of the Mediterranean sea he knew lay just west of the airport. Was he high enough? Were there obstructions? Did Arafat have the ability to send an aircraft to intercept them? A missile to blow them out of the sky?

His eyes darted from instrument to instrument looking for something familiar, anything that would show him where he was and where he was going.

In the center of the panel he saw the small screen that he knew pilots called a situation display. It showed a loss of altitude he must quickly rectify or they would crash into unfriendly earth. He moved the wheel accordingly and watched the readout change for the better, helping his contracted chest muscles relax a little so he could breathe again.

After a moment of flying in the darkness, eyes still scanning the instrument panel and screen, he knew his chances of getting safely back to solid ground without the pilot were about one in a hundred. He reached over and shook the unconscious body. His hand was repulsed as it touched the sticky ooze of blood. Mohammad's eyes darted between the lifeless form, the instrument panel, and the dark sky while he forced his free hand to slip through the ooze, searching for the wound. He found a jagged hole in the pilot's lower neck pumping blood in spurts down the man's back and onto the seat. With his blood-covered hand he ripped away a piece of his own shirt, pushing the cloth against the hole in a futile attempt to shut off the flow.

The pilot remained unconscious, forcing Mohammad to take several deep breaths, sweat gathering and dripping quickly down his forehead and into his eyes. He must think.

The compass! His eyes found it on the panel. It read northwest. "That means we're headed across the Mediterranean toward Europe." He looked out of the side window and below the plane. Nothing but pitch-black darkness. They must be over water.

But it wasn't the way home. He turned the wheel gently to the right, watching the compass needle slowly change until he was headed northeast. "That will keep us near land," he said aloud, grateful for the sound of his own voice. "Or where land is supposed to be."

His heart began settling down, his mind clearing a little, allowing him a more critical look at the instruments. The one that read fuel concerned him. The pilot had intended to refuel in Tunis, then at a "private" field in the deserts of

Egypt. A place unknown to Mohammad. A place at which he would never arrive even if he did know where it was—the fuel would be gone first.

He saw the altimeter—5000 feet. Only ocean underneath him. No obstacles that high to concern him or end his journey prematurely. Only lack of fuel would do that.

He thought it through—alone, he was finished. He needed the pilot.

He took a deep breath and flipped the switch marked "auto pilot." The plane's computer took control, leaving Mohammad free to take a closer look at the unconscious man beside him.

He checked for and found a pulse, then looked for the first aid kit he knew must exist. He felt under the seat and found it, unlatched it from its secure position, and opened it. He wrapped a bandage around the wound, stopping the flow of blood, then took a capsule of smelling salts in hand and snapped it in two, placing it under the pilot's nose. The Israeli's head jerked, his eyes fluttered, then opened.

"What . . ." he moaned. "Where are we?"

"You are the pilot," said Mohammad.

The pilot struggled to sit up, trying to remain conscious through the haze of shock, pain, and loss of blood. He blinked away the blur and found the instrument he wanted.

"Five miles from the coast." His eyes scanned the instruments. "And about enough gas to get us to . . . Tripoli, Lybia." He gasped with pain, gritting his teeth. "Got any friends in Tripoli? Hopefully better friends than the ones you went to see in Tunis."

"None. Will they let us land?"

"You bet, but we'd better plan on staying a while and eating prison food. They don't like Israelis, even mercenary ones like me." He smiled. "Without money to buy our gas, and our freedom . . ." The pilot thought a moment, his head propped against the seat and windows.

"Catania, Sicily. We can make that," he said.

Sicily. Politically neutral, at least in most things. Yes, it might be a chance. Mohammad nodded agreement.

"Okay, you'll have to fly. I'm too weak, and my left arm seems paralyzed." He forced a weak smile. "Probably something I ate.

"Let off the auto pilot and turn left. Do exactly as I tell you."

Mohammad followed the instructions and watched the instruments, making sure he didn't fly the craft into the ground. After a few moments they were headed west and a little north. The pilot laid his head against the window and closed his eyes. Mohammad noticed the cloth was full of blood again and wondered if the man would make it far enough to show him the finer points of a safe landing.

He pushed the thought aside and replaced it with another. Sabrila had set him up. Someone knew what he had been up to in Palestine and had used the information to get him out of the way. The *who* was obvious. Ibrahim and those for whom he must be working.

The *why* was a little more difficult, and something he'd need time to work out. If he survived this, he'd keep a low profile until he knew what was going on.

He felt the plane hesitate, then again. The pilot's head jerked up, his eyes focusing on the fuel gauge.

"We're losing gas. They must have shot a hole in the tank. We'll never make it to the coast. You know how to swim?" asked the pilot.

"No, I am from the desert, remember. I—"

"Life jacket-parachute's behind the seat, and a small life raft. Get them ready." The Israeli took the mike from its hanger and began broadcasting the Mayday, giving coordinates.

The plane flew on for another fifteen minutes. Mohammad had strapped a parachute on the pilot and one on himself and had prepared the life raft to be dragged out of the door when he was forced to leave. He couldn't remember ever feeling such fear. He had never minded the thought of dying for Palestine at the sting of an Israeli bullet, but the idea of drowning or dying as shark bait made him want to throw up.

The engine sputtered.

"Pull the cord on your chute after the count of two, no longer," the pilot said. "We are only a few thousand feet up. You will hit the water in a hurry. Move it! Go on, move it!" he said again as he saw the reluctance on Mohammad's face.

Faisal shoved the door open as the engine sputtered again, then looked back at the pilot. "You also . . ."

"I'll be there! Get!"

Mohammad closed his eyes as he took a firm grip on the packaged life raft and went through the door, the sudden feeling of free fall and cold air taking his breath away and shoving his stomach into his throat. He pulled the cord and felt it unfold then hit, the impact nearly jerking the raft from his vise-like grip. His body swayed like a pendulum, and he wondered how long . . .

His body hit the water with a thud, the pain of it shooting from his feet to his brain, where it joined the fear created by the water around him. He panicked, grabbing at the straps of the chute and forgetting to pull the cord that inflated the life jacket. He felt his body being pulled into the black depths, his lungs gasping for air but filling with water. His flailing hand caught on something and jerked it free. He felt an upward sensation as the life jacket inflated, lifting him until his head sprang through the waves, his mouth spewing forth the salt water while violently trying to force air past it to his lungs.

He bobbed twice, then felt himself start to sink again and knew he must get free of the ropes and the chute before they dragged him back under. He grabbed at the straps and forced his fingers to pry them loose, releasing his would-be death trap and allowing him more buoyancy.

His mind began to calm and at the same time he began to feel the cold. He looked around for the life raft that was supposed to unfold and inflate upon impact but couldn't see it in the darkness. He wondered what had happened to the pilot. They both had known he would never free himself from the plane in time. Both had known that trying to save him would have meant death for both of them. The Israeli had been a brave man. Mohammad wondered how long it had taken him to die.

He saw the light of dawn on the far horizon, casting a dim shadow across the waves as they surrounded him. He felt something bump against his head and jerked around, afraid it might be sharks, only to find the raft. He crawled into it, exhausted, letting himself lie in its bottom, catching his breath.

A half hour passed before he could force his body to kneel and search the endless sea in all directions. Looking for the wreckage, the pilot, possibly . . .

Nothing.

He watched for a long time before tumbling back into the bottom of the small rubber island, shivering, overcome by a body that cried for relief only unconsciousness would bring.

He would be free of this. It would end. He would return to Israel. Somehow, someone must pay for this betrayal.

Only a few knew what he had been doing since returning to the West Bank, of his protecting his people from the PLO, their worst enemy.

Back when he discovered that he wanted to be free of Arafat, he also had known he could never leave the PLO, at least not alive. He was privy to the machinations of the inner circle, their murderous methods and self-aggrandizing robbery. His leaving would be considered a threat to them and the deception they practiced to remain in power. They could not afford to let him or anyone who rejected their leadership live.

So, he used the system. When West Bank Palestinians began to see for themselves that the PLO no longer had their best interests at heart, and began taking their destiny into their own hands, factions within the PLO determined that they had need to send several insiders back to reassert control. Although Arafat had disagreed, he had little control and finally assented, as long as one of his most trusted men was sent as well. Of the inner circle, Mohammad was one of a very few whose identity was not actually known to the Israelis. They knew his name, but they had no knowledge of the face that went with it. He used that fact and this opportunity to free himself from close proximity to the men he now hated most. Within days he had returned to the West Bank and his people as Arafat's special liaison—a handsome term for "enforcer."

Because of his position, Mohammad was trusted, so Arafat allowed him to select men he wanted to go with him. Of course, other factions also sent "teams," each assigned certain responsibilities and assassinations as lessons to West Bank leadership, but the teams did not deal with one another.

Upon his return to Nabulus on the West Bank, Mohammad went directly to leadership, honored members of the Nabulus community, and told them everything he knew of PLO intentions. They immediately believed him and spread the word, saving many lives, although for some it was too late.

It was then that his new life had begun. He made a secret alliance with West Bank leadership, promising to protect them from the PLO and again work for peace, this time without murder.

Now, five years later, Mohammad was still a double agent.

Considered by the PLO as their man on the West Bank, he was given orders to control and kill in order to keep PLO authority strong. Instead, when they ordered a murder, the individual would simply disappear and be given a new identity while word was funneled back to Tunis, and through the media, that the person had been killed by some unknown party. He learned to play the game, and he taught others how to play as well. West Bank leadership learned to deal with Arafat, making him believe they were in total support of him, seemingly accepting his guidance and instructions. Then, through means of their own, they worked for peace within Palestine and Israel. Mohammad was their protection. Slowly Mohammad Faisal's self-respect had returned.

Now his secret life was a secret no longer.

He bit his lip as he kneeled again and scanned the Mediterranean's bleak, endless waves. By the time he was found it would be too late. The American that Sabrila Hassan was after would live only hours.

CHAPTER 14

9:00 A.M., Tiberias on the Galilee

Lev Zafit watched from his private balcony, checking, making sure. Yes, it was them. He walked quickly inside his office and picked up the phone, calling his contact.

Who wanted these people was of no concern to Lev, but it did pique his curiosity that the interest was so intense.

The conversation was brief. His instructions were simple: follow and do not lose them; then, when they were close to Jerusalem, call a number he had been given, using a specific code name.

Lev Zafit was a Jew, but a Jew of a different color. As a young man he did not agree with the Zionist theory of occupation. But, knowing his future would be grim if his views were known, Lev kept his opinions to himself, hiding them from his parents, friends, and neighbors, and later his wife and children.

When it came time to serve in the IDF, Lev had been lucky. A minor birth defect of his heart gave him time without combat, then early release. He returned to college, got married, and was given a job at the Tiberias Hotel he now managed.

Over the years, Lev met with small groups who felt as he did, mostly Jewish intellectuals at first, then with more fanatic Jews and Arabs who considered themselves a resistance force. They had gone on a number of "night raids." Simple things—graffiti, slashed tires on military and police vehicles, simple theft of government property.

In June of 1980 Lev took an extended business trip to Europe to be given further training for managing one of Israel's largest hotels on the shores of the Galilee. While in France he arranged to meet with a member of the PLO's leadership, just to talk, and to listen to their story and their recruitment pitch.

Lev shook his head. It had all been a lark; an egotistical, rebellious lark! One that had trapped him into a lifetime of betrayal and personal self-hate!

He had been a part of the Arab underground for more than ten years now, and responsible for providing valuable information to groups such as the FRC, Abu Ibrahim's revolutionary group, who raided Jewish settlements along the Galilee based on what he told them.

The death of other Jews in these raids had given him sleepless nights, but rationalization fringed with fear of consequence had helped him shove it aside, not to mention the rather healthy amounts of money he received for his work. He could practically retire a wealthy man now, at the relatively young age of thirty-four. But he had often asked himself, retire to what? And where? In Lebanon, or possibly Damascus? And with whom? His wife and children . . . He shuddered at the thought.

He went to his small office and called in the assistant manager, giving him several instructions, telling him that he was going to Jerusalem for several days on business.

As he threw his bag in the back of his small sports car he saw the couple and their guide leave the lobby and move to the Volvo. He slipped into the leather seat and followed. This would be his last, he thought, as he looked at his wife standing in the window, watching. Somehow he would make his contact understand that he could do it no longer. Somehow he would free himself from the hold that was strangling the life out of his very existence.

He slammed the gearshift into second, allowing only a large truck to separate him from his quarry. Lev Zafit was a trapped man.

10:00 A.M., Jerusalem

The Englishman hung up the car phone, then spoke to Sabrila. "I have another dozen little surprises for the Israeli occupation forces, dearest." He lit a cigarette. "And the Czech, Zalinka, thinks he can convince Mohammad's second-in-command, Nabril Al Razd, to help set the trap you want for Minister Hoshen. Once Mohammad's death is verified, of course, and for the right price."

"Al Razd will convince Saad Khourani to ask Minister Hoshen for a meeting?" Sabrila asked.

Pike nodded. Zalinka was going to make it look as if the West Bank leader had trapped Hoshen and that both of them were killed in the ensuing gun battle. "Relax, Sabrila. It's being done. Do you have the rifle Zalinka requested?"

"Yes, it is in the trunk of a small American car in the parking garage of safe house 11. It is the very best, and has both regular and infrared scopes. In the hands of a man with Zalinka's talents it can kill at six hundred yards." She handed him a set of car keys. "You are going to make a very nice replacement for Mohammad. You may even get me to think you are worth the exorbitant amount of money you require."

"Of that, you can be sure. By the way, I checked my Swiss account this morning. Thank you for being so prompt with the first half of my fee."

He paused. "Have you heard anything more about Faisal?"

"He has disappeared into the depths of the Mediter-ranean. The plane left radar shortly after it turned toward Sicily."

"I'll let Zalinka know. Everyone else is happy?" Pike asked.

"Everyone. Have you followed the instructions from ANGEL? About the Americans?"

"I'm working on that. It's apparent that your leader went to a lot of trouble in getting the Danielses here. We wouldn't want them to go home without a proper party in their honor."

"Then I will make arrangements for the news release."

"You're sure they spent the night at the hotel in Galilee?"

"It is your turn to relax, Pike," she smiled tightly. "I am sure. Although they did not stay at the hotel we were originally told, another agent found them. ANGEL gave me the information only an hour ago."

"We will know when they arrive in Jerusalem and where?" he smiled.

"Yes."

"How are you getting this information?" Pike asked.

She looked at him quickly. "It is not necessary for you to know this. Why do you ask?"

"Relax, Sabrila, I'm not an agent trying to pry some kind of incriminating information from you. I just get concerned about sources I have no knowledge of. I don't trust them."

"This source is impeccable, Pike. Believe it."

Pike shrugged obedience and Sabrila breathed deeply, putting her head against the back of the seat.

"Why Daniels?" Pike asked.

She shrugged. "He is American, a member of the peace team. His father-in-law is a U.S. senator. His humiliation will be felt by many in important places. Beyond that, I don't attempt to read ANGEL's mind, nor do I ask questions that do not concern my ability to do as I am asked."

She downshifted as they came to an intersection and stop sign. They passed through Abu Gosh. At one time her grandparents, her brothers, and their families had lived on an estate only a few miles from the town, farming and raising hundreds of olive trees. Her grandfather had been an important man. There even had been talk of making him leader of a nation that would be formed to keep the country from being split. It was his right because he was the leader of the House of Hassan, and all Arab Palestinians paid allegiance to him at the time.

But not now, not anymore.

Sweat began to bead on her forehead, the memory causing a sharp pain at the base of her skull. Soon it would be hers again. ANGEL's promise to her. Payment for Sabrila's family's humiliation, and their deaths.

Her face muscles tightened. Because of the Jews she had

no family. No one except ANGEL and INFERNO. Her grand-parents had died broken people in Jordan. Her father and brother had given their lives fighting Jews as members of the Palestinian Liberation Army. Her mother had died of a broken heart.

Sabrila had never forgotten. Would never forget. She would have her revenge on Israel. She would have her heritage back.

Soon.

CHAPTER 15

11:00 A.M., Jerusalem

When the knock came at the door, Macklin was guzzling orange juice directly from the carton, his wet hair dripping down his neck, a towel held tightly around his waist.

He opened it a crack, shocked at finding Ruth Levona. "Uh, Colonel, I'm, uh . . . a little unprepared for a formal visit this morning . . ."

"Get dressed, Colonel," she said, smiling. "I'll wait in the living room. We have to talk." She started to push on the door, forcing him into a rapid retreat down the hall and to the bedroom.

He dressed quickly. When he had returned to the Aman yesterday—after a complete fourteen hours of much-needed sleep—he found that the Syrians had said nothing about the raid into their territory, although Assad had put his air force on full alert. Intelligence analysts felt that it was sure proof Assad was behind the manufacture of the warheads at the factory, and everyone else had agreed. Macklin didn't think so, but it didn't matter. The target remained the same, regardless of who was behind it.

After that, things had more or less come to a standstill. The informant and his family were still in the hospital recuperating from being scared half out of their wits. The man wouldn't be ready to talk to them until today. The end of the day came when David Stein showed up and had a discussion with Ativa. The rest of them sat around the outer office tensely awaiting the results. After Stein left, Ativa broke the ice by telling them all to report early to continue their planning of the Duma project. It was still on.

Then Ativa had grabbed Macklin by the arm and had taken him over to Levona, telling them to clear up their differences or he'd personally have them drowned in the Mediterranean.

They had gone to dinner.

Macklin grabbed his shoes and socks and went down the hallway. Ruth was on the patio. He plopped himself in one of the chairs and started with the socks. "What's up?"

They had ironed out their differences, making their apologies, each promising to let the other do his or her job. But Macklin had come away somewhat unconvinced. Ruth Levona was a strong-willed woman with an agenda. A very private agenda.

"I wasn't up-front with you last night." She turned and faced him as he leaned back in the chair, his second sock still in his hand. "I want Badannah. He was the one responsible for my parents' deaths. He led the raid on Nahariyya."

Macklin forced himself not to look shocked. "You sure?"

"He bragged about it over Lebanon radio for months. He was young then, a new leader in the Palestinian resistance. He became Syrian later, when it was advantageous to join Assad's new government."

His first reaction was to tell her she was endangering the lives of the entire team. Feelings like that couldn't do anything but cloud her decision. He didn't say it.

"The decision to save Imad was the right one, I believe that. But my presence on that chopper was because I wanted to be in on Badannah's humiliation, and if possible, his death."

The chill in her voice gave Macklin goose bumps. "Why are you telling me this? Shouldn't Ativa—"

"Ativa knows. He trusts that I can control my personal feelings. I . . . I'm not so sure anymore. I need your help."

"My help? How . . . ?"

"I must remain a part of this team but I can't let my personal hate cloud future decisions. You can't let me."

Tom could see the fear in her eyes. Fear of losing control. He stood and took her in his arms for the second time. The first had been at her apartment door the night before. She had felt good then. Warm and soft, as she felt now. Their kiss had melted him like putty.

Ruth pulled him tight. "Last night . . . in your arms . . . I realized how much I need you, Thomas Macklin. I'm tired of fighting shadows alone." Ruth leaned into him, locking her fingers behind his neck. Tom pressed his hand on her back and her lips to his, sending a tingle clear to his toes. As their lips slowly parted, their bodies remaining close, Ruth placed her head firmly against his shoulder.

To Tom her plea was a simple one to fulfill. Any assault on the complex at Duma would be his to manage. She would simply stay out of it, even if he had to tie her to a chair or lock her up in the local jail. He would do it. He loved her too much to do otherwise.

Macklin couldn't see how deeply rooted her hate had become. After all, love *is* blind.

1:00 P.M., Tel Aviv, Israel

General Chaim Ativa was a stocky, powerfully built man. His black hair, streaked with gray in front and lightly around the ears, was attached to a tanned face. As he stepped into the elevator he took a handkerchief from his pocket and handed it to Macklin.

"Colonel Levona's lipstick looks good on you, Colonel Macklin." He punched a button. "But not nearly as good as it does on her."

Macklin handed the hanky to Ruth. "Please."

She smiled, the scarlet blush giving her face and neck a sunburned look.

"Glad you two could finally show up." Ativa went on. "And friends, too. Come with me to the intelligence section. Your informant has just given us some information I think you should look at, Colonel Macklin."

Ativa reminded Macklin of a retired boxer. His nose lay flat against his face, giving the appearance of having no bone from bridge to tip. His eyes were black slits in muscled flesh. His shoulders were shoved up against his head, making it appear as if he had no neck. Macklin found it interesting that he could see clearly over the general's head to what was in front of him.

"Have we received any further indications of changes at the factory?" Ruth asked.

"A few trucks . . ." Ativa shrugged. "Some movement. Hopefully we have enough time to pull this off."

"Information from the informant, General?" Macklin asked.

"Yes. It seems Badannah laid a nice little trap for anyone approaching the factory. Would you like to see how it was going to work?" He stepped from the elevator and strode down the hall.

The two colonels were right behind him, Macklin stuffing a used handkerchief in his back pocket.

They walked through a doorway whose steel door needed only Ativa's voice to activate its magnetic locks. The informant sat in a comfortable chair looking haggard and worn out. Ativa greeted the translator, then asked him to wait in the hallway.

"Colonel Levona, you speak Arabic fluently. You'll interpret for us. Ask this gentleman to tell you about the underground bunkers."

When Ruth had translated the informant's excited explanation, Macklin caught himself wondering at the intelligence of whoever was responsible for the factory's security. "Too inviting," he said. "We never go in the easy way. No fun." He smiled at Ativa, then turned to Ruth. "Ask the guy if he can shed any light on what they'll do now that we know about their little scheme."

Levona translated. The Syrian shrugged, then seemed to brighten.

"He says he was only the contractor, he doesn't know anything about the factory." She hesitated only a second. "But, he was warned to get out of Duma by his cousin, the sergeant responsible for the factory's defense. A Sergeant Khalis. He would know."

Macklin paced, rubbing his chin, thinking. "Does he know where the sergeant lives?"

She translated. "Yes."

"Good. Is it on a base, in town, with other military personnel, separate?"

He waited while she spoke the fluent and beautiful

tongue. His experience in Riyadh, Saudi Arabia, helped him pick out a few words.

"He lives in the town, in an apartment house. Many of the leaders do. Badannah lives a few blocks away. He says Khalis is afraid of Badannah."

Tom glanced at Ruth. The mention of Badannah's name had no visible effect.

"General, if you will allow myself and the interpreter outside to spend an hour with this man, I want to get detailed information about the sergeant and his surroundings. I think I have a plan to get inside the factory without being discovered." He checked his watch. "Ruth, could we pull the team together for a meeting later tonight?"

Ruth nodded. "I'll make the calls while you talk to the informant."

"When you're finished, please join us in my office," Ativa said, moving to the door.

"Yessir. Shouldn't take long. Oh, and sir, if you could get the latest satellite pictures of Duma and the factory. Detailed as possible?"

The general opened the door for Colonel Levona, a slight grin on his bulldog face. "Nice to see I won't have to drown the two of you in the Mediterranean."

Macklin sat slumped in the couch in Ativa's office, his stockinged feet resting on the coffee table covered with papers, his eyes scanning a newly marked map of Syria. The satellite photos and the information the informant gave, along with a recent map of Duma, had helped him come up with the final version of a plan of attack. He was confident it would work. As he slapped the photos down on the coffee table the door swung open and Ruth came in.

"The team coming together?" he asked.

"All but Merriame. The funeral . . ."

Macklin looked at his watch. "Four o'clock today. I forgot."

"Will you go? It will be a different experience for you, but I think we should."

"As much as I hate 'em, I'll go. He died for his country . . . and for that child. He deserves to be honored."

"They are preparing a second team. Chaim Daliyat."

Macklin sat back in the chair. "On whose orders?"

"Hoshen's, by way of Stein. A backup. In case it gets too hot in the kitchen and someone has to fire some of the cooks."

"Meaning us, I suppose."

"Perceptive, aren't you?"

"How hot is it getting?" he asked.

"On a scale of zero to a thousand degrees, about five hundred. General Ativa says there is evidence of desertion at the factory."

"Daliyat," Tom said. "I know his work. The Israeli media's fair-haired boy, isn't he?"

"Political aspirations, but that's the least of my concerns. He plays games. I don't trust him. Twice important enemies of Israel have escaped his grasp under peculiar circumstances."

"Think he is on the take?"

"Just playing the odds. I just don't want him on this job."

"Then we'd better get moving. I know it's your job to do the planning and I don't mean to step on your toes . . ." She slugged him in the arm. "Take a look at this," he said, handing her his written proposal.

"What is it?"

"My plan to get what we want, if they don't leave Duma too soon."

She began reading and he let her, the minutes ticking slowly by. When she put it down he leaned forward.

"Well, what do you think?"

She looked at the proposal thoughtfully. "If he follows the same pattern every day . . ."

"Our informant says he never varies. The market he uses, the stores he shops, the places he stops for a drink, the time he arrives at his apartment, the time he leaves it. This man is such an animal of habit I am almost embarrassed for him." He smiled.

Levona's look was one of worried admiration. "This is a Syrian and terrorist stronghold, Tom. Hundreds of things could go wrong."

"I admit timing is critical, but, with the exception of the method of retrieval, it isn't much different than our operation in Kuwait City a few months ago. I—"

"That one put you in the hospital, remember!" She shoved the papers at him irritably.

"This is different, Ruth. I have confidence in this information. We didn't get this from Mossad or the CIA. Your informant knows this target personally. He certainly isn't a planted agent. He would never endanger his family like that. No, things are different from—"

"I'm just worried, that's all," she interrupted. "It'll work. Let's just hope we get the chance to try it!" She stood and went to the window, her arms folded against renewed anxiety. After a moment she checked her watch, then returned to the couch. "I have another responsibility this afternoon, after the funeral."

She took off her shoes and pulled her legs under her, putting her arm across the back of the couch behind Macklin, relaxing, feeling comfortable. "Ativa is concerned about a couple of members of the advance American peace commission. They arrived early to do some sightseeing in the Galilee. They foolishly asked for only one person to guard them. Hoshen agreed to it. Ativa questions their sanity." She shrugged. "Anyway, they are supposed to check in at the Mount Scopus Hotel at six o'clock this evening. When they arrive I will meet them and the agent with them, and make arrangements for their continued safety. You can come along."

"Umm," Macklin said, his mind still with the Duma project. "Will you be able to get the piece of equipment I asked for in that plan?"

She nodded. "We will have to make some alterations, but it will be ready."

"And the explosives?"

"Yes, but why so particular?"

"The stuff is extremely volatile. If we're forced to blow the place up and chemical weapons are kept there, this stuff will burn the poison into oblivion so fast it won't be able to kill innocent bystanders."

She stood behind him and began to rub his tense neck muscles, sending a message to his brain that enough was enough. He laid the papers on the small table by his chair.

"That, dear lady, is not something they taught you in basic training."

"My mother used to do it for my father each night. She taught me."

He closed his eyes, letting his mind empty of numbers and lists and concentrate on Ruth's soothing touch. After a few minutes he took her hand and led her around the couch to sit beside him. She put her arms around his neck and they kissed. After a moment he pulled slightly away and looked into her dark eyes. "An Israeli, an American. Jew, Christian. Intelligence operative, special operations leader. You think this relationship has potential?" He smiled.

She returned the smile, rubbing the back of his neck with her hand. "Definite possibility. We'll move to a deserted island, start our own government, create new jobs without the pressures, and find a religious belief we can both handle." She pressed her lips to his again as the door swung open and Ativa walked in.

He seemed to ignore their presence, sat at his desk, and began working.

Macklin quickly stood, grabbing the papers from the table and walking toward the door. "Uh . . . Lieutenant Gad and I have some detailed planning to do. I told him I would meet him in the operations room." He opened the door and was gone, leaving Ruth with a foolish grin on her face.

Ativa looked over the top of his glasses at her. "Negotiating a political alliance with the Americans?" he asked, his eyes dropping back to his work.

Ruth reached for her shoes. "Something more important. I'd like a little time off when this project is completed. Any objection?"

"None," he said without glancing up. "About time you found a good man. Would have preferred a Jew, though." He ducked, her pen slamming into the credenza behind him.

"Watch it, Papa Ativa. Next time I won't miss," she said, smiling, then closing the door behind her.

2:45 P.M., Ein Karem, Israel

The cemetery was on the side of a mountain near the small village of Ein Karem a few miles west of Jerusalem. Every Baptist knew the name as the place where John the Baptist was born. The road wound down sharply from the Jerusalem hills into a beautiful terraced valley rich in olive trees and vineyards.

Macklin recognized the church sitting just to the right of the main road. His parents had a picture of it on the wall of their home. "The Church of St. John," he said, pointing. "Run by Franciscan fathers and supposedly built over the grotto where John the Baptist was born."

"How do you know this?" Levona asked.

"My parents consider it one of the holiest churches in Christendom. They have a picture of it at home, next to one of Jesus being baptized by John in the river Jordan. There is a Greek inscription above the door that says, "*Hic Praecursor Domini Natus est.*"

"Here the forerunner of the Lord was born," Ruth translated. "John was considered a great prophet by the Jewish people, and feared by our leaders. Some of both groups even claimed he was the Messiah. Because of it the people flocked to hear him, and the leaders flocked to have him thrown in prison or killed."

They drove through the small town, then took a left up a small incline to a synagogue. Ruth added the Mercedes to a half dozen other cars parked in a paved lot next to it. She turned off the key and faced him.

"We are early because I must explain some things to you, or maybe you have questions?"

"Yeah, I can think of one real quick. Imad hasn't been dead twenty-four hours and already he's getting buried. It seems a little . . . uh . . . rushed."

Ruth smiled. "It is based upon scripture. In Deuteronomy it says, 'Thou shalt surely bury him the same day.' When it can be done, we keep this law. In your Christian burials there is usually a viewing of the body, is that correct?"

"Yes, out of respect for them. To sort of say good-bye, I guess."

"Not with Jews. Two rules direct most of what we do. One is called Kevod Hamet, or treating the dead with respect and reverence. The other involves Kevod Hechai, or concern for the living. We think it breaks both of these rules to view the body in its decaying and unnatural state."

"A rule I like. I always hated viewings, still do. Mine will be strictly closed casket."

"That is another thing. There will be no casket. The body will be wrapped for burial and possibly placed in a simple pine wood box to be taken to the place of burial. It will not be embalmed, nor will you see cremated remains."

"For the same reasons?" Macklin asked sincerely.

"Partly. Embalming removes the blood from the body. We believe the blood to be an integral and necessary part of the whole. It should not be discarded as waste. To do so is to desecrate it. Also with cremation. The scriptures say dust to dust. Fire is considered a destructive power that prohibits the body from a possible resurrection.

"You will not see this, but Imad will be buried in a plain white garment with no pockets, called a shroud. The white is symbolic of purity, and it is simple and without pockets because the dead present themselves to God without their pride and possessions of this world."

"Where will he be buried?"

"In the ground near here. He, like all Jews who live in Israel, are luckier than those who are buried in America or some other distant country."

"What do you mean?" Macklin asked.

"It is our belief that gilgul neshamot, the rolling of the body underground to Israel, must take place when the Messiah comes and they rise again in life. In attempting to avoid the long journey, Jews of the Diaspora often have their bodies brought here for burial."

Macklin looked at her quizically, a slight smirk on his face. He removed it when he saw she was very serious.

He cleared his throat. "I didn't think you believed in a resurrection."

"Some Jews don't. That was one reason why some disagreed with Jesus so violently. He taught of resurrection. Then, when he told them not only would there be a resurrection, but as the Son of God his death would begin it, they called him a blasphemer. In those days people were put to death for blasphemy."

"But if he was the Son of God he wasn't a blasphemer."

She smiled. "No, he would not be."

"During the services you will see several other things, Tom, minor things, that are different. The mourners will be very vocal, and Sergeant Merriame and her parents will perform what is called the Keria, or tearing of the garment. It is a sign of their anguish. The parents tear the garment on the left side because the left side is closest to the heart, and Imad, their child, is closest to their hearts. Merriame will tear hers on the right. When they do this they will say, 'Baruch ata adonai elohainu melech ha-olam dayan haemet.' Blessed art thou, Lord our God, the true judge."

Another car pulled in beside them and Lieutenant Gad and a blond, tanned, and pretty woman got out.

"His wife. They have a baby as well.

"One other thing before we go. Your presence here is what is important to Merriame, not your words. The Talmud says: 'The greatest reward is bestowed upon all who know how to be silent in a house of mourning.'"

"Keep my trap shut, is that it?" Macklin smiled.

She smiled back and handed him a small cap. "It is called a yarmulke. It is for covering the head while in the synagogue where we meet before going to the grave site.

Macklin put it on. Ruth reached over and adjusted it, then kissed him gently on the lips. "I want you to understand my people."

He put his hand behind her head, kissing her again. "If this is the reward I get every time you teach me something new . . . I am ready for a full day's tutoring." She punched him playfully in the shoulder while drawing back, getting out of the car.

"We will walk from here. Ready?" she asked, checking her hair in the mirror, then her eyes. Did the hatred of funerals show? She had attended too many.

CHAPTER 16

3:00 P.M., Central Israel

The Volvo turned back on the main road to Jerusalem as Mike leaned over the seat and spoke to Raffi.

"Thank you, Raffi," she said. "They are special people. I pray only the best for them."

"Reuben is considered a fanatic by some. Israel should be full of such fanatics. At least he tries to do it peacefully. We have many who use weapons, and who go way beyond what God would want. They are dangerous to everyone."

"This Gush Emunim is a popular movement in Israel, isn't it?" Jerry asked.

"Very, and gaining momentum. As you heard Reuben say, they believe they must prepare all of Israel for the coming of the Messiah. Until it is prepared he cannot come. Does this help you understand why so many refuse to give up settlement on the West Bank?"

"Yes, it helps." Jerry looked back at the village, feeling somewhat depressed. How could you fight the reasoning of a Reuben Ben Shami? And yet, it was contrary to the reasoning of the Arab gardener he had visited with in Tiberias. He believed that the Palestinians would quit fighting and live peacefully if only the Israelis would give them their rights.

He leaned his head back against the seat. In the last twenty-four hours he had talked to enough Jews and Israelis to make his head swim, yet he was no closer to a real solution than he had been when watching the news on CNN at home. Was there a solution? He was beginning to think not.

He had realized one thing. The leaders were a big part of the problem. This included their unwillingness to let the people work things out, buy and sell the land, settle peacefully together. On the one hand you had Jewish leaders forcing Palestinians from the land, on the other hand the PLO was killing Palestinians who tried to sell it or leave it, or who gave any indication of trying to solve things peacefully. The people were caught in the middle and were suffering for it.

Mike turned to Jerry. "Tired?"

"Exhausted. You?"

"Tired, and still a little nauseated. Must be something I ate in Tel Aviv yesterday. I'm ready for Jerusalem.

"I have enjoyed seeing Israel, Jerry, especially the Galilee. This morning as the sun came up . . . it was so peaceful."

"The place where Jesus walked." He sighed. "I was hoping . . ." He hesitated, taking her hand. "Has it been a disappointment?"

She smiled. "I felt peace at Galilee, Jeremiah, and at that synagogue in Nazareth, and on Nebi Samwal. But I know there isn't physical peace here, probably never will be." She glanced out of the window. "No, not a disappointment. I feel what I came to feel. The Savior did walk here. This is a promised land, thank goodness. If it weren't, the people probably would have killed each other off long ago."

They rode for some way in silence.

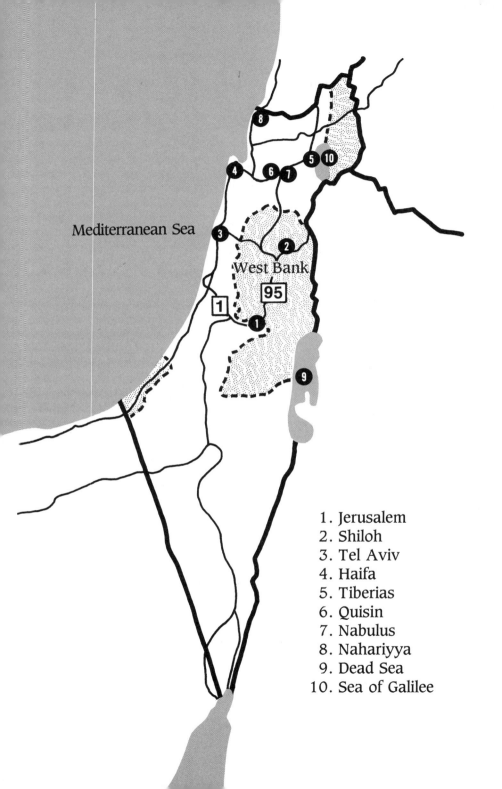

Mediterranean Sea

West Bank

95

1. Jerusalem
2. Shiloh
3. Tel Aviv
4. Haifa
5. Tiberias
6. Quisin
7. Nabulus
8. Nahariyya
9. Dead Sea
10. Sea of Galilee

"I would like to stop at the Garden Tomb," Jerry said. "It will help me get my perspective back, okay?"

She nodded assent. Talking to the people was pulling him apart. He had spoken of the garden often. The place where he had made peace with the Savior after the hell of Vietnam. "Yes, that's one place I wouldn't miss."

"You hear that, Raffi? The Garden Tomb for a short visit, then the Mount Scopus Hotel and a hot bath."

Raffi nodded, his attention diverted to the rearview mirror. He had seen the red sports car when they turned onto the main road just below Shiloh. The man looked Israeli, and the license plate indicated he was. But why was he parked, using binoculars to look in the direction they had just come from? If he was an agent, he wasn't very subtle. Raffi was making the turn onto modern Highway 67 when the red sports car closed space again. Enough was enough. He pushed his foot to the floor and let the Volvo go all out.

"What's up?" Jerry asked.

"Straight road, fast car, sleepy passengers. A great temptation." He smiled. "Actually, just making up some time."

He looked in the rearview mirror. The red car was gone or lost in traffic. Maybe it turned north, he thought.

Then again, maybe not. He would take a longer route once they were in the city. If the red sports car was tailing him, he would lose it. Then he would get to a phone.

4:00 P.M., Jerusalem

Lev Zafit stood at the phone booth, his eyes glued to the entrance of the Garden Tomb as he dialed the numbers written on a small piece of paper, then waited for some time as the call was routed through several foreign exchanges. The last operator spoke in Arabic.

"Yes," said a woman's voice, making him hesitate. He looked at the number and remembered his contact's instructions. He hadn't said the voice would be his own, nor that it would be male.

"TIBER," he said, giving his code name.

"ANGEL," came the reply. He looked at the paper again. It was the correct response.

"They are at the Garden Tomb. Just arrived."

The phone clicked off. Zafit hung it up, absentmindedly ripping the paper into small pieces, throwing it into the street. What will happen? Would others simply follow the Americans, or was something worse intended? His morbid sense of curiosity held him to the spot. He looked down the street. Finding a small restaurant, he decided he could watch from one of its outdoor tables. He had never witnessed what actually happened after one of his calls.

Zafit walked nonchalantly to the eating place, taking a chair at one of the tables near the front. The waitress reminded him of his wife. The same trusting eyes, at least. He gave his order, then waited, thinking.

He and his wife had moved to a relationship bordering on divorce, and if it hadn't been for their strict orthodox upbringing, it would have ended that way years ago. Their marriage had been made by the local matchmaker. Then Lev had known that he loved this beautiful Jewish girl. They had been happy together, having several children while he struggled to the top managerial position at Tiberias's best hotel. But over the years they had drawn apart. She had sensed the change after his return from Europe and had questioned him about it, thinking possibly he had been involved with another woman. He had no recourse but to let her believe that—it gave him some sort of cover for his impatience and self-hate. Then, when he had actually started working for the PLO as an operative and there had been deaths as a result, his tense anger and confusion had caused her further concern, which in turn had caused her to question. He had responded by becoming aloof, passive, and business-like, emotionally moving away from her and then from his children.

He would leave her some day. Not because he was not fond of her, but because he could not face her when it was discovered what he had been doing, how many Jewish lives he had been responsible for ending. And he would be discovered. It was only a matter of time. He had been careless lately, forgetting to care, and he had strong feelings that he was being watched.

He ordered another drink, keeping his eyes and mind on the entrance. It was difficult through traffic, with buses pulling up now and again, unloading tourists.

When the food came the smell reminded him that he hadn't eaten and he pulled his thoughts to the mundane activity of lifting a fork. His eyes went to the entrance less often, his mind diverted from his subversive activity. To the average man sitting nearby, Lev Zafit was just another Israeli enjoying an early supper.

Sabrila picked up the phone before the first ring finished, then did nothing but listen. The Englishman watched the expression on her face change to elation. She slammed the phone back onto the receiver in exultation.

"The Garden Tomb! Are your men ready?"

"A phone call. They are in a safe house only a few blocks from the garden. What about the police? That section . . ."

Sabrila smiled. "They will have to respond to a sudden emergency in another sector. Do it," Sabrila said. "ANGEL's orders."

Pike's mouth hung open. Yes, indeed, ANGEL had powerful contacts. He picked up the phone and dialed the number.

Raffi waited as the operator connected him with Ativa's private number. From the window of the holy site manager's office he caught glimpses of Mike and Jerry walking the paths of the garden. As best he could, he watched others for the telltale signs of enemy surveillance. No one looked suspicious. Raffi decided he'd keep his distance unless he felt they were being threatened. He knew this was sacred ground for the couple and wanted to keep himself apart, letting them say and do as they wished.

"Raffi! Where are you?" Ativa exclaimed in Hebrew.

"Garden Tomb," Raffi responded.

"Hang on." Raffi waited until the line clicked on again.

"Stay put. I've ordered men there. Should arrive inside ten minutes."

"Good. I think we'd better get them under protection at the hotel. I may have been followed from the Galilee."

There was a brief hesitation. "Are you sure?"

JERUSALEM

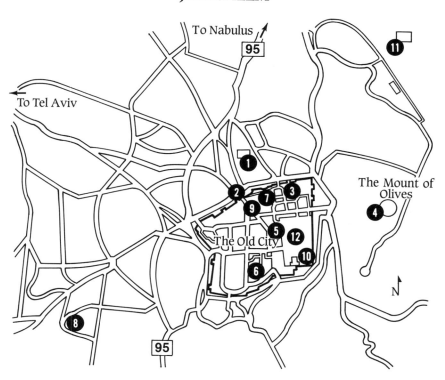

1. Garden Tomb
2. Damascus Gate
3. Muzra's Shop
4. Orson Hyde Memorial Gardens
5. Western (Wailing) Wall
6. Macklin's Safe House

7. Entrance, Zedekiah's Cave
8. Presidential Residence
9. Al Wad Street
10. Al Aqsa Mosque
11. Haddassah Hospital
12. Temple Mount

"Of course I'm sure, but I haven't seen him since entering Jerusalem. Maybe I lost him." Raffi was nervous. The kind of nervousness that warned of impending action. He rubbed the handle of his pistol—now in his belt, under his jacket—reducing the tension he was feeling in the pit of his stomach.

The phone was silent.

"All right. Don't wait for my men. Get the American to the hotel as quick as you can. Move, Raffi. I'll have men meeting you there. They'll cordon off the entire ninth floor and keep an eye on our guests." Ativa hung up.

With the adrenaline pumping, Raffi scanned the garden as he moved from the administrator's office into the main lobby. Watching, looking for the enemy he knew might be there by now. Jerry and Mike stood near the entrance, waving to him. They looked tired, ready to go. He must not let on that there was possible trouble.

Then he saw them. Two men in the crowd, moving close to the couple, guns drawn. The room was long and narrow, one side full of windows. He started to run for the far exit, keeping his eyes on the assailants through the windows. He would never get there in time. He pulled his gun as he saw the shocked look on Jerry's face, a gun shoved tightly into his back. Raffi pushed half a dozen tourists aside and raised his gun, taking aim. Too many people saw it and panicked, screaming, running for cover, getting in his way. The Daniels couple were shoved through the exit as Raffi saw another assailant out of the corner of his eye. He dived for cover behind a low wall as the woman fired her automatic and dashed for the exit, pinning Raffi down. The firing stopped and he was on his feet again, running around and jumping over people, yelling at them to get out of the way and stay down. As he got to the gate he saw the enemy pushing Jeremiah Daniels into a blue Mercedes, another wrestling with Mrs. Daniels. He fired the Makarov, hitting the man in the hip, giving her a chance to break free. He had only enough time to dive for cover again before the other men splintered the gate with bullets.

As he rolled through the bushes and then ran for the wall Raffi heard sirens, more weapons, an explosion, the squealing of tires. He leaped for the top of the high wall, grasping the wrought-iron railing there, pulling himself up only to see the Mercedes moving into heavy traffic.

Mike was nearly trampled by the sandals of half a hundred people running for cover, but she regained her feet and dived for the weapon her assailant had lost when he went down screaming in pain. She turned to fire but panicked as the Mercedes sped from the curb. She ran down the walk trying to get a clear shot at the tires, the driver, anything that might stop them, keep them from taking her husband. People froze, then prostrated themselves on the ground, covering their heads as if flimsy hands would keep bullets from vital gray matter. Under different circumstances Mike would have found their pell-mell, frantic actions laughable. Not now.

Several darted into traffic, risking life and limb to escape the scene, causing drivers to slam on their brakes, creating a momentary traffic jam through which the blue sedan had to work its way. Mike hardly noticed the sound of the automatics and explosions as she raced after the car. She lurched between two vehicles and into the street, trying to shorten the distance between her and the fleeing sedan.

She heard a popping sound like distant firecrackers, then she felt stings as particles of pavement exploded off the street and bit into the flesh of her ankles and legs and tore her clothes. She kept running, involuntarily covering her head with one flailing arm. Then someone grabbed her, forcing her to the ground, her tears and sobs wracking her chest as she yelled for Jerry. She kicked to be free until she could kick no more—her strength spent in the fury of her hate and desire to rush after those who had stolen her most prized possession and rip out their hearts. She saw the darkness out of the corners of her eyes; then it spread, blocking off the view of the street, then filling her mind as she lapsed into unwanted blackness.

Jerry Daniels forced his eyes away from Mike as she ran after them, the anger deep in his stomach where the sweating terrorist pressed a gun while the sedan crashed against vehicles and forced its way through traffic, desperate to be free and away.

Jerry had never wanted to kill before. Now he wanted. He wanted to reach out and grab the man by the throat and strangle the life out of him!

"Do it, American! Do it, so I can kill you!"

The hate exuded from his captor's stale breath, his eyes flames of fire. Jerry realized the man was having an adrenaline or drug rush and was out of control and dangerous. He concentrated on calming his own nerves, keeping himself from doing something foolish. He must think his way free.

"That is better, American." The assailant smiled tightly, pushing hard on the gun. "Mohammad Faisal wanted us to pay you special welcome to Israel."

Raffi saw Mike as he plummeted from the top of the wall to the concrete below. He ran after her, grabbing her, and bringing her to the ground, covering her head from the gunfire. As she passed out he pulled her to safety behind a vehicle. A woman tourist was taking up space there as well, a curious and excited expression on her face. Raffi ripped out his identification. "Can you watch her while I try to stop them from taking her American husband?"

"You got it, deary!" the lady said, scooping up Mike's head in her arms. "Go get 'em!"

Raffi gave her a thankful grin, jumped to his feet, and raced down the street. He could cut them off by going through the alley.

Raffi had never run so hard in his life, dodging cars and people walking the sidewalk who were unaware of what had taken place only yards from where they stood. He exploded from the alleyway and glanced in both directions. The Mercedes was racing in his direction at high speed. He lowered the pistol and fired.

Jeremiah heard the thump and saw the windshield shatter, then the driver's head jerked back toward him. The car jolted, out of control, slamming his Arab assailant's head into the side window. Jerry used his right hand and grabbed hair while knocking the pistol free with his left. As the car careened over the steps that led down to Damascus Gate they were knocked into a fighting rabble in the backseat. When it bumped to a stop Jerry was on top, the assailant unconscious beneath him. He tried to catch his breath, thinking it was over, when the door was nearly ripped from its hinges. Jerry's hand flew toward the man who stood there before he realized it was Raffi.

"Come on!" Raffi yelled, turning to watch for the enemy as Jerry scrambled to his side.

People were scattering in every direction, screaming and yelling in half a dozen different languages. Raffi pointed toward the gate. "IDF troops should be there. Go!"

Jerry took the steps three at a time, Raffi on his heels, their eyes peeled for men who might try to stop them. Jerry reached under his jacket before he remembered that the assailant had taken his pistol.

He heard the gunfire and felt the wind of bullets forcing him to the stone pavement, then scrambled for cover behind a small cart near a bunch of traders' tables. He glanced behind him.

Raffi was lying in the street, his gun arm shattered, the pistol gone, lost under the feet of a hundred people running for cover. Jerry saw the crowd open as two men with automatics scanned, looking for him. He kept low, moving behind the tables until he could reach Raffi's good arm, pulling him to safety, leaving a trail of blood. He ripped a section of his shirt and wrapped it quickly around the Israeli's arm.

"Go!" Raffi said. "Run! They want blood! You must run!"

Jerry glanced over the top of the tables. The assailants were still some distance off but coming in their direction. Where were these troops Raffi was so sure should be there? Where were the police?

His eyes darted up the street in both directions. He understood the problem. Other terrorists were blocking the area, already committed to fighting anyone who came their way. Now that battle had ensued they would probably fight to the death.

He grabbed for Raffi's belt, loosening it. He stuck Raffi's arm in the opening, then tightened the belt again as Raffi gritted his teeth against the pain. "Come on!" Jerry said.

"I'm not leaving you. They'd just as soon kill you as look at you."

Jerry put an arm around Raffi's shoulder, lifting, supporting, moving behind the row of tables, keeping low, getting closer to the gate that led into the Old City.

He looked over his shoulder, saw one of the assailants looking in his direction, then yelling, pointing. "They see us! Run, Raffi!" They bolted past the tables, the assailants yelling in Arabic for everyone to get down. As they dashed past the opening and around a corner he heard the guns fire, then the ricochet off the stone walls.

Raffi half stumbled, took two steps, then fell, sprawling on the stones of the street. Jerry thought he had been hit, but found no more wounds. The pain simply had been too much. He grabbed him and hoisted him over one shoulder, standing erect, the hair on the back of his head standing on end, his mind aware that at any second the gunners would have them in the deadly sights of their weapons.

He looked desperately for a way to go, to hide. He heard the screams as he stumbled behind a crate against the wall of a building, gasping for breath. He peered around the corner of the box to see the crowd opening with the sweeping motion of the assailants' Kalishnikov rifles. People ran in all directions, creating enough chaos to keep Jerry's hiding place safe for about thirty seconds.

Jerry's mind focused on the blood running from Raffi's arm onto the ground. The blood! They would see it and follow it! He panicked as he looked at the small pool of red where he was standing. He searched the faces of the crowd, trying to find anyone who might help them, but saw only fear, people cringing or running quickly away, knowing that the two men with the deadly weapons were hunting Jerry and Raffi.

And then, suddenly, "Mister!"

Jerry's muscles went taut as a hand touched the middle of his back. He spun around, his fist ready to deal a painful blow. The young boy jumped back, his hands coming up automatically to protect himself, a package falling to the ground, spilling.

"Wait! I can help you," the boy said as he scrambled to shove the few articles back in the sack.

Jerry looked around the edge of the crate again, ignoring the dirty little urchin.

"Mister! Come!" the boy said in muffled tones of fair English. "I have a place . . ."

He looked at the boy—the dark eyes were pleading, then darting in the direction of Jerry's approaching enemies.

"They come! Please, follow . . ." He started down the narrow street, keeping to the wall, motioning with his hand, the assailants' view now being partially blocked by the large crate.

Jerry followed, looking over his shoulder. He saw one of the men look in his direction, recognizing their now fully visible forms. The killer raised his weapon, firing. Jeremiah ducked to one side, and the bullets careened off the rock wall. He saw the boy turn into another narrow street. In five steps Jerry was on his heels, the near miss and sound of bullets giving his legs new strength.

The street was nearly empty, and Jerry knew that at any second they'd be sitting ducks. He started to run but the kid grabbed his arm and pulled him toward a door, flinging it open before them. Jerry lurched inside, his good eye adjusting quickly to the darkness. He saw an old man sitting in one corner, rocking gently in a rustic chair. The man's head jerked up as he tried to identify the people interrupting his thoughts. The boy spoke to him in Arabic, the old man cocking his head to hear, then nodding as he went back to his rocking. Jerry realized that the old man was blind.

"Wh . . . what about the blood. A trail . . . they . . . they'll follow!"

"Come," the boy said, ignoring Jerry's words.

"But—"

"Come! They will not hurt the old one unless they find you here!"

Jerry took a deep breath while getting a new grip on Raffi, mustering up the energy to lift again. He followed the boy through another room and out of a back door into a second narrow street, where they turned and went deeper into the city, passing several shops as people scurried out of their way. Jerry stopped long enough to get a new grip on Raffi while checking their back trail before continuing to follow the boy, who had disappeared into another street.

When Jerry caught up, the boy stood at the head of a third street, motioning for Jerry to hurry. "Now you must stop the blood," he said, looking at Raffi's dripping arm.

Jerry looked into Raffi's half-open, pain-filled eyes. "Sorry, my friend." He grabbed the wound and pressed. Raffi screamed, then passed out. Jerry half dragged, half carried him along the street and finally through an old archway. The boy flung open a door and they entered another house.

Except for several pieces of old furniture and a Persian rug, the first room was empty. Jerry caught his breath, placing his shoulder against the wall, releasing the pressure hold on Raffi's wound.

"Not yet!" The boy flipped back the rug, keeping Raffi's blood from staining it, then went through another opening. Jerry followed, finding himself in what seemed to be a bedroom.

The boy shoved a bed mat aside, then took a small knife from his pocket and began prying the floorboards free one by one. Jerry laid Raffi on the floor, looking around the room for something to stop the flow of blood. A gown of satin hung from a hook on the wall, beautiful and hand-embroidered. He reached for it, then decided he'd use his belt instead, making a tourniquet. It was hard to believe this was all happening, and he wondered why a man had to endure such an experience once in a lifetime, let alone twice! But at least he had the answer for which he had come to Israel. He and Mike were not safe. Probably never would be.

When he had the belt tightly in place he ripped a piece of cloth from his shirttail and used it for a bandage, stopping the flow of blood from running down Raffi's arm and onto the wood floor. He ripped another longer strip from Raffi's shirt, wiped the blood from the Israeli's head wound as carefully as he could, then bandaged it.

The boy finished removing the boards, then a large stone beneath them, revealing a dark hole. "You must go that way," he said, pointing.

"Where does it go?" Jerry asked wearily.

"Zedekiah's Cave, but you must not go into the grotto. You will get lost. Wait for me here."

Jerry got on his hands and knees and looked into the hole, his eyes trying to adjust to the darkness beyond.

"I can't—"

The boy tapped on his shoulder, then handed him a large Rayovac flashlight. "American," he smiled. "Made to last a long time."

Jerry flipped the switch and shined the light down the hole, surprised to find a floor only a few feet below.

"Wait in there. I will try to bring others."

Jerry nodded. The opening wasn't large enough for him and Raffi to enter at the same time, so he took Raffi's good arm and lowered him to the floor below, then followed, still standing with his head in the upper room.

"A doctor. Tell them we need a doctor."

The boy nodded while kneeling and picking up the stone. Jerry fell on his knees, exhausted, glad for the flashlight as the boy lowered the stone in place. He turned the beam on Raffi's still unconscious body and checked both vital signs and bandages.

Jerry sat on the floor, placing his back against the wall, giving his mind and body a moment to recuperate. The light hung loosely in his hand, its beam bouncing off the stone floor and walls of a passageway that got larger only a few feet away, falling deeper into the earth.

After long minutes Jerry lifted the flashlight, letting the powerful beam extend into the tunnel and find the wall at its far end. He had picked himself up to investigate when Raffi moaned.

"What . . . Where are we?"

Jerry touched his shoulder, careful not to shine the light directly into Raffi's stunned eyes. "The boy . . . he brought us here. He said this is Zedekiah's Cave."

Raffi put his weight on his good arm and with Jerry's help gingerly lifted himself up to a sitting position, placing his back against the rock wall. He felt the bandage around his head first, then gently touched his broken arm.

"You passed out from the pain. The bullet shattered your arm. You've lost a fair amount of blood."

"Umm. I feel like I've lost it all. My head . . . I see two of you."

Jerry laughed lightly. "If there were I'd send the other guy for help!"

Jerry started to rise. "I'll check out the passageway. Rest a few minutes."

"Solomon's quarries."

"What?" Jerry said, willing to let himself down again.

"This is Solomon's quarries. Same thing as Zedekiah's Cave. This entrance shouldn't be here. I—"

"Just be glad it is. Those guys with the automatics didn't intend to take us back in one piece."

"We usually have soldiers at Damascus Gate. If they had been on post . . ."

"Never mind. I'll be back in a minute. Shut up and rest."

Jerry started down the passage, the flashlight searching for what lurked in the darkness. The floor angled steeply toward what seemed to be a dead end, then veered sharply right. As Jerry turned the corner he ran into solid wall, banging the flashlight and dropping it. He caught his breath, but the light stayed on.

"Good ol' Rayovac!" he said to the darkness.

He bent and picked it up, noticing a crevice in the wall near the floor. There was a time, he thought, when I could have slid through that space! Maybe . . .

He stuck his hand in the hole and felt a rock at arm's length. With effort he shoved it off to one side. Taking a deep breath, he wiggled into the opening, shining the light in the space beyond. Two or three feet away were several large rocks blocking a view of what seemed to be a large grotto. Zedekiah's Cave. He thought about going farther, then decided he'd better return and check on Raffi. He wriggled back into the tunnel, got to his feet crouching, and went back up the tunnel, wondering how quickly he could move Raffi into the grotto if their enemies discovered the blood trail again.

Not fast enough, he decided.

Raffi raised his hand against the bright beam of the light.

"How ya' doin?" Jerry asked.

"Sleepy," he said softly. "I worry about this child who went for help. I think maybe we should go back . . ."

"Not a chance, Raffi. You left a trail of blood a two-year-old could follow. Those boys with guns could be waiting within ten feet of this place."

"They must want you awfully bad, Mr. Daniels. To follow us from the car was suicidal and they knew it. You have very powerful, very deadly enemies. I am surprised they did not just kill you at the garden gate."

"I humiliated some people. Killing me was not their intention. Torture, humiliation, years of it, then death. That's more in keeping with the way they do things."

"Then staying here may be better. Your escape has humiliated them again. This time they will kill you on sight."

"Can the boy be trusted?" Jerry asked.

Raffi shrugged. "He is Arab." He paused. "Possibly we could escape . . . through the quarries." He gritted his teeth against the pain.

"Relax, Raffi. Ain't no way I can get you into the quarry. Entrance is too small. I'll trust the kid."

128

"He is an Arab," Raffi said coldly.

"Umm. Who saved us from killers," Jerry answered, shutting off the flashlight, conserving the batteries. "Tell me about the caves. Not exactly a tourist attraction, I take it."

"Too dangerous, and they're beneath the Old City, under some holy sites."

"They could hide an army," Jerry said.

"Yes. We don't wish the enemies of Israel to come here. That is why this entrance must be closed." Raffi adjusted his position. "All other entrances are locked and guarded. We also do unscheduled searches of the caves."

"Why did the boy call it Zedekiah's Cave?"

"A legend. When King Nebuchadnezzar conquered Jerusalem in 586 B.C., all authorities fled the city, but King Zedekiah was trapped. His men told him of the great cave beneath Jerusalem and said there was a passage there that led to the plains of Jericho. They led him to an entrance very near where the Damascus Gate now sits and began their journey through the dark interior of the earth."

Raffi took a deep breath, clenching his teeth against the pain, then continued. "At the very time when Zedekiah entered the cave, some of Nebuchadnezzar's men were sent into the wilderness to hunt for food. They chased a deer into the brush. As they waited, wondering where it would come out, they were astonished to hear voices and footsteps. They prepared their weapons and trapped King Zedekiah as he came through the exit on the far distant plains of Jericho. Immediately they took him to their king. The Bible teaches us what the good king did to him."

"Plains of Jericho are a long way from here," Jerry said, smiling in the darkness.

"Yes, but it is a big cave," Raffi laughed lightly.

"I love a good legend," Jerry said.

They chuckled together.

"King Solomon cut stone from these caves to build the temple. He left behind a huge labyrinth of caverns. They have been used for many purposes since then. Possibly Zedekiah did use them for escape, or at least to hide himself and his family."

Jerry thought of Mulek, Zedekiah's son, who escaped the destruction of Jerusalem and death at the hands of the Babylonians even though the rest of his family did not. Possibly this place saved him, or others like him.

Jerry felt tired. He let his eyelids droop, then shut. Soon the boy would return, then they could worry. Right now . . . a little sleep. That's what they both needed . . . just a little sleep.

CHAPTER 17

5:15 P.M., Hadassah Hospital, Jerusalem

Levona watched the light change and then stepped on the gas, moving the Mercedes quickly through the intersection. Both she and Macklin were listening intently to the announcement being repeated over the radio.

The attempted kidnapping took place near the Garden Tomb earlier this afternoon. Aman forces intervened, leading to a bloody battle in which two Israeli soldiers and three of the kidnappers were killed. Five bystanders were wounded. The American's bodyguard managed to free him from the captors' vehicle and the two fled into the Old City through Damascus Gate. The kidnappers apparently pursued them. At this time military officials are not sure where the two men are. The two kidnappers are also at large. Officials say that the Moslem quarter is extremely volatile, but that they are preparing to thoroughly search the area.

We read you the communique once again, emphasizing that at present we cannot verify the terrorists' claims. It reads:

"Quote. The Revolutionary Council for Palestine has struck a blow for justice today by kidnapping Jeremiah Daniels, a member of the American Peace Commission. Daniels is an enemy of the Arab people, responsible for the death of members of its international army for Islam—and an enemy of Arab freedom from Western decadence.

Daniels was in Israel under the direction of the American CIA. His mission was to work with Israeli officials in the continued effort of Western imperialism to thwart the effort of Arab peoples to be free of Israeli oppression. We have documents that Daniels carried to Israel which show that the two nations never intended to talk peace with the Arab world but, in fact, were in the process of laying out plans for war.

We warn the decadent American president and the Israeli leaders that we will kill Daniels and his Israeli protector unless they accept responsibility for these actions and confess their intentions to the international press. Close quote."

Assistant Minister of Defense David Stein has stated: "The attack is believed to be under direction of Mohammad Faisal and the PLO. Two prisoners have been interrogated and both have admitted that they work for Faisal, a member of the inner circle of Yasser Arafat's PLO, and suspected of being in hiding on the West Bank."

Stein has also stated: "The Revolutionary Council for Palestine is Mohammad Faisal's organization of West Bank PLO fanatics."

Macklin turned down the radio as the broadcaster launched into another story. "Are you sure of your information?" he asked as Ruth swung the car into a reserved military parking stall in the hospital parking lot.

"Very sure. They claim they have Daniels, but we don't believe it is true. We think he and his Israeli guard, a man by the name of Raffi Ben Shami, escaped into the Old City."

"But they could have been recaptured."

Ruth shut off the ignition, turned half in the seat, and faced Macklin. "Yes. The police in the area were diverted by a false report of a riot a few blocks further south on the other side of the Old City. Only Ativa's men arrived to help Raffi."

"Who—?"

"I don't know who diverted them. We may never know, but the Old City is completely surrounded now. The terrorists cannot get them out even if they did recapture them."

"Comforting thought. They can shoot them instead."

Ruth looked out of the window, trying to avoid Macklin's stare. "It is probably their intention. The news release was sent to the radio station at the moment the attack began. They expected to be successful in getting Daniels. Now they must kill him so that he cannot deny their allegations."

"Well, the allegations are at least partly true," Macklin said with a stiff laugh. "Jerry was responsible for the death of an Arab terrorist. The statement just forgot to mention a whole lot of details about why!" He shook his head. "I can't believe Jeremiah would come to Israel! Whose fool idea was that?"

He turned back to Ruth. "What about the second part, Jeremiah's involvement in the CIA and having documents to give your government? Did you find out if any of that was even remotely true?"

"None of it. Daniels and his wife are here as a part of the American Peace Commission, by appointment of the president of your country. There are no secret papers or military agreements. Both Israel and the United States will officially have to deny those charges."

"It's easy for me to accept that. Jerry would be the last person in the world involved in anything run by the CIA."

"How was he responsible for the death of an Arab?"

Macklin took a deep breath, then began explaining how Jerry had thwarted TERROR1, a terrorist plot in Jackson Hole, Wyoming, and how, in their desperate attempt to save their plan, the terrorists had tried to kidnap Senator Freeman. "Mike . . . Mrs. Daniels, who is Freeman's daughter, was seriously wounded. The Arab known as Winters was killed, and the one called Owens is rotting in an American prison somewhere."

"But these people were not the ones behind what happened in Wyoming?"

"No." He explained the plot to destroy the American economy. "Fillmore Duquesne was responsible."

Ruth's face lit up with recognition. "That is why the American industrialist was killed. He failed his Arab friends."

"That's right. The others involved have all been taken care of as well, by their own people. When it was discovered that they were trying to replace the leaders of their own countries they were either shot or thrown in prison, their property and wealth confiscated."

"I understand. This kidnapping may have been revenge, then."

"By whom? All the main players are dead and buried, or wasting away in some rotting hole, penniless. They haven't the means or the money to carry out something like this."

She smiled. "Relatives. In the Arab world when one member of a family is humiliated, the whole family feels it. A son, a daughter, brother, sister. Someone could have come after Daniels."

"Well, whoever they are, they're mighty powerful!"

"Yes." Her brow furrowed. "Their connections extend into Israel."

"Yeah. Come on. I want to see Mike."

She grabbed his arm. "You can't. You're not supposed to be in Israel, remember?"

"The devil with that!" he said, pulling away and opening the door. "I'm gonna visit her, Ruth, and we, you and I, are going to find out what happened. Then, if possible, we're going to help them."

She joined him as he walked quickly toward the entrance. She smiled. "Now you know how I felt about Imad."

"Yeah, I know."

"These two are important to you."

"Very good people, that's all."

He opened the door for her and they went to the elevator. "This could end peace talks, Tom. The international press . . ."

"I know. Let's just hope Jerry's in a position to knock the wind out of their sails."

"Mrs. Daniels? Mrs. Daniels? Can you drink this?"

Mike was confused at the unfamiliar voice, then felt the hand behind her head, lifting. Then liquid touched her lips, moistening her dry mouth and throat. She opened her eyes, focusing, trying to remember.

"Where . . . where am I?"

Her head was lowered back onto the pillow, the shadowy figure in white moving away; another, in tan, replacing her.

"You are in Hadassah Hospital. I am—"

"Jerry!" She tried to throw herself from the covers, but the tan dream pushed her shoulders, forcing her back.

"Please, Mrs. Daniels. We want to help. Please, relax."

Mike let her body stop struggling. "Jerry! He . . . Ohhh, you don't understand! They took him from me! The Mercedes

. . . Mohammad . . . he said . . . the name was . . . Mohammad." She struggled again, trying to be free of the bed. "I must find Jeremiah."

Macklin stepped from the shadows and placed his hand on her arm. "Mike."

"Colonel Macklin?"

"How ya doin', lady?" He held her hand tightly.

Mike wiped the tears away with her arm, then reached for a tissue. "How . . . what . . ."

"A long story. This is Ruth Levona. She's with the Aman, Israeli Army Intelligence."

Mike looked at the pretty lady in front of her, then back at Macklin. "Jeremiah . . ."

"We don't know, Mrs. Daniels," Ruth said, glancing at Macklin and wondering how much she should say to a woman who may have become a widow. But then, she had done it before, hadn't she? It really wasn't so hard. You just shut off your heart, refuse to feel. You control.

"Two of Ruth's people were killed in that battle, and three of the group who took Jerry," Macklin said. He told her about the news release. When he was finished, tears were running down Mike's cheeks again, her teeth biting into her lower lip.

"We . . . we took a horrible chance. We couldn't hide . . . Jerry . . ." She raised up and put her arms around Macklin's waist, the tough exterior melting away to reveal her fear, the tears flowing.

"How could this be happening again? We thought it was over. We thought we were safe." She caught her breath, trying to get control. "No, that's not true. We needed to find out if we were safe." She slammed her fist into the mattress. "We should have stayed in Jackson. We . . ."

Ruth felt the anguish and desperation, the love. She took Mike's hand and squeezed it. "No, you were right, you can't run. You have to face them. You can't let them control your life."

After a few minutes the sobs died into sniffles. "I'm sorry I'm such a baby, but . . ." Mike tossed the soaked tissue aside, grabbing another from the small box.

"Can you tell us anything? We must know what these people looked like so we can—"

"Mohammad! When they grabbed us at the gate, one of them made a point of mentioning the name Mohammad."

Mohammad Faisal. Ruth knew the name well. The PLO's

henchman on the West Bank. A shadowy figure Israeli intelligence didn't even have a picture of, let alone a knowledge of his whereabouts. Had PLO leader Yasser Arafat authorized the kidnapping in an attempt to stop the peace talks because he and his group had been refused participation? Or was Stein correct in his news release? Had Faisal really left the PLO and started this group called the Revolutionary Council for Palestine?

Ruth Levona hated Faisal almost as much as she hated Fami Badannah. Both had caused her personal grief. Both were sworn enemies of Israel who had murdered Israeli citizens. In her opinion, both deserved nothing more than hanging from the neck until dead. But she didn't believe Mohammad Faisal was stupid enough to try something like this, nor would he drop the PLO. Like all members of the inner circle, Faisal relied on its money and power for sustenance. Like a man addicted to heroin, the Faisals of the world couldn't give up their evil habits easily. No, a bigger evil was behind this than Mohammad Faisal. That was the evil she wanted to destroy.

"You are sure of the name?" Ruth asked.

"Very sure. Who is he?"

"A West Bank terrorist," Macklin put in.

"You are Senator Freeman's daughter, aren't you?" Ruth asked Mike.

"Yes."

Levona turned to another woman soldier standing near the door. "Contact the senator. He may want to fly here until we have this resolved. Do it now, please!" The girl fled from the room.

"You . . . you swing a lot of weight for a"—she looked Levona over—"a hundred and fifteen pounds." She forced a smile.

"Practice. Now, before you fill us in on the details, you must understand why we are keeping you in the hospital. You were not injured, but in the doctor's thorough physical he discovered that you are pregnant and spotting a little. The excitement—"

Mike's grin was from ear to ear. "Pregnant! Oh . . ." She suddenly realized what Levona was saying. "I . . . I didn't lose the baby?"

Levona smiled. "No, no. The spotting is very light, but we want to make sure you don't, so you must rest here tonight."

"Congratulations," Macklin said, wondering if Jerry would ever know.

Levona hesitated a moment, then decided she'd go ahead. "Were you followed to Jerusalem?"

Mike grew serious, thinking. "Raffi did act strange, speeding up the car, watching the rearview mirror. But he said he was just behind schedule."

"They must have known where you were. Have you had any other contacts with other people outside of Raffi?"

Mike thought, then brightened. "At the hotel in Tel Aviv! An Englishman here on business, and an Israeli business associate, a woman. She looked Arabic, but said she was Israeli, from a Jewish family that immigrated here in 1950 from . . . Egypt, I think."

"Did Raffi know this woman?"

"No, but he did take pictures of both her and her English friend. He asked us about them, then told us not to worry. He made sure we weren't followed out of the city. He stopped along the way and mailed some film. I thought it was the pictures of the man and woman."

"I will check. What about this Englishman?"

"Alistair . . . Benson. From Hampton, or Hampstead, something like that. He joined us for breakfast at the hotel in Tel Aviv . . . two days ago."

Alistair Pike, Levona thought. Back in business. An outside hired gun. Whoever was behind all this was careful about keeping everything outside of their own organization, hiring very expensive help. Not a Mohammad Faisal trait. He did everything with men who had served in the PLO for years and returned to the West Bank with him. He refused to trust outsiders.

She shook her head lightly. Why was Mohammad's name used?

She made a note to find Raffi's missing pictures and determine who the woman was.

"Tell me about the rest of your visit," Levona asked. "Your trip to the Galilee."

Mike launched into it, telling about their trip to holy sites, then the kidnapping. By the time she finished she was drained.

As Levona shoved the notepad into her attaché case the girl slipped through the door, returning from her ordered chores. She spoke quietly to Ruth.

"Colonel, please, don't whisper!" Mike said, upset.

Levona returned to the bed and stood next to Macklin. "Your father is out in the mountains. A woman named Charla said the senator and your brother were checking on their cattle. I assume Charla is your sister-in-law. She will have him call as soon as he arrives at the house." She touched Mike's shoulder. "I will be back. Has anyone else been here to speak with you?"

Mike shook her head, her mind somewhere else.

"A guard is posted outside your room for your protection. We will go and speak with the man in charge of your husband's rescue and let him know what you've told us so he won't burden you with more questions."

"Then you're not directly involved in finding Jerry?" Mike asked.

"No. Colonel Macklin asked that we come as soon as we heard on the radio what happened. Ironically, we were to meet you at the hotel this afternoon."

Mike looked at Tom. "Thank you. One of these days we'll get together when someone's life is not at stake." She forced a smile.

"You must rest, Mrs. Daniels," Ruth said. "You have good news for your husband when we find him. You don't want to do it looking a mess!" She smiled.

"You will let me know . . ."

"Please don't worry. Everything will be fine. Becka will be here for a while. I will see you soon."

Tom kissed Mike's hand as Ruth moved toward the door. "We'll find him, Mike. He'll be all right."

She smiled again, accepting the hope he tried to give.

As they stepped to the elevator, Tom had a question for Ruth. "You seemed awfully deep in thought in there."

"Things are not making sense. We know that Mr. Daniels was not CIA and the terrorists' allegations have no basis. That means someone is using him to discredit peace talks."

"Faisal works for the PLO," Macklin said. "Must be them."

"Possibly, but I don't think so. The PLO's predicament is very serious right now. At present the United States is blocking PLO involvement in the peace talks and Arafat is trying to change that. A mistake like this could destroy any chances of U.S. support."

"Unless they see there is no chance," Macklin said. "Wouldn't they want to stop peace talks then?"

"Stop them, yes. Take the blame, no. I can see them forming a group such as the Revolutionary Council for Palestine to hide their involvement. But why, then, would they use Mohammad Faisal? Why would his name be used so easily?"

"I see what you mean. Who then?"

"We have many choices." She looked at her watch as they entered the elevator and started down—six-fifteen. The elevator stopped and the doors opened, several people around them getting out.

"What will be your American government's official position on Daniels?" Ruth asked.

"Deny the charges," Tom said as they walked into the parking area. "One, because they aren't true, and two, because they don't want anyone knowing the truth about what happened in Wyoming. It would frighten a lot of Americans if they knew something that big and potentially deadly had happened so close to home."

"They may not have a choice. The Arabs are already privately demanding information, making behind-the-scene threats to end peace talks, based on the terrorists' claims."

She started the motor and pulled from the garage.

"Where're we going?"

"Aman headquarters. We must talk with David Stein."

Macklin noticed her wrinkled brow of concern. "What's wrong?"

She shrugged. "You remember in the news broadcast that Assistant Minister Stein said two of the terrorists incriminated Faisal as the leader of the kidnapping attempt?"

"And you've said you disagree."

"Yes, and Stein knows what I know. He is too quick to accuse."

"How come?"

"Politics."

"Umm. You have that problem, too."

"That is why we are going to Tel Aviv," she said. "I must talk to Stein. Hopefully he will reconsider his position."

"If not?"

"Stein is politically responsible for the Aman, but he has little clout. Hoshen, as Minister of Defense, controls things. We will go to him."

Sabrila took a deep drink of the amber liquid, pleased with their success.

"It went well, Alistair, don't you think?"

"You don't have the American." He swallowed half a glass-full.

"We don't need him," she said coldly. "The damage has been done."

"But you wanted him, ANGEL wanted him."

Sabrila said nothing.

"I have an idea," Pike said.

"I'm listening," she said, the chill still in her voice.

"If he gets away, set him up as Hoshen's killer."

Sabrila lit up. "And Khourani. Very good, Pike. Tell Zalinka to hold off for a day or two. Let the American think he is safe. Then we can get to all three of them."

"You're sure Mohammad is dead?"

"Sure. He can't save Khourani. Do it. I'll clear it with ANGEL later. She will agree." She smiled. "This will work very well, Pike. Having Daniels, a suspected CIA agent working against peace talks, kill the leader of the West Bank coalition and the Israeli Minister of Defense . . . Wonderful!" She laughed. "What place have you decided to use in making Daniels look like a murderer?"

"The holy mount, of course."

Sabrila smiled. "You really are worth the money. And the marksman?"

"Only the best," he said. "Anything else?"

"Only one. Is your man still in place in Jackson Hole, Wyoming? The one you had watching the Danielses and the senator's family?"

"Yes. He decided to take a couple of weeks' vacation and spend some of his hard-earned money. Why?"

"We still have unfinished business there. Will he help us?"

"For the right price he'd kill his own brother."

She laughed lightly, then gave him the instructions.

"Your ANGEL is really out for revenge, isn't she?" he said. "All this big talk about freeing Palestinians is rhetoric."

"It is both. The senator and his family interfered in ways that are unforgivable. They must pay. Simple as that."

"Umm." He handed her a piece of paper on which he had written a number. "Sorry. I'm out of this one. I don't relish killing innocent women and children like you seem to. You make the call."

He stood. "I need some fresh air, and some sleep. I'll finish helping you with things here, Sabrila, but that's it. I won't be involved in Jackson." He headed for the bedroom door, leaving her alone in the room.

She waited a few minutes, then picked up the phone and placed the call to a number in Teton Village. Alex Manners was in and cooperative. She promised she'd deposit a check for a hundred thousand dollars in a Cayman Island bank account, fifty thousand up front, fifty when the job was done. He promised to do it within the week.

Sabrila made one other phone call. This time it was routed by way of Italy through Greece, the United States, back to Israel, and went to a scrambled private line at Aman headquarters in Tel Aviv.

"This is Sabrila." She listened. "Yes. My phone is protected as well." She listened again. "A temporary setback even if he escapes." She explained her plan, then listened again. "Yes, I will call ANGEL tonight. Don't worry, we will soon have all three of them out of the way. Have you taken care of the other one?" She listened. "You must do it soon." She listened again. "I realize it must be subtle . . . But the sword—" The line clicked off and she hung up. INFERNO was a hard man, but he was also in charge. If it were her she'd just kill the remaining obstacle and be done with it.

But a little more time, a little more caution, couldn't hurt. After all, INFERNO had been in place for twenty-five years. Waiting, ever so patiently waiting. She could wait the few extra hours he said he needed. It would all work out the same, and soon, very soon, the House of Hassan would be in place.

CHAPTER 18

6:00 P.M., Wailing Wall, Jerusalem

Lev Zafit had walked the streets of the Old City for nearly two hours. Since watching the attack on the Americans his mind had gone blank and his system had shut down. Lev had never seen the product of his betrayal before. He had never seen men shot down, innocent strangers screaming, frantic, terror in their eyes, their hands shaking so badly that they couldn't control themselves.

Lev sat on the low wall bordering the sidewalk, his head in his hands, the vision of battle still racing through his mind. The cars speeding to the curb, people scattering in every direction, then police rushing in, only to be pinned down in a hail of bullets. One was struck down as he jumped from a burning car, choosing to dodge bullets over the sure death awaiting him in the flames. It had been a no-win situation. The decision had ended his life.

Then the explosion of the vehicle, turning the street into an inferno of flames and smoke! He had seen it all! And had panicked.

Fear had forced his legs to turn and run, distancing himself from the havoc his betrayal had caused, and from the consequences he knew awaited him if even one Israeli policeman recognized the guilt Lev knew must be written all over his face.

Lev lifted his head, taking a deep breath, wishing he hadn't stayed. The fruits of his treachery filled his mind with all of the past deaths he must have caused; with bloodied bodies, and graves dug by families deprived of loved ones. All because he had sold out for money.

He was a traitor! A murderer!

He stumbled away from the wall and mindlessly wandered, his self-hate hot in his breast. He deserved nothing more than death, to be hung from a tree, food for insects and birds, his bones picked clean, while his spirit festered in Hades.

As he tried to shake off the nightmare of what he'd done, he found himself at the Wailing Wall. Stepping close, he began going through the motions of prayer, earnestly striving for the proper order, asking that God forgive his sins. In his mind he saw the gate on the other side of the temple mountain from where he stood, the golden gate, the one through which the Messiah would come and punish the wicked and destroy the enemies of his people. Lev knew he was one of those ripe for destruction.

He wondered how long he must burn. How long would it take for payment? King David had committed adultery and killed only one man. He, Lev Zafit, had been responsible for the deaths of dozens! David had paid all of the days of his life, tormented by what he had done, praying that God would not leave his soul in hell. At least God had promised David that he wouldn't. He, Lev Zafit, would receive no such promise.

He prayed harder, his body moving rhythmically, his heart becoming involved, supplicating, trying to feel something from God, tears bouncing off his cheeks and landing on the stone of the ancient wall.

Nothing. What more could he do? How does one pay for taking a life? Many lives?

His legs became weak and he fell on his knees, his shoulders slumping, his head falling into his lap.

Lev was not a man of courage. He couldn't look death in the eye and spit. It frightened him when he thought of the hell his own people would put him through if he told them what he had done.

And what of his family? The humiliation! His children would be ostracized, his wife forced to change her name, move their family to another place! Was it right, putting them through such sorrow and bitterness for his sins?

The faces of the dead swooped into the darkness of his closed eyes, ghosts of his evil deeds throwing themselves at him. His eyes flashed open, his body tense, arms lifted to ward off the spirits of the dead before he realized that it was only his imagination.

Or was it? Could he live being haunted like this, the spectre of evil deeds constantly before him? No, it would drive him insane!

He closed his eyes against the pain and anguish, rocking back and forth, saying the words, praying for the strength to free himself from the abyss of his own hell.

As he hung up the phone David Stein took the last cigarette out of a pack and tossed the wrapper toward the waste
can, adding it to others of the same brand lying in a ring
around the octagonal receptacle. As he struck a match a
knock came at the door. He checked his watch—7:15 P.M.—
then lit the cigarette.

"Yes."

The door swung inward and Colonel Levona stood in the
opening, Macklin at her shoulder.

"Colonel Levona," Stein said, putting on his best smile.
"Colonel Macklin. Please, come in." He took a deep drag on
the cigarette, then snuffed it out in the overflowing ashtray,
enlarging the gray ring surrounding it and getting the dust
on his fingers. He rubbed his hands together, brushing it off,
then pointed to chairs. "Please, sit. It is a surprise to see you.
I suppose you are here for an update on what intelligence
tells us is happening in Syria?" He forced a smile.

"One of our team filled us in a few minutes ago. Apparently there's a lot of activity at the factory. They may be leaving."

Stein nodded. "Too early to tell what it means. They
could be adding additional troops for protection . . ."

"They could be moving," she said.

He shrugged. "Maybe. General Ativa says you are ready
with your plan." He looked at Macklin, fishing for information.

"Yes, we're ready," Macklin responded warily.

"Good. Would you . . . care to share . . . anything you
need?" He smiled.

Ruth interrupted. "We came here on another matter.
General Ativa is handling our needs on the Duma project."

Stein waited, a surprised look on his face. Macklin got
the impression he didn't like Ruth much.

"We have talked with Mrs. Daniels. She and the kidnapped American are friends of Colonel Macklin."

Stein's frown was hard, his eyes cold. "That is not your
responsibility, Colonel. Between Aman, Mossad, and the
Jerusalem police, we have more than enough people working
on the Danielses' attempted kidnapping."

"We understand that, Assistant Minister," Macklin said. "However, they are American citizens and personal friends of the president of the United States. My visit was to get enough information—"

"Colonel Macklin, your embassy has been informed. They will see to Mrs. Daniels's needs and will inform Senator Freeman and the president. You have other duties. And, I might remind you, your presence here is not to be known." Stein forced the hard face into more agreeable lines. He needed information. "What did you discover in this diversionary trip?"

"Mrs. Daniels says Mohammad Faisal's name was mentioned," Ruth said. "Several times."

Stein responded carefully. "We captured two terrorists. They say the same thing." He leaned forward, placing his forearms on the desk. "They also tell us the kidnapping was sponsored by the PLO."

She shook her head adamantly. "It is wrong."

He looked at her cautiously. "What do you mean?"

"Are you saying Faisal started this group, the RCP, the ones claiming responsibility for Mr. Daniels's disappearance?" Ruth asked.

"Yes, the PLO is behind the whole thing. Everyone knows Arafat is angry because he wasn't allowed to participate in peace talks. But because of his earlier statement disavowing terrorist tactics, he can't be directly involved in terrorist activities or his position worsens in the eyes of the world, especially with the Americans. It makes sense to me that Arafat would use another group, a new one to which he had no previous ties. It would leave himself and the PLO free to denounce the act and declare his innocence of any wrongdoing. He has done it many times."

"But you see, that is the problem. Everyone knows Faisal is PLO. Arafat would be a fool to use him if he intended what you say."

Stein felt the trickle of sweat roll down his side. He must keep calm, find out what they know. "You have another explanation?"

Ruth tossed her attaché case in the direction of the couch. "Let's not play games. The other option is obvious. Another group, determined to discredit Israel, the United States, *and* the PLO. A group or individual who is trying to stop peace talks while wresting control of the Palestinian people away from the PLO. Someone who desires to be the new Palestinian leader, possibly to make a major bid for the leader of all Arabs. Someone who very much wants a violent solution to our presence in this land. This effort to use Faisal and the PLO is a smoke screen, a cover for their movements. They are betting on our fixation on the PLO, knowing how quick we are to focus on anything or anyone with PLO connections, leaving them free to accomplish something worse than a kidnapping."

Stein fought the desire to let his mouth fall open. He had to fight panic. He stood and walked to the window. He must get control. "Worse?"

"Surely you can see that this is only the first step. Leaders of the Arab nations have made no formal denunciations of us and the Americans. They are only privately asking for explanations, leery of an unknown group who say they have documents. They will wait for something more. This enemy, whoever they are, will give it to them, and it will leave no question in anyone's mind about the Americans being untrustworthy, and our working with them against the Arabs. You know how paranoid these Arabs are right now. If something like what I propose happens, they will run from peace talks and never return.

"Iraqi leaders are certainly looking for an excuse to force the United States from the region. Iran, Yemen, possibly Syria, as well. Even Saudi Arabia might welcome a safe way to be rid of them, now that they have what they want. If whoever is behind this is successful, they will unite the Arab world again, against *us*. We will fight more wars against a more united Arab front!"

Stein felt his hand start to shake. She had everything but names! How could she? How . . . ? He was boiling inside. It was everything he could do to keep his exterior unruffled. He turned on Levona.

"It is all supposition. The PLO is behind this, Colonel! We have proof! Witnesses. Faisal did not intend his involvement to be known. Do you think the men we interrogated volunteered the name to us? Hardly!"

"Mrs. Daniels—"

"Was to be taken with her husband. If she had not escaped she couldn't have told you anything."

Macklin could see Stein's anger was about to boil over and scald all of them, but he had a question of his own.

"How did the terrorists know where the Danielses were?"

"What?" Stein said, his train of thought intruded upon.

"*How*, General Stein, did the terrorists—"

"Our understanding is that the terrorists followed them from the Galilee."

"How did they know they were in the north? Isn't it true that only a limited number of your people knew where they were?"

Stein didn't speak. He must not be careless, turning against these two would be the worst thing he could do. Levona was respected by Hoshen, well-liked by Ativa. If she went to either of them it would be out of Stein's control. He must keep it here, in this room.

"Umm, I see what you mean," he said, letting his face reveal the change a sudden revelation would bring.

"Mrs. Daniels told us that an Englishman and an Arab-looking woman passing herself off as an Israeli befriended her and her husband in Tel Aviv," Levona added. "She said Raffi took pictures of them and then made sure they weren't followed from the city."

"But they were followed from the Galilee," Macklin said. "And what about those pictures, Mr. Stein? Where are they? Who are these two mysterious people? What role do they play?"

Stein sat at his desk. "I can't answer your questions, but I will find out. You think, then, that we have a breach of security? That someone inside told the terrorists of where the Danielses were?"

"Yes. And we think your news release was a little premature."

"I can see that now. But Minister Hoshen—"

"The minister made that decision?"

"Yes, of course, but once I tell him about this . . ." He was in control now, playing the game he had played so well for the last twenty-five years. He stood and returned to the window, acting the thoughtful Israeli. He turned and faced Levona and Macklin. They had gotten too close, but he had planned for just such an occasion.

"I'm going to share something with you. It is extremely confidential." He watched their eyes. He had them. "General Ativa has been under surveillance by a special team of operatives from the Mossad. We suspect that he is a collaborator."

Levona's mouth dropped open. "Ativa? But that's impossible!"

"I understand your feelings, Colonel." He reached into a desk drawer, pulling out a file folder. Opening it, he removed two pictures. "These may help."

Levona took them and Macklin gazed over her shoulder. In the photo three men were sitting around a table looking at some papers.

"Ativa meeting with a man you all know," Stein said. "At least by name."

"Who? I . . ."

"Mohammad Faisal. We think the papers you see in Ativa's hand are the names of our undercover agents on the West Bank."

Levona sat down.

"Who is the other person?" Tom asked.

"A doctor, a go-between. We watch him, but he is not important to us now. The point is that Ativa is probably your insider."

"Does Hoshen . . ."

"Yes, the minister knows. When the pictures came to me via one of our Arab undercover operatives, I went immediately to Minister Hoshen. He is responsible for the surveillance orders." He took the pictures back and closed the envelope, lifting it for dramatic effect. "There is more here, and it all fits very well with what you are telling me. It may give us enough to have Ativa removed."

Levona was visibly stunned, her world falling apart. Ativa had been like a father to her ever since . . . ever since she could remember. Macklin pulled at her arm and she got to her feet. They moved to the door.

"Not a word, Colonel," Stein said. "Understood?"

Ruth nodded.

"One other thing. For now the government has released our official position on the matter of the kidnapping. It will stand until we have Ativa. It shouldn't take more than a day, maybe two. Will you cooperate?"

Ruth nodded again as she closed the door behind them.

Stein was pleased with himself. His preparation had paid off. Even though he hadn't planned on releasing the information on Ativa for another twenty-four hours, now was just as good. He shoved the file back in his desk and leaned back in the chair, chuckling to himself. The look on Levona's face! Her world was shattered!

The smile turned to a nasty grin. Soon she and her friend Macklin would be gone as well. Part of the fallout created by Ativa's downfall. Unwittingly, they had placed the last nail in Ativa's coffin. And in their own.

All he needed was an excuse to take them off the Duma project. ANGEL was providing that. The factory would disappear. Levona and Macklin could be held responsible for jeopardizing Israel's security. As new head of Aman, he would see that they were properly disciplined.

And with Daniels well on his way to becoming America's latest fiasco . . . the killer of Israel's minister of defense and of a prominent West Bank leader . . . Stein had to admit, Sabrila's new plan was genius.

He reached for another cigarette. If things went as planned, Daniels's death would become a temporary wedge between American and Arab interests. It would give them enough time to take power.

He coughed as the smoke hurt his lungs. He would quit the habit someday. Right now, he owed it to himself. Everything was on schedule. Mahmoud Salamhani deserved a reward.

CHAPTER 19

7:30 P.M., Jerusalem

Jerry was lying in a filthy room, his hands and legs tied to a post that held up shelves filled with endless rows of eerie, olive wood carvings of Christ on the cross. The room was dark and hot, the sweat running down Jerry's emaciated body, his face bruised, dried blood caked around his swollen mouth and eyes.

The terrorist entered the room, a gun in one hand. He smiled wickedly, laughing, kicking Jerry, goading him, punishing his already defeated body.

The assailant's face was of ashen-colored stone, the

anger etched in flesh like cracks in rock. Words gushed forth, harsh words, vulgar, filled with hate.

He lifted the gun, its black barrel glistening in the dim light, the finger gently squeezing the trigger. The gun jerked, the explosions like loud claps of thunder. One, two, all six bullets moving in slow motion through the thick, dank air. Moving toward Jerry's spent body.

Mike screamed and awoke with a jolt, sweat dripping off her brow, her already nauseated stomach wanting to convulse, the fear gripping her paralyzed muscles.

Her eyes focused on the small light at the head of the hospital bed, her mind and body revolting at the reality of the dream.

After a moment of gaining control, she threw off the damp cover and put her feet to the cool floor.

"Oh, Jerry, where are you?" she asked the empty room. "Where?" The sobs wracked her body as she dropped to her knees, pleading with the Lord for comfort, for knowledge that her husband was all right.

Moments passed and her sobs became sighs, which were in turn replaced by an idea—then calm determination. She stood and went to the sink, filling a paper cup three times, drinking. She opened the closet and withdrew her clothes, quickly dressing. She couldn't stay in the hospital any longer without going crazy. Colonel Macklin's call hadn't been encouraging, and her father said that all he was getting was political double-talk from both Washington and Israel. He would come as soon as he could, but he was at least a full day away. By then, Jerry might be dead.

Mike knelt again. She must find Jerry. She asked for guidance, pleaded for her husband's safety and freedom, and for the ability to slip from the hospital undetected. Then she remembered the baby. There had been no further spotting, but she asked for protection for the little one as well. As she stood she felt determined. Her mind had committed her body and spirit. She would find Jerry, somehow, somewhere, in the Old City.

Mike asked the cab driver to take her to a particular type of women's shop, then stuffed a twenty-dollar bill in his pocket. "Hurry!"

He screeched away from the curb, turned the corner, and pulled over, a big grin on his face.

"Keep the change," she said, returning the smile, knowing she had been taken.

In less than fifteen minutes she found what she needed and paid for it. Going into a change room she quickly slipped into her new clothes and added a little dark makeup to her already tanned skin. When she was finished she looked in the mirror. Some might discern the difference, but with the headcovering, veil, and long dress, very little but the eyes could be seen, and hers were dark brown. She thought they looked very Arabic.

She quickly shoved most of her regular clothes into a sack she would discard later. Taking her ID, money, and traveler's checks from her purse, she pushed it all into the four pockets of the rolled-up Levi's she was wearing under the dress, then threw the purse into a nearby trash can.

Taking a deep breath she left the room and strutted through the store. The saleslady gave her a wary look.

At the street she hailed another cab and asked to be dropped at Damascus Gate. Her heart was pounding. She was alone in a city she hardly knew, and she was afraid. But she refused to let anything get in the way of finding her husband before her nightmare became a reality.

They passed the Garden Tomb. Police vehicles and soldiers still roamed the area, getting thicker as the taxi neared Damascus Gate. Mike saw the car where it had come to a standstill on the steps—the blue sedan from which her husband had fled.

"Go to another gate. Stephen's Gate," she told the driver. He wiggled his way through traffic, several policemen checking his identity card and peering in the window at her, then letting them by.

The taxi stopped and she slid out, paying the driver with a ten-dollar bill.

Moments later she approached Stephen's Gate, her heart pounding, soldiers between her and the entrance. They would stop her. Already she was thwarted. Then came the disturbance. Two soldiers threw an Arab to the ground and began to search him, another started running down the street, two other soldiers in hot pursuit. No one was watching. She slipped past them and quickly found the shadows, walking rapidly into the nearly empty streets.

Jerry awoke with a start, his hands flailing about in the darkness of the unfamiliar chamber in which he sat. Raffi reached over and touched him.

"Shhh."

Jerry's mind rallied, focusing on the muffled words of Arabic coming from the room overhead. Raffi tensed, backing even farther into the darkness. Jerry scrambled after him, standing, then grabbing the Israeli's shoulders, pulling him down the tunnel away from the light.

"What is it, Raffi?"

"Palestinians!"

His mind already working out a way he could get Raffi through the narrow hole into the cavern, Jerry pulled harder. Raffi yelped with pain.

In Jerry's anxiety-laced fear he had pulled on Raffi's broken arm. He released his grip and tried for a better hold as a set of legs lowered through the hole. They'd never make it. He dropped Raffi roughly, aimed his body at the half-evident form, and ran, hitting the man's lower torso as if it was a sawed-off tackling dummy. He felt the resistance as the man's body hit the side of the hole, then the body went lax and the forward motion carried both of them into the darkness. Jerry scrambled for the rifle where it clattered on the rock-solid bottom of the tunnel, not realizing that his only competition for the weapon was lying unconscious on the floor. He grabbed it, swinging about and pointing it at the ray of light through which he knew the next assailant must come. He was sweating, afraid. Afraid he would be forced to kill again.

He heard a whack, then something large hitting the floor above. Then silence. A shadow moved across the opening and Jerry's finger tensed on the trigger. Then came a voice.

"American?" It was a young voice.

Jerry breathed a deep sigh and he put the gun on safety. "Yeah. What happened up there?"

The boy dropped through the hole, stooping, then moving out of the light. "As I returned I saw them come from another building into this one. I followed. When that one came down through the hole the other was watching." He smiled. "We hit him with the stone. He sleeps now."

Jerry grinned. "You saved our lives twice today. I won't forget . . . We?"

"The doctor. It took me a very long time. He was delivering a new baby." The boy shrugged. "I waited." He moved aside from the hole as another set of legs lowered into the cavern and a man emerged. "Although the Israeli forces search for you, they are cautious in the Old City, afraid of causing riots. It will take them several more hours to enforce a curfew so they can move about freely." The boy looked at the sleeping terrorist. "Like this one, others hide, waiting to hear of where you are. They will kill you for the reward."

"Reward?" Jerry asked.

"Yes. Someone has offered ten thousand American dollars for each of you—dead."

Jerry looked at the boy, who was stooped a little, making his tall skinny frame fit in the tunnel. He wore a long-sleeved shirt two sizes too small, and a wornout pair of cotton pants, two sizes too big, held up by a piece of rope. His feet were sandaled, the dust of the day's walking wedged in between his calloused toes.

His hair was uncovered, thick, and pitch black. The two-time savior was thin-faced with round eyes and a smile that flashed full across his face, showing a row of perfect, white teeth.

The doctor bent over, taking the light from Jeremiah's hand and flashing it on Raffi, a wrinkled brow of concern across his bearded face.

He moved to where Raffi sat and began inspecting his wounds. "I am Doctor Daoud Jamel," he said as he opened his black case. "The boy is Raoul. He is an orphan, but a good boy. You were lucky he was the one to help you. Unlike some in my country, he thinks all men are alike. You are the American I hear about in the news. You are supposedly held by terrorists." He smiled, as he cut away Raffi's shirt.

"What news?" Jerry asked.

"Israeli radio says that a West Bank faction of the PLO kidnapped you and, although you escaped, recaptured you and are holding you and this man somewhere in the Old City. The American government is threatening to withdraw their acceptance of the PLO and have even condemned West Bank leaders for being involved." He smiled again, stooping as he looked at Raffi's arm. "It was all announced very quickly after your disappearance."

Jerry got the message. Too quickly, in the doctor's opinion. "Why has he not been taken to an Israeli hospital?" he asked Jerry.

"A couple of men with Kalishnikov rifles wanted to give him more than a broken arm," Jerry said firmly. "I decided we'd stay out of sight, trusting the boy. I went to sleep."

"Children," he said. "If we adults could only be as trustworthy"—he looked at the boy now sitting on the floor, whose big eyes were taking everything in—"we might have peace in this land."

Jerry felt dizzy, took a few steps, and joined the boy, exhausted. He held the light while the doctor cleaned Raffi's wound and prepared the arm for setting.

Jerry guessed Dr. Jamel was about five feet ten inches. He carried two hundred pounds, much of it around his midsection, and had gray hair streaked with black, and a black beard streaked with gray. He wore a white shirt rolled up at the sleeves, over which was a suit vest that matched his pants. The black shoes were scuffed but of good quality. Jerry had the feeling that the good doctor knew his business and took very little guff from his patients.

"The terrorists have released a communique."

"And?" Jerry prompted.

"They say you are CIA and that you came here to plan war against the Arab world. They claim to have documents that prove this."

Jerry laughed lightly. "I wouldn't give the CIA the time of day any more than I would the PLO!"

Jerry adjusted his position, feeling a twinge in his back from carrying Raffi. He wondered if it was a disk or a muscle problem.

Raffi was lying on the cold stone, his eyes closed, his pale skin stark against the blood staining his clothes.

"Your Israeli . . . His arm may never be the same again. The bone is shattered by the bullet. We must get him to a hospital." He said something to the boy and Raoul disappeared through the opening. "Raoul will tell the police and get an ambulance. You had better tie up those men—and get me a blanket from upstairs to keep this one warm."

Jerry struggled to his feet and completed the tasks. Then he plopped down and took a deep breath.

"How do you fit into this, Doctor? You're Palestinian and yet . . . "

"I am a doctor," he smiled. "I help the injured, no matter who they are or how they got that way. They do not stay and I do not help them escape. They come, they go. Arabs and Israelis."

He knotted another stitch. "Like many Palestinians, I do not hate Israelis, but all of us are frustrated by what seems to be a political structure bent on denying our existence as a distinct nationality, even though most Israelis do not agree with the position their government takes. Our frustration is a breeding ground for violence. My people look for freedom and a way out of poverty and oppression. They throw rocks, destroy, even kill, and they get hurt." He shrugged.

"The Israelis would put you in prison."

"Some, yes. But as I said, not all Israelis agree with the official position you Americans see in your newspapers. If I go to prison for this—so be it."

The doctor began putting away his instruments and medicines.

"Do you support the PLO?"

"These days few people in this land support the PLO, Mr. Daniels. They make many empty promises while leaders amass great personal wealth. They hid this for many years, but now the people know that while they suffer in poverty and humiliation in the occupied territories, the leaders spend millions on exotic parties, lavish homes, very expensive automobiles and, some, sexual indulgence. These millions could be spent freeing Palestinians, at least feeding them. Many feel that the PLO does not want them to be free. It would cost the leaders their luxury and force them to return to a land plagued with problems for which they have no answers.

"But, until recently, the people of the West Bank have had no one else to whom they could turn. West Bank leadership will try changing that, and it is not a small thing. The PLO and all outside factions do not want the West Bank seeking peace on their own. They would lose the cause for which they are paid by corrupt Arabs of other lands who still want to use us for their own purposes, and they would be shamed, their promises unfulfilled." He laughed gently. "There are so many who want to represent Palestinians, and all of them insist their way is *the* way of defeating the Israelis. But most of them are organizations that want to use the Palestinian problem as a launching pad to fame and fortune, like the PLO has."

He sighed deeply. "The Italians have the Mafioso. You Americans have your CIA. We have the PLO and a dozen others."

The doctor smiled. "I am just a foolish old man who loves this land and all of its people. But I have faith in them. I believe that if the people were allowed to decide their own destiny, peace would come very quickly." He sighed deeply as he closed his case. "But, I am afraid it will never be. Wicked men will not allow it."

He looked at Raffi. "Help will arrive soon. It is best that I not be here." He moved toward the hole. "You see, although I am on a mission of mercy, I fear for my safety at the hands of this man I hardly know. Thus it is in the land called holy." He lifted himself up through the hole and disappeared.

The walk in hot clothing made sweat trickle down Mike's back, even though the evening was cool. The side of the road was dusty, causing grit to collect on her sandals and feet, agitating the tender skin between her toes. The taxicab driver had brought her to a turnoff, telling her it was only a short distance to the garden gate. She walked some distance before realizing he had dropped her at the wrong intersection. She backtracked nearly a mile, her temper fuming just below the surface, adding more sweat and grime to her skin.

She leaned against a stone wall, wiping her forehead, tired and depressed to the bone, the nausea holding near the back of her stomach like glue.

Mike pushed on the gate, walked through, and closed it behind her. Making sure she had stopped bleeding before leaving the hospital had given her peace of mind concerning the baby, but she wondered if all the walking . . . She didn't think so; in that part of her system she felt no pain.

The walk sloped gently down between rows of shrubs, trees, and flowers, creating a peaceful, cool environment that immediately began dissipating her worried feelings. Vandals had been at work breaking down rock walls and fountains, but it looked as if workmen had been busy making repairs. At least it was private, and quiet.

She came to a small, vandalized amphitheater recessed into the mountain. High rock walls on two sides offered complete privacy while still leaving the west open to a magnificent view across Jerusalem. She removed the head scarf and veil, the breeze immediately cooling her damp hair and skin. Unbuttoning the top two buttons of the high-necked, Arab dress, she flapped it a little, letting fresh air cool her upper torso.

Sitting down, Mike looked out across the city, catching her breath and gathering her thoughts. It all looked so peaceful when one stood back and gazed across its buildings, roads, and high walls. From where she sat, even the temple mount with its bustling masses of pilgrims, worshippers, tourists, and soldiers looking like ants seemed without a care or problem. Yet actually it was just the opposite. There was turmoil in Jerusalem tonight. The world was looking for her husband.

Her hand went to her hair, ruffling it, letting it dry in the cool of the evening breeze, her mind forcing its way through the maze of uncertainty that clouded everything.

She had done all she knew how to do. Searching the city, wandering aimlessly through its streets, was exhausting, frustrating, fruitless . . . and frightening. Scared faces, soldiers, hundreds of closed doors that would never open for her, people she couldn't talk to.

She had come to Orson Hyde Gardens to regroup . . . and to rest.

She laughed a little at her overzealous determination of several hours earlier. Her thoughts had been of strutting into the city in her Arab garb and walking directly to the place where Jerry was held. She had just known it would happen.

It hadn't. And wouldn't.

The tears gathered in the corner of her eyes again. "Oh, Jerry! Where are you?" The nightmare flashed through her mind, the vivid images of a beaten, bruised, and defeated Jeremiah Daniels wrenching her heart.

Standing, she moved to the southern side of the enclosure, looking around the garden from the open side of the amphitheater. The breeze slightly rustled leaves and branches. A few birds flitted about from tree to tree, calling one another above the quiet but perceptible buzz of insects as they moved among the shrubs and flowers.

The noise of the city was dull in the background, hardly

noticeable. Her eyes went to the road above the garden, then found the gate. From there they moved across each of the paths. She was alone. No other human walked the garden's peaceful paths.

Turning again, Mike went back into the small, circular amphitheater as far as she could, its high stone wall rising fifteen feet above the floor. She took a deep breath, then lowered herself onto the bench, stretching out, giving her legs a much-needed rest, her body a moment of rejuvenation. She needed a clear head, a chance to think things through.

She closed her eyes tight against the day, wishing it away like a bad dream, hoping that if she were pinched she'd simply wake up and find herself back in Wyoming, with Jerry beside her.

Her mind flew from one event to another, looking for hope in the nooks and crannies of the past twenty-four hours. Her hands tightened into fists. Thinking only created fear and panic. She adjusted her position on the hard bench and laid her wrist across her forehead, letting exhaustion pull at her eyelids. She needed rest, that's all. Then she'd figure out what to do. Then . . .

The sun fell farther toward the western horizon, but the garden remained empty except for her womanly form made tiny by the oversized stone bench on which she was lying. Her chest began moving regularly, exhaustion claiming its due.

City lights started coming on a few at a time, then by the hundreds. The last of the sun's rays glinted off the dome of the Mosque of Omar on the temple mount. Minutes passed, then half an hour, and finally three-quarters of an hour. Exhaustion eliminated dreams and Mike rested, recuperating from her desperate search, reviving her worn-out will.

An hour had passed in peaceful sleep when deep in the recesses of her mind a warning light went on and her eyelids flashed open like blinds attached to an impatient hand. Sitting bolt upright, she scrambled away from the sensed danger, her eyes focusing on the two shadowy, undersized forms before her. The wraiths jumped back, quickly scuttling to the dark side of the amphitheater, jabbering rapidly to one another in Arabic.

The darkening sky startled Mike nearly as much as the children had, and created a moment's disorientation and panic. She slid farther away from the cringing forms, trying to gather her senses. As her mind woke up she remembered where she was, but she was still afraid of the intruders. Then came recognition—and relief.

The two children, dressed in the traditional Arab gelebeah linen gowns, stood with wide eyes. One was a girl who looked as if she might be between six and eight; the other, a boy, tall and thin, a white cap resting on the crown of his head, a few strands of black curly hair protruding recklessly from underneath. Mike guessed at age twelve.

Warily the boy moved his slim body in front of the little girl, jabbering some sort of warning as she peered around his left side. They both stared unblinking at Mike, eyeing her carefully from head to foot.

"Hello." Mike smiled, relieved.

No answer.

"Do you speak English?"

The boy nodded, forcing a brave and defiant expression to wrinkle his brow.

"Are you from close by?"

There was no reaction this time, but Mike's eyes picked out a small satchel of belongings lying on the bench close by.

"My name is Michaelene Daniels. My friends call me Mike." She leaned forward and they took half a step backward.

"You . . . the name is for a man!" the boy said, a bit haughtily.

She smiled. "The nickname, yes, but it is easier to say. You can call me Michaelene if you like."

He nodded again. "Why you are sleeping here? It is dangerous at night."

"It was not my intention, but it seems my body decided to take a vacation."

He looked at her quizzically.

"Never mind. I was tired. It was quiet and peaceful. I couldn't help it." She smiled.

The girl spoke, her small girl voice sweet to hear in the Arabic language.

"My sister . . . she says she saw you on the television in the merchant's store window. You are a celebrity?"

Mike laughed, thinking of the events of the past day. The broadcast had carried pictures of both her and Jerry.

"No, I—"

The girl spoke again in Arabic.

158

"She says your husband is in trouble." He looked at Mike, his head cocked to the right a little, wondering if this could be true.

"Yes. People tried to kidnap him, but he escaped into the Old City. I . . . " Her eyes darkened as the anxiety returned. "I don't know where he is right now. I am looking."

The girl was talking anxiously in Arabic again, pulling at her brother's gown, determined.

"What is it?" Mike asked. "She seems excited."

He spoke firmly to the girl, then turned to Mike. The girl spoke hurriedly again and he spoke even more firmly, roughly brushing her hand off his sleeve.

"She doesn't know what she is talking about! We beg . . . we get our food in the city, then sleep in places like this at night. She said she saw one of our friends . . . " He hesitated.

Mike's stomach churned. "Go on, please! One of your friends. Did they see my husband?"

It was evident that the girl understood what Mike was saying and spoke again.

"Yes . . . maybe," the boy translated. "She saw Raoul, an errand boy, leading two Israelis into the old Mullah's house. She watched and they never came out again." He shrugged his shoulders. "One was hurt."

Mike stood, walking to them, kneeling, talking directly into the small set of eyes peering around the boy's sleeve. "Could you tell me where? Could . . . would you help me find that place?" Her eyes went to the boy's, which grew stern as he backed away a step.

"You are American. Husband also. I am Palestinian." He poked himself proudly in the chest. "You are my enemy. I cannot help you." He folded his arms across his chest, indicating the firmness of his position. Mike sensed that he wasn't as adamant against Americans as he tried to make her believe.

The girl stepped from behind him and began scolding in harsh tones, shaking her finger at him. He flushed, his eyes darting back and forth between the girl and Mike.

He nodded, speaking in conciliatory tones to the adamant little waif. Mike put her hand over her mouth, stifling a grin, not wanting to make the boy's embarrassment any worse as he struggled for a way to save face.

"You pay us, then we try!"

Mike quickly reached under her gown, searching her

pockets for money. She had only several dollars' worth of change, and realized that it had been some time since she had cashed a traveler's check.

"This for now. I will give you more later. A hundred American dollars, and some food."

The boy's eyes grew large. Mike could tell he had never been offered such a generous amount for his services.

She stretched forth her hand. "Shake?"

He grasped her hand and pumped it several times. "You make a good deal. The services of Rashid Tafiq are well known and very dependable." His smile was from ear to ear.

"That is your name—Rashid?" she asked.

"Yes. And my sister is Issa." The little girl was standing fully in the open now, her eyes bright with excitement.

"Issa, I am so happy to meet you. I hope we can be friends." She took the little girl's hand. "You are an answer to prayer."

The frail frame bent at the waist, bowing respectfully,

"Does she speak English?" Mike asked.

He brought his fingers together then lifted them apart slightly. "A little." He smiled lovingly at his little sister. "She understands much." Mike could sense the special bond between the two apparent orphans.

"Please. Sit down while I get ready. Rashid, where are your parents?"

He shrugged, looking toward the distant city. It was not a subject he would talk about easily.

"Why do you wear Arab clothing?" he asked. The girl understood the question and waited curiously for the answer.

"I was afraid. An American in the Old City, alone, a woman." She shrugged. "I was afraid someone—those who are responsible for my husband's disappearance—would recognize me and I would never find where he is being held."

He nodded sternly. "The Old City can be dangerous. I will protect you this time. But wearing the clothes will help." She was putting on the veil and head scarf. "You look like an Arab."

The little girl quickly added something that made the boy flush again.

"She says a very pretty Arab."

"Thank you, Issa." Mike said, taking the thin face with the large and beautiful oval eyes between her outstretched hands. "Now! Let's go find your friend!"

Rashid had his package of belongings flung over his shoulder, dangling from a self-made cloth rope, and started up the walk. "Come. I will lead the way."

Issa took Mike's hand and began moving after her brother, her small, warm palm sending a chill of love directly into Mike's heart.

Thank you, Lord, she said to herself. Thank you for hope . . . and these children to lead me.

Mike stood at the door, perplexed at the two boys speaking excitedly in their native tongue. The taller of the children, a boy named Raoul, had only just returned to his house. When they had first arrived Mike had been disappointed to find he wasn't home, but the old grandfather had said something to Rashid in Arabic, indicating that the boy would return soon. Then, when Rashid told her that he had been there earlier with an American, Mike knew she must wait.

The Arabic was even more rushed now, and Issa began dancing about anxiously. She grabbed Mike's hand and started to pull her down the street, the boys moving before them, still talking hurriedly. Rashid stopped in mid-sentence, a smile from ear to ear. "Your husband, he has been found, Mrs. Mike!" he said, grabbing her other hand and pulling her on again. "We must hurry. The police have come to get him!"

Mike's legs suddenly found added strength and she raised the dress above her dusty, sandaled feet and ran with the children down the cobbled street, the new boy speaking hurriedly in broken English as he ran at her side.

"I find . . . I hide them . . . Bad men with guns . . . "

Mike's heart sank and she stopped abruptly. Facing Raoul and taking his shoulders in her hands she asked, "Is he . . . are they . . . all right?"

"Yes . . . " She saw his eyes smile, looking past her. She turned around to see Jeremiah some distance away, but coming toward them, encircled by the police. His face was grimy but as handsome as she had ever seen it. She couldn't go on, her heart thankful, near bursting. The children ran to the police, talking to them excitedly. The new boy shouted at

Jerry and drew his attention, then pointed up the street toward Mike. At first Jeremiah's face showed confusion, then bright recognition. He burst from among his protectors and ran up the street toward her, grabbing her in his arms, wrapping them tightly around her, swinging her in a full circle.

"Jerry! Oh Jeremiah! Are you all right, are—" He muffled her speech with a hard kiss, then another.

The children clapped while the police stood in perplexed wonder. Jerry pulled away, looking at his wife carefully, touching her face as she touched his.

"Turned Arabic, have you?" he said, appraising her gown.

"I'll tell you about it later."

Jerry stooped down and took Raoul's hand. "I thought you had deserted me."

Raoul looked sheepish. Mike introduced Rashid and Issa. She could tell Jerry's heart was touched.

"Will you all join us for supper?" Jerry asked.

They looked at one another, smiling, then nodded excitedly.

"Then come on," he said, putting his arm around Mike's waist. "I'm starved."

Mike brushed the tears away lightly from her cheeks. "I . . . the children—"

He touched her lips. "Shhh. We'll get it all explained later. Right now, I just want to hold you."

Mike wrinkled her nose at him. "And get to a hot bath."

The police encircled them again as they moved up the street. Mike reached out for Issa, taking her hand and pulling her along. The two boys talked excitedly, then followed them through Damascus Gate to the waiting car beyond.

CHAPTER 20

7:30 P.M., Tel Aviv

Lev Zafit undid another button on his shirt. What little air there was in the small room was heavy and smelled of his own sweat. The sleeves on his starched shirt were moist and soiled where he had wiped gathering beads of salty perspiration from his face and neck.

Except for him, the room was empty now. But he knew his interrogators watched from beyond the two-way glass, enjoying the suffering of a traitor.

He didn't care. He wanted them to whip him, hang him from a tree, make him suffer. At least in that there was some cleansing, some payment. There was no other way to be rid of the ever-present, burning guilt that even sleep didn't dispel.

He heard the click of the latch in the door behind him and raised his head, wiping the tears quickly with his sleeve.

The bulldog general with the soft eyes came around to the head of the table and sat in the chair opposite Lev. The man was all business, but in a gentle sort of way that penetrated Lev's defenses. His voice was uneven, gruff, but not harsh. A deep resonant sound, almost methodical while staying humane. Lev found himself liking the general, which added to both his guilt and his desire to talk.

"Lev," said the interrogator, "when you made your call from the phone booth, why did you trust the person on the other end of the line?"

"My control agent gave me the phone number I should call and a code name that would be used by the woman I was to contact."

"A woman?" Ativa asked, leaning forward. "And this woman was on the line?"

"Yes."

"And the code name?"

"ANGEL."

Ativa sat back. "Who is your controlling agent?"

"I have never met him. I only know his voice and the code words we exchange. Even when we attended the same training meetings abroad, his identity was always kept from me."

"How was this done?"

"Disguise, or we talked by phone."

General Ativa eyed the traitor. He wasn't lying. This was a man overwhelmed with guilt, wanting to be free of it. They would learn much from him.

"We have notified your wife. One of our people will be with her for a while. We do not want anyone getting word of where you are, for your protection as well as your family's." He moved forward and placed his arms on the table, leaning toward Zafit. "You need rest. You'll be taken to a cell and given something for sleep. We want you rested, able to remember even the smallest detail. We want your help." He knew Zafit would go for the carrot. Forced traitors always jumped at the chance for redemption.

Zafit's head jerked up, his eyes hopeful. "Help? But what can I do?"

Ativa chose his words carefully, using them to bring Zafit hope while still reminding him of his precarious position. "Everything you tell us, every detail, will help us find who forced you into this. We know how they work. We know that you had no options and that you were a reluctant spy for them. What you did cannot be condoned, but you can help repair the damage and possibly stop even worse things from happening to Israel." He smiled. The Zafits of Israel were the easiest to deal with, as they should be. Everything he said was true, but Zafit was also guilty of treason, and for that he would go to jail. How he felt about himself day in and day out while living there would be determined by his cooperation.

Ativa stood and the door opened, a uniformed guard entered and grasped the traitor's arm, firmly but without malice.

Zafit quickly stood. "Thank . . . " He cleared his throat. "Thank you. I . . . " The tears came without warning. "I . . . "

Ativa nodded with understanding, then motioned to the guard. As the door closed behind the two men, Chaim Ativa sat down. A few seconds later Colonels Levona and Macklin joined him.

"I see what you mean, Chaim," Ruth said. Tom pulled up a couple of chairs across the table from the general.

"How did you get your hands on him?" Ruth asked, sitting down. "He surely wasn't at the scene of the kidnapping."

"He was, but that isn't where we found him. He saw it happen and apparently decided he'd call it quits. He turned himself in to a friend of mine at Jerusalem police headquarters, who notified me. No one else knows we have Zafit." Ativa shrugged. "Traitors often do that. They can't handle the guilt anymore once they see what their information does to people. They want to cleanse themselves. This is one way of doing it."

"I wonder how many more Lev Zafits there are in Israel," Tom interjected.

Ativa smiled. "More than we are willing to admit." He turned to Ruth. "Let's forget Zafit for a moment. You said your need to see me was urgent."

Ruth looked down at her hands. How did one ask an old friend if he was a traitor?

"Chaim, David Stein has evidence implicating you as a collaborator with Mohammad Faisal. He says—"

Ativa smiled. "I wondered how long we could keep up the charade."

Ruth's muscles went limp. She wanted a denial, not a confession.

Ativa fixed his eyes on hers, leaning forward. "I have met with Faisal, many times—not as a traitor to Israel, but as one who is working to save her from destruction."

"But how . . . ?"

"Faisal has turned against the PLO. He works to protect West Bank Palestinians against PLO assassins, and to bring about peace. We have been working together for some time, but I was sworn to secrecy. His life, and the lives of his people, would have been worthless if the slightest hint of collaboration were to fall into the blundering hands of the press."

"You make that sound past tense," Macklin said.

"Mohammad has disappeared. It is feared he is dead. His people have gone into hiding. I am protecting some of them in safe houses here in Jerusalem."

Ruth stood and faced the wall, her arms folded tightly, confusion in her voice. "He . . . he is a terrorist, Chaim. An enemy of Israel. You know the law forbids contact with him without government sanction."

He nodded, his face fallen. Of all the people he wanted to understand, Ruth was the most important. She had been like a daughter. "Yes, you are right. I have broken the law. For that reason alone I may lose my position as head of Aman. I also realize it makes me look like a collaborator, but much good has come from it. We have stopped nearly twenty assassins, prevented many deaths because of Faisal's information." He paused.

"And what have you done with these assassins? Why don't the rest of us know of their arrest?" Ruth asked tightly.

A slight grin appeared on Ativa's face. "Some died trying to escape my men. The rest are safely tucked away in our prisons."

"Then you have proof of your innocence," she said, turning back to him.

The smile remained. "Yes, I have proof. But do you need it so badly?"

She sat down and took the older man's hand. "Chaim, this can destroy you!"

"That doesn't matter right now, Ruth. We have saved lives. We have shown West Bank leadership that we care more for them than we do for silly rules that prevent us from having peace in this land. Isn't that more important than even my position?"

"Slow down, folks!" Macklin said. "Broke the law? Saving people's lives is breaking the law?"

"In Israel, yes." Ativa answered. "Every man in Israel feels that he can talk sense into the Arabs. Every Arab thinks the same of us Jews. It adds great confusion to have individuals bargaining, promising, dealing for our country. It has also done much harm, causing tremendous disunity. So a law was passed forbidding anyone from speaking for Israel, even communicating with her enemies on their own. Some have disobeyed the law." Ativa shrugged. "For it they are tried and imprisoned."

"But surely in this case . . . "

"My case is no different than any other. I knew that from the beginning. I may not go to prison, but I will be dismissed from office and forced to retire, regardless of the good I may have done." He took a deep breath. "Stein is only doing his job. And Minister Hoshen. If they don't, they also could be out of work." He paused, smiling. "I retire in a few years anyway. The lives we saved were more than worth the risk."

Ruth smiled. Ativa had a thick crust and a rough exterior. Few people really knew his heart. She knew. Because of one loved dearly by both of them, Ruth had come to know Chaim Ativa as few others did. He harbored, and hid, a heart of pure gold behind that exterior. Because of it, he had always put the lives of people before politics and paper pushing. That was why she trusted him. Even in this.

"You say *we*. Are others involved in your little operation?" Ruth asked.

"Several trusted men," he smiled.

She returned the smile. "Stein is building a case against you. He intends to knock you and your gallant intentions off their white horse."

He grinned again. "How long do I have?"

"Twenty-four hours. Maybe thirty-six."

"Then I must spend my last hours wisely. Mohammad contacted me before he left, warned me that there would be an attempt on the life of an American diplomat. I thought immediately of the Danielses, but Raffi had them out on the road somewhere and they couldn't be reached. When he called from the Garden Tomb, I felt relieved, and sent men immediately. They were only minutes from preventing the kidnapping altogether. But at least they created enough confusion to allow Mrs. Daniels time to get away, and probably saved the American's life. He and Raffi were found only a few hours ago, safe, in the Old City. Raffi is in the hospital, Daniels and his wife and three children are on their way to a safe house. They will remain there as long as there is danger of another attempt."

"Children?" Macklin asked.

"Yes, but it is a story that confuses even me, Colonel. You will have to ask them to share it with you next time you see them." Ativa smiled. "They are unique people."

Macklin smiled. That he knew.

"Mohammad left for Tunis. He did not say why, only that he would contact me upon his return. His plane went down over the Mediterranean, and he is believed dead." Ativa hesitated, a hardness in his eyes. "He was betrayed. Someone must have found out what he was doing. Unlike my own case, his enemies did not give him a chance at a fair trial." He rubbed his eyes gently, trying to dispel the ache. "The man who told me of Mohammad's disappearance is Faisal's most-trusted lieutenant. Within an hour of Mohammad's flight out of Israel, he was approached about a plot to assassinate several of the West Bank's most influential citizens, people Mohammad had gone to great lengths to protect because of their willingness to talk peace with us. They had formed a coalition against the PLO leadership. He was offered a great deal of money."

"And?" Ruth asked.

"We are moving them to safety. Then he will disappear."

"They had to have Mohammad out of the way to reach them, kill them, and stop peace talks," Ruth said.

"That is why I wanted you to see Zafit. The traitor is not aware of it, but I believe he was part of the same plot."

The two colonels looked at one another, confused. Ativa moved to clear it up.

"It is clear from the terrorists' news release that Daniels is being used to discredit American influence and cause Arab nations to doubt our intentions. Whoever is behind the one attempt is behind the other." He paused again, shaking his head. "If Mohammad had only told me more. Names . . . " He shook it off. "We do have Zafit. And something that may interest your devious minds."

He leaned forward, placing his elbows on the table, interlocking his fingers. "You remember that Zafit said the name of the person who took his call used the code name ANGEL. Any recognition?" he asked. "Have you ever heard that code name used, Colonel Macklin? Anywhere, anytime?"

Macklin shook his head.

Ativa turned to Ruth.

"No, never," Ruth said

"When we began closely watching Duma eight months ago we discovered the name. It popped up again while doing surveillance on Iraq's second-in-command, General Dabib. We heard it again in a phone call over satellite used by Syria's General Shaath. Both transmissions were coded but we deciphered them. Both dealt with meetings—places, dates, and times—held during the last six months. All arranged by this ANGEL."

"I assume you watched those meetings," Macklin said.

"We tried, but couldn't get any operatives inside. We did get close enough to make a list of attendees. Four more military leaders from Arab nations, along with terrorist leaders Abu Ibrahim and Ahmoud Hassan, and several of their bodyguards."

"A meeting of the devil's worst. Anyone else?" Macklin asked.

"The usual kitchen help and pretty young ladies. Several

carloads," he smiled. "And a heavily veiled woman we have yet to identify."

"ANGEL!" Ruth said.

"That is my guess," Ativa replied. "And I believe she is responsible for what is going on here. But there is one other bit of information."

"I can hardly wait," said Macklin.

"After your rescue at Sahles, General Shaath of Syria apparently panicked. He made a call on an unprotected phone to a residence in Damascus. One of the listening posts was attuned to him. He talked with the person we believe was ANGEL. She calmed his anxious heart and said everything was under control. The factory was being taken care of—sorry, Ruth, unfortunately she didn't broadcast her intentions. She did say she had met with INFERNO, in Israel, and that they would have Megiddo's Sword within three days. Shaath's ruffled feathers were smoothed and he promised to use his influence on Assad to have Syria's air force on full alert to protect the factory against any immediate attack from Israel, but that he would need more money. They parted friends."

"If she knew what phone he was using, she'd probably have the man's throat cut. When did you intercept all this?" Macklin asked.

"Early this morning."

"Not much time to find this guy, then, is there?"

"What is Megiddo's Sword?" Ruth asked.

Ativa smiled. "There is a medieval Christian legend about a powerful sword. It is said that the angel Gabriel created the sword on the forge of God for the Christian Messiah to use in his last great battle at Megiddo, the Christian Armageddon. Lucifer, the devil, stole it from heaven and delivers it to those who sell their souls to him. The leader of the Turks supposedly used it in battles against the Christian crusaders when they came to reclaim the Holy Land. With the sword in his hand he was invincible, his enemies falling before him like stalks of grain before the scythe. Supposedly it was recaptured by the leader of the last crusades, who then buried it in the Mount of Olives, where it awaits the hand of the Christian Messiah on the day of his return. He will use it to cut asunder his enemies, those who have come to drive the house of Israel from Jerusalem."

"What do you think it is?" Ruth asked.

"That, dear lady, I do not know. The key is to find INFERNO and let him tell us."

"How?"

"As you see, all of these events are related. All intended to stop peace and overthrow Israel. Zafit is the key. He has a controlling agent and that agent might also control INFERNO. If we find the one, we may find the other. Second, INFERNO is an agent with the capability to access our most destructive weapons, possibly our nuclear arsenal, and things our scientists may be . . . "

His hesitation alerted Ruth. "What is it, Chaim?"

He shook his head. "Nothing, really. We have a new weapon, but it is not finished, has never been successfully tested. It will never be operational within ANGEL's time frame."

"But maybe we should check it out." Ruth said. "Possibly—"

"I wouldn't know where to begin. To my knowledge no one person knows exactly what it is. Even the scientists themselves don't have access to all of the information about it. Each carries out his part of the overall development without having the slightest idea what the others are doing. Only five men in the entire country know the whole picture."

"Any of them suspect?" Macklin asked.

Ativa shrugged. "Money does strange things. I suppose one of them could be INFERNO, but even they can't make the weapon operational."

"Why not?"

"Once the weapon is ready, I understand that it will take five sets of separate codes combined into one whole to make it work. Only one, maybe two, people will have access to the combination set."

"Who?"

"It hasn't been determined yet. The codes aren't even written."

"When will it be done?"

"I am not privy to that classification of information at this point. It could already be done, for all I know." He shook his head, trying to think it through. "To my knowledge they are still months away." He took a deep breath. "It is foolish to pursue this, but I will check it out, discreetly. In the meantime we must pursue INFERNO in other places. If we stop him, the weapon he is after makes no difference. Agreed?"

Ruth and Macklin looked at one another, then each nodded.

"All right, Chaim," Ruth said. "But let us know what you find out. It makes me uncomfortable to know so little about something as powerful as this weapon must be. What do you want us to do?"

"Find the woman and the Englishman that made contact with the Danielses in Tel Aviv. Raffi says he has never seen the woman before, but he thinks the man is—"

"Pike. Alistair Pike," Ruth said. "Mrs. Daniels helped with that. What else?"

"You should know that Mohammad was also contacted by these two. We need to find them before they do more damage here. They also may lead us to INFERNO.

"Pull your team together. They can be trusted. Have them access our main computer banks. Begin a background search of anyone you suspect of being INFERNO. I will let you establish the parameters. Find a way to access Mossad files without their knowing. See if you can get a line on ANGEL's identity. That may tell us something."

Ruth nodded, knowing his requests would not be easy to meet.

"I am going to find Zafit's controlling agent. To do that I will travel to Tiberias incognito." He smiled. "Stein can carry on his investigation as he wishes, but he will find it difficult to have me arrested if he can't find me. Maybe I can stay free long enough to find INFERNO for you.

"Be careful, both of you," Ativa said. "This agent will not take kindly to discovery, and if he finds we are after him, he will warn ANGEL and run. We will not catch up with either of them."

"What are your plans for Zafit?" Ruth asked

"Move him to a safe place. He may remember more later, or possibly we can use him. Set a trap."

Ruth leaned back against the chair. Chaim Ativa had always been a rebel, but he had been an honest one. He had given his entire life to Israel, and his family. His wife had died of heart disease in middle age, his son . . . No, Chaim Ativa was not a traitor. She had been right in coming to him and ignoring Stein.

"I'll get my team together, Chaim," Ruth said, getting up from her chair.

Ativa looked at Macklin as he stood to join Ruth. "I have

one other thing. Could you excuse two old friends for a moment, Colonel Macklin? I need to speak with Ruth about a personal matter."

Macklin looked embarrassed, then: "Sure . . . I'll, ah, wait in the hall. Just outside here . . . " He went to the door, closing it behind him.

Ruth sat down and Ativa took her hand. "I am sorry about Eytan Merriame, but you made the right decision. Luck was not with you, that's all."

"I . . . have wrestled with it, Papa Ativa, but I am in control now."

"Yes, I can see that. You were always good at controlling your feelings." He sat back, staring, a worried look on his face.

Ruth had always been able to talk to Chaim. He knew better than anyone how she felt inside. "More may suffer the consequences of my choice, even if it was right. I am not handling that very well. With everything that has happened in my life . . . "

He patted her hand. "You cannot turn back time, any more than you can change your destiny. But you can stop the hate, you know that."

"I can control it. I can't stop it."

He rubbed the top of her hand with his thumb. "Tell me about your American." He nodded toward the closed door.

She flushed a little. "He is a good man."

"You love him. I can see it in your eyes." He smiled gently.

She nodded. "I only loved one other as much."

His blue eyes flashed a twinkle. "And he loved you. I visit his grave, but not so often anymore. He was a good son."

"I know." Her face grew serious, wrinkles of hate forming around her eyes. "The man who killed him and my father is responsible for the factory in Syria. I still hope for a chance of sending him to hell."

Ativa squeezed her hand again. "Would that rid you of the hate?"

She looked away.

"Ruth, I am glad that Colonel Macklin has come into your life. Dov is gone. He would want you to be happy. He would want you to love."

"I . . . I will never . . . forget him." The tears welled up in her eyes. It seemed that her emotions were out of control a lot lately.

"I know, Ruth. But don't let his memory, or the hate of those who killed him and others you love, ruin your life. If you do, they win."

Ativa looked at his watch. "I must leave. I have a lot to do in Tiberias tonight."

She kissed him on the cheek. "Be careful, Papa Ativa."

He opened the door and she walked to where Tom stood. As they went down the hall, Ruth had the sudden urge to return and hug her father-in-law. She ignored it as foolishness, but did turn to see him standing in the doorway. She waved, then walked with Macklin into the warm night, goose bumps dancing across her flesh.

The agent called INFERNO stood at a window overlooking the temporary holding and interrogation buildings at the back of Aman headquarters. He watched as Ativa and two others loaded a man into a car. A man he knew and controlled through an agent in northern Israel. His brow wrinkled as he realized the consequences of Ativa's discovery. The agent who controlled Lev Zafit knew Stein's true identity. They had worked together for years. It was through Abdel Shomani that Stein had found out about the meeting between Ativa and Mohammad Faisal, and it was through him that pictures of that meeting had been taken. If Ativa found Shomani . . .

He shook his head slowly. And things had been going so well . . .

After watching the car leave through the guarded gate of the courtyard below, INFERNO opened the desk drawer and from Ativa's file removed a set of pictures, sticking them in his pocket. Sabrila and the Englishman had been careless when making contact with the American at the hotel in Tel Aviv. Luckily, the photos had crossed his desk before reaching Ativa. He would see that they were now placed in Ativa's office—where they would be found by an investigative team trying to verify the guilt of their recently deceased Aman leader as an Arab agent.

He didn't like the idea of killing. He had never done it before, but he had no choice now. He had laid the groundwork for Ativa's removal long ago. Admittedly, it hadn't called for violence, only incrimination as an Arab spy. But Ativa was too close now. He left Stein no choice.

He pushed a button on the intercom connecting himself with his secretary. "Miss Obessen, I apologize for needing you so late; thanks so much." He waited for the usual conciliatory reply, then went on. "I will be going to Jerusalem tonight. I will stay at the Hilton so I can be fresh for meetings early tomorrow morning with Likud party leaders. I won't want to be disturbed while working with them concerning several crucial matters. Can you clear my calendar?" The positive response came. "Good, and Mrs. Obessen, this is a private, very confidential meeting. Take the usual precautions about where I am, will you?"

"Yessir."

He lifted his finger. Tonight he would not be in Jerusalem.

11:30 P.M., Near Nabulus, West Bank

Ativa shifted the car into low gear as he turned onto Highway 36 out of Nabulus. Darkness enveloped the narrow road, making the turnoff he searched for difficult to find.

He had spent the last few hours interviewing people who knew or were remotely associated with Lev Zafit. The first three were short, fruitless conversations with frightened people who thought the Aman was after revenge, looking for bodies to feed the fire a traitor's arrest had started. The sixth, interviewed only an hour ago, had borne fruit. The Tiberias shopkeeper had seemed unusually tense, palms sweating, eyes averting. After fifteen minutes of questioning, the general knew he had something. After half an hour he had discovered that the man had participated in raids on nearby Israeli settlements with Arabs who had come across the border from Lebanon. Chaim called Jerusalem and had one of his aides do a complete search through General Command's memory banks. He discovered that the man worked for Abdel Shomani.

Shomani was an Arab Christian whose family became displaced from their property in 1955 during Israeli attempts to scare the Arabs from the land. Somehow Shomani had ended up in an orphanage in Haifa run by Catholic sisters. He didn't stay long, preferring a life on the streets among the Arabs of Nabulus, using his wits to feed himself. He had done well, working hard, saving his shekels, finally getting enough to open a small souvenir shop in Nabulus. By the middle eighties he had built it into a comfortable living. He expanded from there into several other businesses as well.

What Ativa found interesting were records of airline flights showing Shomani taking trips outside of Israel, which coincided with Zafit's trips, each within a day of Lev's departure and return. Palestinians who left Israel were watched very carefully, and few went abroad, simply because of the hassle of Israeli restrictions on their passports. Some were even afraid, with good cause, that if they left Israel they would never be allowed to return. Shomani seemed to have no such fear. In fact, he seemed to come and go as he pleased. It looked as if he had friends in influential places.

Ativa wanted to talk to Abdel Shomani.

He passed the road just as he saw it, pulled over, backed up, and made the turn. Shomani's house was several miles northwest of Highway 36 at a place called Qusin. Shomani's success had allowed him to purchase a small farm there, where he was raising olive trees, producing olive oil for sale in his shops in Nabulus and several other West Bank cities. Oil of very good quality. He paid above-average wages, hired more help than he really needed, and was loved by the Arabs who worked for him.

Ativa wondered how Shomani had maintained his comfortable living amidst the turmoil between Arab and Jew. Too often, Chaim's countrymen were quick to take away quality Arab lands or property. It shamed all Israel when such things happened, but many fanatic Israelis, willing to use weapons against the Arabs, were settling on the West Bank, forcing the Arabs off the land they had owned for generations.

But they hadn't taken this choice piece of property.

He downshifted, working his way up the hill. At the top he turned into Shomani's lane. The lights shone on modest but well-kept buildings, fences, and a yard. He pulled up to an adequate, neat home with a number of lights in the windows on the first and second floors. As he got out of the car and walked to the door he heard music. He knocked, waited, then knocked again. He tried the latch. It slipped freely, the door swinging partially open.

"Abdel Shomani?" he called in Arabic. There wasn't an answer. Chaim removed his American-made .45 from its holster, then pushed the door further open.

The quiet, laced with muffled strains of Bach, made the general's hair tingle and his heart pound.

The entry was small, stairs on the left leading to the second floor, a hallway in front of him going to what looked like the kitchen. A closed door was on his right, a double pocket door, the kind that slid into the wall. Gently he slid it just enough so he could see into the well-lit room. A glass, its liquid spilled across a Persian rug, came into view, then the hand that had recently held it.

Sliding the door aside completely, Ativa squatted by the body and checked for a pulse. There was none. He rolled him over, and, although the picture sent by fax was of a younger man, he knew it was Shomani, dead only minutes.

His muscles tensed and he released the safety catch on his gun, beginning a search of the house. The first floor was empty and showed little sign of recent activity, although odors of an evening meal—lamb, he thought—were strong in the small kitchen-dining area. The back door was slightly ajar. Ativa switched off the light, then checked through the window. After several minutes he flipped open the door and bolted quietly into the garden area. There were no shots but he waited, listening, his heart thumping loud against his rib cage.

Nothing.

He slipped into nearby trees and shrubs, sweat gathering in his palms. He felt vulnerable, as if eyes stared at him through the underbrush, waiting for the moment to nail him.

Minutes passed. Nothing but shadows and a gentle breeze blowing in the darkness, rustling leaves on the trees. Satisfied, but careful, he returned to the house, then to the den. It was going to be a long night.

He continued his search, careful to stay clear of windows. Climbing the stairs, he found three small bedrooms. Two looked as if they belonged to children, but were empty and didn't look as if they had been used regularly. He remembered Shomani had a son and daughter, both with families of their own. The merchant's wife had died a few years earlier of a lingering disease, so he wasn't surprised to find only masculine items in the third room.

He returned to the body, emptying pockets of the Italian-made slacks and sports coat. He found the usual items—wallet, keys, and change, along with a small penknife. He went through the wallet, placing each item on the counter. Then he noticed that one of a half a dozen bottles was tipped over, its contents on the counter and floor. It looked as if the Arab had been shot while getting his last drink of Irish scotch. He knelt again, checking for a bullet wound in the back of the neck. It was there. Twenty-two caliber, he estimated, and professionally placed by someone Shomani knew. The Palestinian had been immediately paralyzed—if he had lived at all.

He went to the desk and carefully looked through the scattered papers. Nothing. The drawers were next. In the bottom, left-hand drawer he hit pay dirt. Shomani's personal calendar for the day read "meeting with I—11:00 P.M.—discuss his escape."

He checked his watch—11:10—then looked at Shomani. "I" had come and gone. He laid the calendar on the desk and picked up the phone.

It was then that he felt the cold steel firmly pressed against the back of his head.

CHAPTER 21

11:30 P.M., Syrian desert

Mohammad glanced out of the small window of the Cessna as the last rays of sun were creating dark shadows in the hills and valleys only a matter of feet below them. His knuckles were white from grasping the seat, the memory of his unplanned swim in the Mediterranean still fresh in his mind.

A small Greek trawler had fished him out of the sea and delivered him to Catania. From there he phoned his most trusted friend, Nabril Al Razd, for passports and money.

Nabril had told him that Sabrila's hired help tried to enlist him in a conspiracy to kill Saad Khourani, leader of the West Bank Coalition for Independent Representation at Peace Talks. Nabril, with the aid of Mohammad's Jewish

177

contacts, had moved Khourani and others into deep hiding. Mohammad would leave them there for now. He didn't know what Sabrila was up to, and he wanted Khourani and the other members of the coalition out of harm's way for a while. He would thank Ativa for that when the time came, but for now he must pursue another lead.

Mohammad cursed himself for the hundredth time. He had been careless, overconfident, believing his help of West Bank Palestinians was unknown to his enemies. His stubborn refusal to use means of communication other than face-to-face talks had nearly cost him his life.

The tires skidded against hard ground, the plane's propeller creating a dust storm around the wings and body, battering them with small particles of sand and rock.

As the plane slowed, then stopped, the prop winding down and knocking to a halt, Mohammad could hear nothing but the sound of wind blowing across the desolate expanse around them.

Mohammad and Nabril jumped from the Cessna and began pushing it to an opening between large rocks. In less than ten minutes it was covered with camouflage cloth and hidden behind netting.

They were fifty miles from Duma, making Mohammad grateful for the sound of the jeep approaching down the ravine. He saw the dust billowing up behind the tan and brown vehicle, two occupants huddled behind the windshield, out of reach of flying sand in the quickly increasing furor of a growing dust storm.

As the vehicle halted, the passenger jumped from his perch and walked to Mohammad. He bowed as he removed the covering of his kafeyeh, revealing his young face.

"My brother, you honor us with your visit. Come. We must hurry from this place. The storm rises."

"Labib," Mohammad said, kissing the younger man on both cheeks. "Thank you for your cooperation. I know it is dangerous for you. I gather all is well in the house of Assad?"

Labib smiled. "Unfortunately, my uncle the president is well, and I am still forced to feign allegiance to him."

Mohammad put his arm around his friend's shoulder as they started for the jeep. "Someday, Labib, Allah willing, you will lead this country into a new freedom."

As they climbed in, Mohammad began to question.

"Where is Ibrahim, Labib, and this mysterious woman you say has come to your country?"

"In Damascus. Exactly where, I am not sure. But strange things have been happening, Mohammad. Fami Badannah's garrison at Duma is receiving large amounts of armament. Unusual items such as Exocet and Stinger missiles, and mines."

"You think Ibrahim has something he wishes to protect?"

"Rumors fly in the wind more numerous than the dust grains of this storm, Mohammad, but several I hear many times, from usually dependable sources."

"And what do they say?"

"That Ibrahim is working with the woman, and that she has purchased the help of two rogue German scientists, spirited from Iraq by Ibrahim when things turned for the worse there. That they are very close to nuclear and chemical warhead capability for the improved SCUD missile."

Mohammad's back straightened. "And do the rumors speak of their intention?"

"They use them against Israel."

"Use them? You mean as a bargaining chip. Surely—"

Labib shook his head. "No, *use* them, Mohammad."

Mohammad looked into his friend's eyes and saw fear there. "Does President Assad know?"

Labib's face was hard as granite. "He must. How else would Badannah receive such support. He at least turns the other way, probably for money.

"But surely he understands the danger. If Ibrahim has SCUDs and uses them against Israel."

"You forget, Mohammad, Assad wishes war with Israel. He cannot start it, but if someone else did, he would be most anxious to join, especially if Israel were already decimated by SCUDs with chemical warheads."

Mohammad thought a moment. "Maybe." Then, "Who is the woman?"

Labib shrugged. "Rumor says she is the heir of the House of Hassan."

Mohammad smiled. Jerisha Duquesne.

After that, they talked little, the dust filling their eyes and nostrils as the jeep bounced slowly toward Duma. After fifteen miles the sun was gone and the road was difficult to see, but the headlamps were not turned on.

They saw the lights of Duma at 1:00 A.M. As they entered the outskirts of the city, Mohammad decided he would get a very close look at the factory, gather information, and take pictures. Then he would return to Israel. It seemed that he and the Jews were fighting a common enemy. One that might destroy them all.

Day Six

CHAPTER 22

6:40 A.M., Hadassah Hospital, Jerusalem

Ruth held Chaim Ativa's cold hand to her cheek while the unsteady beep and pump of machinery carried on their life-saving effort.

The bullets had nearly severed an artery but had not been fatal. IDF forces had arrived within minutes of the shooting and had saved his life, then rushed him to Jerusalem. They found his body next to that of Abdel Shomani, each with a weapon in his hand, the apparent casualties of a violent confrontation.

Ativa had been in surgery for several hours and was heavily sedated. The doctors gave him less than a fifty per-cent chance of survival.

Ruth moved and stood quietly in the corner near the door, watching the doctors and nurses hook up machinery that constantly monitored Ativa's vital signs. She looked defiant and angry; her jaw set like concrete and her eyes a cold black.

Tom took her arm. "Come on, let's get out of the way."

She was reluctant at first, then let her rigid body be pulled out of the room and to a row of chairs in a waiting area. As Ruth sat down she banged her fist against the chair, then folded her arms firmly across her chest.

Macklin sat back, stretching his legs out in front of him, playing with the button of his jacket while measuring what he should say. She picked up a newspaper and wrote down a number. "Call Minister Hoshen," she said unemotionally. "He needs to know."

He looked at the number, then at her, afraid, but unable to vocalize the feeling. He shrugged it off, rose, and walked down the hall to where the phone booths filled an out-of-the-way corner.

No one answered, so he hung up the phone, returning to find Ruth's empty chair. At first he thought she might have gone into Ativa's room, but when he found she wasn't there he hurried to the parking lot. The space that had temporarily housed the Mercedes was empty. He heard the screech of tires on pavement and looked to see the car disappear into traffic.

Macklin stood on the porch of the safe house, the sun sending rays earthward, warming it and dispelling the darkness of night, giving hope, it seemed, to all the world but him.

He had caught a cab from the hospital, returning to Tel Aviv and Aman headquarters in search of Ruth. Nothing. Then back to Jerusalem and her uncle's house, and, finally, the safe house.

The early morning had been full of gut-wrenching surprises. Minister Hoshen had immediately placed Stein in Ativa's office and ordered a full inquiry into what had happened in Shomani's home. Someone had leaked the investigation to the press, citing evidence of Ativa's guilt in Shomani's murder and the possibility that the Aman leader was the highest-placed collaborator in Israeli history.

When Macklin arrived at the Aman, Stein had already made his first momentous decision. Intelligence reports had indicated that the Duma factory was deserted. He was looking for Ruth in order to relieve her of her assignment. The Duma project was being placed in "more capable hands." It had been all Macklin could do to keep from punching Stein's lights out. Instead, he had turned on his heel and left the building. Stein was nothing more than an over-zealous political opportunist using Ativa's frame-up to lift himself to higher dreams. The project, now under his direction, would be fully revamped and carried out, using Daliyat, giving the two political climbers the accolades of people in powerful places. Ruth's team and Macklin were hindrances to Stein's political future. He wanted them out of the way.

For him, for Ruth, for the team, the Duma project was over. And INFERNO was still at large.

He glanced at his watch. Where could she be?

Macklin fell into one of the chairs, staring blankly at the distant temple mount. Who had tried to kill Ativa? Was it INFERNO? Had the general surprised the murderer, or did he know Ativa was coming? If so, how? Only himself and Ruth had known Ativa was going north, and they knew nothing about Shomani. He sighed. It was as if Chaim Ativa had surprised someone. How would they find INFERNO without the general? He didn't know, but they must.

He looked at his watch again. Nearly 9:00 A.M. "Ruth," he said aloud, "Where on earth are you?"

"Locks are for locking," Ruth said from the patio door behind him.

He jumped to his feet and was in her arms in another step. They grasped one another tightly, feelings of love and relief rushing through both bodies. The kiss was hard, then it softened into the pleasure of relief.

"Are you all right?" he asked, pulling away.

She clutched at him. "Just hold me, Tom," she said, digging her fingernails into his back. "Just hold me."

He held her tight, trying to squeeze the distress from her, to stop the cold shaking of her body. "It's all right, Ruth." He rubbed her back with his hand, feeling her arms tighten around him, her softness becoming one with his own flesh. "It'll be okay."

"Is he still alive?" she asked.

"Yes, unchanged."

They stood on the balcony for a long time, holding one another, afraid to let go. He felt her body stop shaking, then gradually relax and give a little, her eyes heavy with exhaustion. Gently he picked her up and went to the bedroom, placed her worn-down body gently on the bed, and wrapped a blanket around her.

He took a pillow and another blanket and returned to the

couch. After closing the blinds against the sun, he stretched out, his body aching for rest.

But sleep wouldn't come. Instead he lay awake for a long time thinking about his life, Duma, INFERNO and ANGEL— and Ruth. He knew now that he loved Ruth more than his own life, and it hurt to see her suffering. He didn't know what had happened, but a light had gone out of Ruth's eyes and it scared him more than when she seemed full of . . . what? Hate? Even that seemed to be gone. Now there was only emptiness. What had happened?

He tossed about on the couch, then put his feet on the floor to go for a drink. As he swigged the last of it, he made up his mind. He'd tell Hoshen about INFERNO, the sword, what Ativa had told them. The minister could deal with it from there. Manlik Hoshen was the man responsible for Aman and its performance. All that had happened was as bad for him as it was for anyone. With each unfortunate event he lost more power, and by now he was probably close to losing his job altogether. Just the opposite of what INFERNO would want. In Macklin's mind, Hoshen would jump at the chance to save his hide; he wasn't the traitor.

Then he and Ruth were leaving the country. If Hoshen couldn't stop INFERNO, at least they'd avoid the havoc the traitor would wreak.

Macklin went back to the couch, his mind eased. He was military. He liked things in neat little packages. Less chance of something going wrong that way. Now he had his package, a plan of action. Now he could sleep.

CHAPTER 23

2:00 P.M., Jerusalem

The house sat on a wooded hill two miles from Jerusalem. When the embassy car delivered Jerry, Mike, and the three children that afternoon, they passed through heavy iron gates opened by a security guard, then drove a hundred yards up a tree-lined driveway before reaching the front of the house.

It was big. At least that was the word Issa used. A two-story stone house with six bedrooms, large living area, kitchen, study, and dining room, and a deck that harbored a large pool. Before the suitcases hit the floor the two boys had stripped of newly purchased clothes down to boxer shorts and had doused themselves in the blue water of the shallow end. They came out only long enough to disappear into a dressing area and change into more modest swimsuits provided by house help.

Mike headed for the kitchen and found a cook already in the process of fixing dinner for their new family. She went back to the living room and joined Jerry, who was watching the boys, and now Issa, through the large patio windows.

"Officialdom called ahead. Dinner is being prepared. Very efficient."

"And very cautious." Jerry pointed at several men in the large backyard, each carrying an automatic weapon.

"It has been a nice day, Jerry. Being with the children, letting them shop. It was wonderful."

"Yeah," Jerry beamed. "I especially enjoyed buying the crib."

She laughed lightly. "An antique."

"True," he answered. "Someone important must have slept in it some time in the past. No one as important as its next owner, though."

"I could have done without the armed escort," Jerry continued, growing serious. "Everything is so . . . unsettled. It makes me nervous."

"The press conference went well," Mike said, trying to cheer him up.

Jerry shrugged. "The press want to think I am as guilty as they made Nixon during Watergate, but they don't have proof. The terrorists haven't come up with their supposed documents."

"They don't have any," Mike said.

"They could get some quality forgeries."

"Did the president ask for your resignation?" Mike asked.

Jerry smiled. "No, but I was tempted to give it anyway. It might defuse the impact of that news release."

"Did he give you the go-ahead on the Wyoming thing? Can you explain what happened? Why a terrorist was killed?"

"Only if the pressure gets worse, and the Arab nations start demanding answers. Right now the state department has them cooling. Most of them have taken a wait-and-see stance. If one more thing happens . . . But, I guess that's why we're in this place."

"Our protection . . . as well as the government's. Why don't they just recall you?"

"Admission of guilt, maybe fear that everything they've worked so hard on will unravel." He shrugged. "At least we seem to be safe."

"Who is responsible for all this protection?" Mike asked.

"It's a little confusing. Last night it was a general by the name of Ativa. But this morning one of the guards with us in the car said that had changed. He was pretty tight-lipped about it, but apparently Ativa has been replaced by Minister Hoshen's assistant, a guy by the name of Stein."

They stood and watched in silence.

"It's them, isn't it?" Mike said. "The people behind TERROR1."

"Yes, it's them. We wanted to know if it was safe. It isn't." He paused. "Maybe it never will be.

"When's Dad coming?" Jerry asked.

She smiled, liking Jerry's use of the word *Dad.* "In the morning. He wasn't sure exactly when."

Jerry was grateful. He needed the senator here, out of harm's way.

"I hope the kids don't mind the guys with the guns," Mike said.

Jerry smiled. "Kids like excitement, especially this bunch."

"I want to take them home," Mike said.

"I figured you did, but have you considered the cons as well as the pros?"

"Yes, some. As much as my heart can stand. Just for a visit. Then they can decide. If they want to come back we'll make arrangements for their care here, especially Issa. A boy might survive on the streets, but Issa needs a better chance."

"Okay by me." He took her in his arms. "Mrs. Daniels, are we nuts or what?"

Mike smiled. "One of us is. I'm just along because I've always liked a circus. Let's just hope we don't get trampled by the elephants."

"Would you consider taking the kids and going home early?"

"You know the answer, Jerry, so why ask?" she said firmly. "I signed up for better or worse, remember."

"You can't fool me, Mrs. Daniels. What you really crave is the action."

She poked him in the stomach. "Right!"

"Anyway, dearest, you are to stay in this place of refuge, play with your newfound family, and from this spot enjoy the rest of our stay in this mixed-up land."

She stepped away and did a mocking bow, her hands pressed flatly against one another and pointing toward heaven. "Yes, oh great one. And should I eat ice cream and pickles? Your wish is my duty."

He stepped forward and picked her up over his shoulder, holding her tightly while heading for the patio door. "No time like the present to get started, then.

"Issa!" he yelled as Mike kicked and screamed, trying to get free. "Catch!" He lowered her into his arms, then swung her once, twice, three times before letting go. Issa laughed and clapped her hands as Mike landed in the water next to her, then came spluttering to the surface.

"I'll get you!" she yelled, splashing water in his direction and across his tan trousers. He jumped away, moving quickly toward the door.

"Sorry, got things to do in the study. Have fun!" He shut the glass door behind him, watching Issa put her thin arms around Mike's neck and slip onto her back. Issa was good for Mike, and good for him, he thought. He watched the boys for a moment. Shy, a little reluctant to move in Mike's direction until she started splashing water on them. Then the Arab tradition melted away and the child took over. Mike would have her hands full for the next little while.

He crossed the room, then the entry, into the comfortable den. The phone was on the desk. He took a device out of his briefcase, picked up the phone, and attached it to the portable scrambler. Then he dialed and waited for the number to go through the necessary exchanges.

"K this is J. You clear?"

"Wait a minute."

Jerry heard the click and ping as Trayco placed a scrambler on his own phone.

"Ready."

"You heard?" Jerry asked.

"Yeah. In the news. Close call. You guys okay?"

"Bruises, scratches. We're safe for now. Aman has us in a well-protected safe house. Take care of things in Jackson like we planned, will you?"

"What about the senator?"

"He's on his way here. I'll fill him in."

"Sorry you were right," Trayco said.

"Yeah, me too. Another favor. Send your plane, will you? We may need a private and effective method of leaving this place."

"Jerry, the woman is in Syria."

"I know it's difficult to keep tabs on her . . ."

"We'll do our best. Let me know what you find out on your end."

"Macklin's here."

The phone was silent. "Why?"

"I'm going to ask him. I need to let him know what's going on. They probably have someone out to get him as well. Watch your backside, Kenny. Watch it carefully."

Jerry hung up.

A tight knot was making his stomach hurt. He had wanted to find out. Now that he had, it scared him, badly. Jerisha was the head of the octopus. By stopping TERROR1 they had only cut off her tentacles. She had grown new ones.

A noise in the hall brought him out of deep thought and he looked up in time to see Mike and Issa running hand-in-hand in his direction, dripping all over the carpet, mischief in their dark eyes. He was struck by how much little Issa looked like his wife at the moment he was about to be overrun.

He tried backing away, toppling the desk chair, tripping, and landing on his posterior, back against the wall. They were all over him, their wetness soaking his pants and shirt, Mike ruffling his hair as she backed away and stood up, her hands on her hips. Issa plopped her wet body on Jerry's lap and put her arms around his neck, laughing at his shocked look. He noticed the boys standing in the doorway, jabbering to one another and laughing as well.

"Rashid, throw me a towel, will you?" Mike said. "The man seems to be a little wet behind the ears."

Jerry took the towel and ruffled Issa's hair, drying it.

"All right boys, upstairs, into the bath," Mike said.

The two looked at each other, mystified. "Mrs. Mike," said Rashid, "we just had a bath in the big pool of water. And you made us bathe last night. Is this all you Americans do?"

She laughed, then explained chlorine and sticky hair. "Now, beat it, you two." They headed up the stairs, looking at things and speaking excitedly in Arabic. "Come on, little lady," she said, looking at Issa. "They have a separate room and bath for you. Time for more bubbles." Issa sat still until she heard the word *bubbles*, then she was off Jerry's lap in an instant.

"Unfair," Jerry said. "She'd have stayed with me if you hadn't said *bubbles*."

"I can't help it if bubbles beats laps," Mike said, disappearing up the stairs.

Jerry sat for a moment, the warmth of Issa's body still making his legs tingle. He was falling in love again.

He shook off the reverie, stood, and lifted the chair back into place before plopping his damp and ruffled self into it. He brushed a few drops of water off his paper and returned to his thoughts, remembering Fillmore Duquesne's haunting words: "They'll kill you when they find out what you've done. It's you that has destroyed them. They'll see that, and they'll send people to hunt you down for it!"

Jerry had been looking over his shoulder ever since.

Fortunately, Kenny had been helping him look. Kenny Trayco, a former member of Red Five in Nam, the elite marine special operations unit, and the man who had saved Jerry Daniels in the jungles of the Delta. Jerry had reciprocated years later by pulling a lost soldier out of a tight spot with the law and helping him find a job and get on the path that had eventually led to a life of fame and fortune as one of the nation's best private guard services. Kenny had helped resolve the mystery of TERROR1, then had stuck to Jerry and Mike like glue, fearing the repercussions that might come from those whose plans they had ruined. Jerry had no better friend in this world.

Using his worldwide connections, Kenny had helped Jerry make a few inquiries. They found out that all of Duquesne's partners had, one by one, been put out of business. Some had been tried and imprisoned. Others had been shot. Some had just disappeared. Then Duquesne himself had been killed. With that, Jerry thought the danger was over for him, that everyone who could hurt him or his family was out of commission. He had been wrong.

At first it was just a feeling of being watched. Then he knew it. Ironically, it happened on the day he and Mike were sealed in the Idaho Falls Temple. A man, the unfamiliar face of an albino, kept hanging around the temple gardens, taking pictures. He had seen that albino before, in Jackson.

Jerry became more cautious, living in constant fear for his life and for Mike's. He refused to let her go anywhere without him or someone else. Someone well-armed and smart enough to protect her. The rest of Mike's family took precautions as well. It had been hell.

That's when he started trying to figure out who was behind it, who was left. After a lot of behind-the-scenes intelligence gathering by the senator and Trayco, they had eliminated everyone but Jerisha Duquesne. But they had no proof. All they could do was keep one eye on her and the other looking over their shoulders.

Neither was easy. Jerisha had become very elusive, flying around the Middle East and Europe. She disappeared more often than not, and they had little idea of what she was up to.

After a particularly bad night of nightmares, he and Mike had decided they couldn't live that way anymore. They had to find out for sure. When the offer came to be a part of the advance peace commission, they decided it was time.

Now he knew. She was after him, probably for revenge. The enemy was no longer faceless; now he could fight it. In time, he'd destroy it for good.

He walked to the patio. The pool looked enticing. He needed to cool off, release his frustrations, his fears.

He removed his shoes and went to the diving board, bounced three times, and threw himself into the air, his arms extended. Then he remembered his wallet.

When he came to the surface the children were standing with Mike on the patio above, laughing.

Issa said something to Mike, and Rashid translated quickly.

"Issa says you forgot your swimsuit."

"I knew I had forgotten something," he said as he threw his wallet onto the nearby grass. "Tell her never mind. I'll wear it to dinner."

He swam. One lap, two, four. He needed to feel the cool water slipping by his aching bones, clearing his frightened, frustrated mind. It slowly dispelled the hard rock of fear in the pit of his stomach, leaving only a pebble.

After ten laps he lifted himself out of the water onto the

tile deck, reaching for a towel hung across a nearby chair. The sun was warm on his back and made him feel even better. God had created a beautiful world. Why did man have to clutter it with hate and violence?

He took a deep breath, stood, and walked to where his wallet lay. Shoving it inside his Nikes, he gathered them with one hand then went up the outside steps to the master suite for a shower.

Mike was standing near the mirror in a slip, brushing out her wet hair. "Frustrated?"

"Frightened," he said, kissing her on the back of the neck.

"Of?"

He decided to keep it to himself. "Of waking up from this dream and finding that I never met and married you."

She turned into his arms. "Not a chance." She kissed him lightly, then again. "You're stuck with me. Get used to it. Now, get dressed. Dinner will be ready in less than an hour."

He headed for the shower, feeling a little guilty for hiding his true thoughts. But there was no need to worry her at this point. She would only feel as helpless as he did, possibly worse. She didn't need it and he wouldn't do it to her.

He breathed deeply, letting the spine-tingling hot water bite into his cooled-down flesh. He wanted to run for the hills of Jackson Hole. Build a fortress and hide. But then, the world of Jackson Hole hadn't been safe from the Duquesnes either.

As he toweled down and slipped on his robe, the phone rang. It was within a step and he had it in his hand before it rang again.

"Hello."

"Mr. Daniels, you don't know me but my name is Mohammad Faisal. Do you recognize the name?"

"My supposed kidnapper; difficult to forget something like that," Jerry said, the knot reforming in his stomach.

"You believe it was me?" Mohammad said flatly.

"What is it you want, Mr. Faisal?"

"I, and others, wish to meet with you. We have much to discuss."

"Like how much I ought to charge you for ruining a perfectly good set of clothes, and how much I'm going to sue you for defamation of character, not to mention mental anguish."

Mohammad laughed. "Mr. Daniels, I know who kid-napped you, and I think I know what they are up to. It is extremely deadly, and our visit may initiate action to save thousands of lives. Doctor Jamel—"

"You have spoken with the doctor?" Jerry's mind was racing.

"Yes, he said you were a fair man."

Jerry thought for a moment. "Nice of him. How do I know you're telling the truth? I've been through one calamitous kidnapping. I don't need—"

"I was afloat in the Mediterranean sea at the time you were kidnapped, surviving an attempt on my own life. The same people who tried to kill you betrayed me to my ene-mies. As with you, they were nearly successful. In fact, they think they did succeed. Our paths cross, Mr. Daniels, because certain parties want to use us to destroy Israel. Many of my people will die as well. I want only to stop it."

Jerry sat on the bed, his mind at full attention. "Who else will be in your group, and what is your main purpose, Mr. Faisal?"

"Doctor Jamel, Saad Khourani—leader of the West Bank Palestinians for peace—myself, and my most trusted assis-tant. We wish you to bring Minister Hoshen, and a represen-tative of your American government, along with whatever protection you feel is needed."

"The Israeli minister of defense is not at my disposal. In fact, he and I don't see eye to eye on a lot of things, and the president isn't about to meet with you or your representa-tives at this point."

"Minister Hoshen can be trusted. The same people who wished us dead also had plans for him and Saad Khourani. I have removed Khourani from their reach. You must warn Hoshen and convince him to meet with us. If we are to stop what I believe will happen, we need Israeli participation. I am not convening a peace conference, Mr. Daniels, only trying to save lives. I want someone from your government who has the president's ear so something can be done."

Jerry paused. "My head says I should tell you take a hike, while my gut says take a chance. I need proof my gut is right."

The line was quiet.

"Mr. Daniels, your embassy will receive an envelope with the proof you seek. Call them and have it delivered to you. If it is enough, and you agree, call Doctor Jamel. He'll contact myself and Mr. Khourani."

"Sounds fair. If, and that is a big if, we decide to do this, when and where?"

"Tomorrow afternoon, the Basilica of St. James, Mount of Dothan on the West Bank."

"A Christian church?"

"You have been there, good. Yes, but the priest is a friend of Mr. Khourani's. They grew up together near Nabulus. He has consented and will keep it strictly confidential."

Jerry thought for a moment. "All right. I'll wait for the envelope. If I believe you are sincere, I'll try making arrangements. One last question, Mr. Faisal. How did you know where I was?"

"Mr. Daniels, many Israelis, some very important ones, seek peace, just as we do."

They hung up.

Jerry finished dressing, a renewed hope building in his chest. If his kidnapping was linked to what Faisal had to say, that meant Jerisha was involved up to her pretty little neck. It might give him a chance at wringing it.

He buttoned his shirt, wondering how he could get hold of Colonel Thomas Macklin.

CHAPTER 24

7:00 P.M., Jackson Hole, Wyoming

Bob stood in his stirrups, straining to make out the pickup that had just pulled into the driveway of the house better than a mile away. It was hard to tell. He dropped back in the saddle, rubbing his eyes. He knew he needed glasses, and Charla had threatened him with an early grave if he didn't get an eye doctor appointment by the end of the month. He still had twelve days.

He nudged his spurs into the bay's flanks and started off the knoll toward the road, the few cows around him scattering as he moved through them. Dismounting and opening the fence gate, he noticed two riders leaving the ranch and heading his way. Whoever had arrived, Charla was bringing him out to the pasture.

He swung into the saddle and pressed the spurs tight in the bay's flanks, moving to a quick gallop. He could see them now. Bishop Hansen.

His heart caught in his throat. Dad had said he would contact them about what was happening in Israel. If it was something bad, he would want the message conveyed by someone who could help them handle it. He nudged the bay to go even faster.

As the three horsemen neared one another, Charla waved and Bob returned it. Her demeanor showed concern, but not the fatal kind, and he reined the bay back, letting him walk to the others.

"Bishop," Bob said, tipping his hat.

"Bob." The bishop reached out his hand as the two men's horses came next to one another. They shook.

"What brings you out this way?"

"I wish I could say it was Church business, but it isn't."

"Israel?"

Charla broke in, explaining how Jerry had gotten away. "Mike is okay. They both are. It was Kenny Trayco who called the bishop."

"Does Dad know?"

"Jerry told Trayco he would fill him in as soon as the senator arrived in Israel," Bishop Hansen answered.

"Why Trayco?" Bob asked.

The bishop pushed his hat back on his head, then turned the horse and started for the ranch house. "Let's head back while we talk, shall we?"

Since Charla had joined the Church and she and Bob had become active six months ago, they had become good friends with Bishop Hansen. He helped them make the adjustments, gave them Church callings, and prepared them for the temple, which was only another six months away. Bob had learned to respect the man like few others.

"You and your family are in danger," the bishop said. "Trayco said you would understand. He is on his way, but he asked me to come ahead and warn you."

Bob tipped his hat back, his eyes scanning the hills around them. Someone could be watching now.

"Trayco says you must prepare yourselves to get away by

morning," the bishop added. Bishop Hansen knew some of what was happening. The day Jeremiah Daniels had walked into his life he changed it. The bishop knew about the constant danger the family lived with because they had saved a lot of lives and stopped some murderers from having their way. Beyond that, he had simply learned to trust them and do what he could for them.

"Does Trayco have any idea who might be watching us?" Bob asked as they walked the horses toward the ranch house.

"No, but they must be close. Have you . . . hired any new hands lately?"

"None," Bob responded.

"Bunch of campers down by the lake, Bob. You remember seeing some of them hiking up in the mountains behind the ranch?"

"Yeah, could be them. I'd appreciate it very much if you wouldn't mention this to anyone, Bishop."

"Not even the sheriff?" Bishop Hansen asked. "Surely—"

"If these folks get any idea that we know what goes on, they may come after us before we're ready, or they'll lie low and come at us when things have settled down. Can't take that chance. We'll get the family to safety, then decide what to do about putting these boys outa commission."

The bishop thought a moment, then sighed, resigned. "All right. But what can I do?"

"Join us for supper. You've done that before and it'll look natural enough. Then go home. We'll make out all right. Did Trayco give any way for us to contact him?"

"No, he said he'd be there when you needed him."

Alex Manners removed the binoculars from his pinkish-white eyes and replaced the sunglasses. He put the wide-brimmed hat back on his completely white albino's hair and pulled back into the shade, thinking.

Just that darned Mormon bishop. He'd seen him before when watching the senator and his son-in-law for Pike. It had been a long, cold watch, beginning in winter and ending long after spring runoff. But he'd kept track of them and earned a smooth twenty-five grand doing it.

He smiled. The call from Pike's woman friend was proof it was going to pay off even better.

He picked up his hiker's backpack and started down the trail. He'd meet Meg and they'd return to their camp at the lake. He'd seen all he needed, and with all the other information and pictures he had he was ready to bring about an unhappy accident at the senator's residence.

Alexander Manners was a third-generation bad guy. His father had been killed in an attempted bank robbery in Seattle, Washington. His grandfather was still locked up in Idaho's state penitentiary and would die there. He had killed two hunters after fighting them over an elk, then mutilated the bodies. The state threw the key to his prison cell into the depths of the Boise River.

Alex was made in the same mold. The difference was that he hadn't gotten caught. An army vet who had been trained in the "finer art" of killing by use of explosive devices, he had kept busy in mercenary activities in a number of places south of the border and in the Middle East. He had even trained terrorists for Qaddafi in Libya for a year, showing them how to kill Americans with explosive devices that airport security and most everyone else would never find.

That was where he'd met Pike. They had worked together on three different operations over a ten-year period. The money was always good, the high life high.

Then he'd been spotted. His albino condition had forced him to do most of his work in darkness, where people wouldn't make note of his appearance. But Pike's last job had forced him to plant a bomb in daylight. He'd been spotted at the scene and the composite drawing was good enough to worry him. He had escaped back to the United States to lie low. Jackson Hole had been his town of choice.

He had always liked Jackson. Fair night life, lots of tourists looking for a good time, and lots of holes to hide in. He'd gotten a condo at Teton Village, using up half of his savings. Over the next six months he spent the rest on a fast car and pretty women, and incidentals like food and beer. Pike contacted him about the same time he had run out of money and was going to have a realtor put his home up for sale. And now with his new job for the woman . . .

He'd given his new assignment a lot of thought. The senator's house was heated by gas. Being too far away from the natural gas lines, they used propane. The tank stood within ten feet of the house. A simple leak, an explosion, a log house turned to kindling—he'd be a hundred thousand richer.

Alex hitched up the backpack and pranced down the trail, whistling. All in all, it had been a good day.

Day Seven

CHAPTER 25

5:00 A.M., Jerusalem

On the fifth ring Jerry's fumbling hand found the phone, knocking it off the hook to the table, then the floor. He rolled over on his back and reached for the cord, pulling the elusive receiver to his palm, then to his ear.

"Hello," he said, becoming aware of his new surroundings.

"Hello, Jeremiah Daniels. Are you presentable for guests?"

Jerry's mind felt the familiarity of the voice, but the barbiturate of sleep slowed recognition. "Who . . . Jim?"

"In the flesh."

Jerry hesitated, confused.

"But what . . . when did you get in? Where are you?"

"An hour ago. I'm at your front gate. What are you two doing sleeping so late? It's nearly sunup!"

"Hang up your saddle, Senator! We don't have a ranch to tend to here. Tell that no-account guard out there he's fired. Letting you interrupt good sleep is unforgivable."

"A thousand pardons. Are you going to have him open this gate or not?"

"I'm thinking."

Mike rolled over and slugged her husband in the arm.

"Mike says no." She slugged him again. "Oops, changed her mind. Tell him you're the pool maintenance man. He'll let you right in."

Mike took the phone.

"Get that daughter of mine out of the sack. It's breakfast time and I'm starved."

"Hi Dad. Fix your own breakfast. I'm still asleep. Let me speak to the guard."

Ten minutes later Jerry was in Levi's and a T-shirt with a silhouette drawing of the Tetons across the front, sitting on the couch introducing his father-in-law to Issa, who had been awakened by all the commotion. After she and the senator got acquainted, Mike took the heart-winning little girl by the hand, guiding her up the stairs for another hour's sleep.

"Your wife is attached," the senator said. "So are you."

"Yeah. If they'll come, we'll bring 'em home for a visit."

"Sounds like fun. Let's see—your house plans call for four bedrooms. I didn't expect you to fill them all at once."

"The best news is yet to come," Mike said, launching herself off the bottom step and onto the couch next to Jerry. "You're going to be a grandpa."

The senator grinned, looking at Mike's bunny slippers. "Jerry, I'm amazed. You said they'd make her think positive. Looks like it works."

Mike took one off and flung it at him, the soft fur landing across his forehead.

He laughed as he tossed it back to her. "When?"

"Seven months."

"Congratulations."

After several minutes of additional small talk about family, home, and health, Jerry leaned forward.

"Glad you came."

The senator shrugged. "Where else would I be? You put your head in a noose, Jerry. Someone was bound to yank on the other end." He forced a worried smile. "I hope you're content now."

"Anything new from the world of politics?"

"One little tidbit. The Israelis are the ones who requested that you be a part of the peace commission."

Jerry smiled. "The Israelis?"

"No offense, Jerry, but when you decided you wanted to

do this, I was the most vocal of a very few in Washington who supported the president's decision to put you on the advance peace team. In fact, several very powerful senators, with favorite candidates of their own, applied a good deal of pressure to have you overlooked and their own choice offered the job. That is, until the Israelis started applying tremendous amounts of pressure."

"I don't get it," Mike said.

The senator shrugged again. "A crazy world, but the fact *is*, Jerry, they and their powerful lobby are the ones who got you this job."

Jerisha's tentacles were longer than even Jerry had thought.

"Some of them have changed their minds. They want you out of here."

"The prime minister?"

"Nah, he likes the ruckus you've created. He thinks it will sideline peace talks a while longer. Give him time to settle more of the West Bank. There are a lot of people who don't want the chance for peace upset. They see something like this as a real problem. It gives the Arabs an easy out, at least a better bargaining position." He cleared his throat. "The president is having to give a few concessions."

"I'll bet. Any particular individual?"

"Defense Minister Hoshen. He's under a lot of pressure right now. All of it I wasn't able to find out about, but he's botched a few major decisions lately. Yesterday, it seems one of his generals was uncovered as an enemy agent for a terrorist group. Killed a man in a gun battle. The general was Hoshen's personal selection for head of the Aman and had access to a lot of information. Some are saying it may have been the source of timing for your kidnapping."

"No wonder Hoshen wants us out. Reduce some of the pressure, at least."

"The president doesn't consider your leaving right now a wise thing. And my sources say it won't make a difference for Hoshen. Too many members of the Knesset want his head anyway. Right now the prime minister is keeping him afloat, not much else."

"Which senators did the Israelis use in Washington to assure my appointment to this position?"

The senator smiled. "I won't mention names, but their initials are Hodgson and Gibbs. Funny thing about that. Two weeks later they both had enough money to pay off bad campaign debts, nearly a million dollars' worth."

"Where'd the money come from?" Mike asked.

The senator shrugged. "Bunch of places. All with legitimate lobbying offices. Whoever siphoned the money to them knew how to do it without getting caught."

Jerisha had money. And access to Fillmore Duquesne's connections. "What else is happening in the good ol' U.S. of A.?" Jerry asked.

"The American press is questioning your sanity for going sightseeing, wondering what the terrorists mean when they say you killed one of their people." He laughed lightly. "Some have even hinted that you were a part of CIA operations during the Vietnam conflict."

Jerry laughed. "They'll have me starting the stupid war before they're through. That's what I love about the American press—freedom of speech means freedom to find two pieces of a very intricate puzzle, then tell everyone you can see the whole picture."

"Can you handle the pressure, son, or would you prefer—"

"The pressure's okay, Jim, but I can't say I haven't thought about the mountains of Jackson Hole."

The senator shrugged. "You were safer in Jackson."

"They would have come, sooner or later," Mike said. "Waiting would have been worse."

Jerry spoke. "How come Thomas Macklin is in Israel?"

The senator's back straightened. "You know?"

"The colonel heard about Jerry's kidnapping on the radio and came to the hospital," Mike said. "I was glad to see him."

"I still have top clearance, Senator," Jerry smiled.

"Wouldn't matter if ya didn't at this point." James Freeman took a deep breath, then told them about Macklin's mission. "He'll receive orders to return to Saudi Arabia today."

"Senator, how much weight can you throw around with our military command?"

The senator sat back. "Why?"

"I want Macklin here. Get him assigned to some post where he has freedom of movement, or get him some time off. Then find him and have him sent to this safe house, along with the Israeli colonel, Ruth Levona."

The senator stared. "You're serious."

"Very. Can you do it?"

"With the Duma project out of their hands they both will

have time coming. Finding them might be the greater problem. What's going on, Jerry?"

"He was a part of TERROR1, remember. He needs to be told what we know. Where are you staying?" Jerry asked.

"The King's Hotel."

"Save the taxpayers' money. We have an extra room." Jerry looked at his watch. "Jet lag will probably nail you in an hour or so anyway, so go upstairs and get some shut-eye as soon as you make those calls. Keep Macklin in Israel if you can."

"You're not telling me everything, are you?" Freeman said, rising from the chair.

"Get some sleep. I've still got several things to think through. We're safe here, Jim. I'd prefer having us all in the same place." He paused. "I called Trayco. He's taking care of things at the ranch. If someone is out for revenge, we need to be very careful, that's all." Jerry decided this was not the time to go into detail.

The senator hesitated, then raised his hands in the air. "I suppose you'll fill me in when you're ready. Where's the phone? I'll get things started on Macklin. Then I have got to catch some shut-eye before I drop. Haven't slept for forty-eight hours." The senator hesitated at the patio door. "Do you think it's . . . safe to call Bob?"

Jerry nodded. "Just be careful. Don't say anything that might reveal what we know. The lines might be tapped at the ranch."

The senator nodded his head in agreement, then disappeared through the door.

"You give me chills, Jerry," Mike said. "I suppose you're going to make me wait, too."

He smiled. "We've talked about it before. You know almost as much as I do. It's becoming more simple all the time. Jerisha set us up. She's got friends here in Israel, and she used Fillmore's Washington connections. She wanted us here for her revenge. It seems we have a small role in a very big play."

"You think Macklin can help?"

"Maybe. When we get all of our heads together . . ." He shrugged. "Who knows?"

He hadn't told them about Mohammad. He wouldn't, until he received the report and decided it was safe to meet with the terrorist. He couldn't help but feel Faisal held a key for them. A key that would lock the door on Jerisha. Once and for all.

He forced a smile. "Relax. We're safe here, and Trayco has arrived in Jackson by now." His mind was diverted by a small presence behind him. He turned to find Issa's dark eyes riveted on him.

He stooped down and she ran to his arms, pointing toward the pool. "Swim," she said. Then she pointed at Jerry and herself. "Swim."

"Sounds good to me. Get your suit on." She broke from his arms and ran for the stairs. He followed, his arm around Mike's waist, an unsettled, nervous feeling rambling around in his stomach. What had started in Wyoming was not over. He would find a way to end it, or they would never be able to sleep safely again.

———————

Macklin awoke with a start, throwing the blanket off and to the floor and sitting erect. Something . . . a noise. When? How long . . . ?

He ran down the hall to the bedroom. Ruth was gone.

He panicked. "Ruth?" he yelled, checking the bathroom, then each other room. He grabbed his .45 from the table, listened at the door, then stepped into the hall. Nothing. He kept to the wall and moved toward the door he knew led to her rooms. He listened again, then tried the knob. It turned.

Gently he opened it. Not a sound. He checked each room. Nothing. His heart hurt. How could she do this again?

His stockinged feet pattered back to his own apartment. He closed the door, deep in thought.

The hospital.

———————

Rashid sat a short distance from where Raoul and Issa played in the pool, using the underwater masks, fetching coins from the bottom. Rashid couldn't play. He was worried.

After four years of survival on the streets of Jerusalem he had developed very quick eyes and ears, becoming sensitive to any opportunity in which he could get work or food for himself and Issa. For a boy of twelve he was extremely perceptive and talented, using his gift for gab and a light heart to turn anything into something good for the two of them.

That morning he had overheard Mrs. Mike and her father discussing the children's future as the two adults sat talking on the patio. He pretended he was out of earshot, but he couldn't miss the words orphanage and burden. Rashid knew Mrs. Mike loved Issa. Possibly, if he and Raoul left, Mrs. Mike would take care of Issa and stop talking of an orphanage.

He was suddenly very sad. Issa was all he had in this world. His parents had left their children's lives years ago, leaving him and Issa to fend for themselves. His mother said their father was killed fighting for the Arab resistance against the Israelis, but he was to keep it a secret or some of their Jewish neighbors might take action against them. He had never told anyone.

His mother had tried making a home for them, but became sick because of work and not eating enough. He had stayed by her side, taking care of Issa, who was only three then, until he awoke one morning to find his mother's eyes staring blankly at the ceiling.

It was the only time Rashid could remember crying. He took Issa and left the house. He knew what would happen if the authorities came and found them without parents. He would have been separated from his little sister and probably never would have seen her again. He couldn't take that chance. All he could picture was Issa being taken into a family that would mistreat her.

They had lived and survived in the streets ever since.

Mrs. Mike was different. Rashid trusted her almost as much as he loved Issa. He knew Issa would have a good home, and much more of everything than he could ever give her.

His heart ached. He wanted to stay, but Issa's happiness was more important.

He and Raoul must leave.

The English copy of the *Jerusalem Post* was sitting across his plate when Jerry came to the table. He glanced at Mike as she stood looking out of the kitchen window, her arms folded.

He flipped it open and read the bold headlines. DOCU-MENT REVEALED! AMERICAN, CIA OPERATIVE? The story went over the details of the kidnapping, then gave a full photocopy of the single-sheet document, committing Israel to acts that could subvert the peace talks. In return? Two hundred million dollars, eventually paid under the table, slipped to the Israeli government by way of the CIA. The U.S. president's supposed signature was affixed; a space for the Israeli prime minister's was still blank. Supposedly, the kidnapping took place before Jerry got that one.

The article went on, offering the prime minister's denials, along with the president's, and a statement at the very end indicating that the document was being reviewed for authenticity.

Mike had circled another article. Minister Hoshen was only hours away from resigning.

"Has the embassy sent our plane tickets over yet?" Jerry asked.

Mike didn't face him. "It's not funny, Jerry. A lot of people will be crying for your blood. American politicians, Arab leaders, Israelis, everyone."

"Has your dad seen this?"

Mike faced him, nodding. "He's on the phone with the president now."

"Well, as they say, those who work in the kitchen had better be ready for the heat."

"I'm frightened, Jerry. Jerisha could pull this off and ruin you, hurt all of us, in the process."

"Knowing what we're up against gives us an edge we didn't have before. We'll stop them. With a little luck." He grinned. "Wyoming-style luck."

"This is not Wyoming, Jerry. They intend to kill you and discredit American efforts by all of this. You're in a foreign country, without the cooperation and protection you need. It's different!"

He stood and walked to her, taking her in his arms.

The senator cleared his throat as he came into the kitchen. "Jeremiah, good morning."

"Senator. Sleep good?"

"Not long enough. You're in the soup, son."

"I can swim."

"If that document isn't proven a forgery right quick . . ."

"I understand. Homeward bound." He moved to his chair. "Let's eat something. I'm starved."

Jerry dished up his plate while Mike poured milk. Jerry tossed a plain brown envelope to the senator.

"That came by courier an hour ago. Interesting reading."

The senator opened the package that still carried the confidential courier seal of Bahrain. After reading for a moment, his eyes jumped to the face of his son-in-law.

"You believe him?"

Jerry nodded. "He gives phone numbers. Call them if you think it necessary."

Mike leaned over her father's shoulder. "What's this?"

"Mohammad Faisal called here yesterday. He wants to meet with myself, Minister Hoshen, and a representative of our government. He's invited Saad Khourani of the West Bank coalition. That envelope tells me he's sincere."

"Keeping secrets?" she said wryly.

"Needed the envelope before it would do any good to discuss it. For all I knew, he was just blowing hot air."

"What does it say?" Mike asked.

"Those are names of—" Jerry began, but the senator reached over and touched his arm, whispering.

"Have you had this place checked for bugs yet?"

"Yesterday, and again this morning by the people at our embassy." Jerry smiled, then looked back at his wife.

"Darling, those are the names of people Mohammad Faisal spirited out of this country and gave new identities to in order to save their lives after the PLO and two other groups ordered them killed."

"Killed? For what?"

"For wanting to negotiate peace without them. It seems Mr. Faisal is working very hard to protect West Bank leadership from his own kind. He's working for peace."

"Then you're going to meet with him?" the senator asked.

"Yes, I haven't any other choice. The man seems to be sincere, and he has information he says will save a lot of lives, maybe help get peace talks going. I have a gut feeling it has something to do with what someone is trying to do to us."

"I'm going with you, as the American representative," the senator said.

"What about the president? He won't like you operating behind his back," Jerry said.

The senator shrugged. "He's not my nursemaid."

"If things go wrong, your career among the so-called elite of Washington will be over. It'll look like a political maneuver."

"I'm getting ready to retire anyway. I just haven't made an official announcement. If this does it for me, so be it."

"You two are thinking of doing this on your own?" Mike asked.

They smiled. "Do you think anyone would give us permission?" the senator asked.

"What about Hoshen?" asked Mike.

"I contacted him this morning. Due to the circumstances, I found the minister to be quite cooperative." Jerry pointed at the article in the paper. "They're calling for his resignation."

The senator read it, then whistled. "It'll take something mighty big to save his hide."

"Someone wants Hoshen out of the way as much as they do us. They had a plan to kill him. Being rid of him politically may suit their purposes just as well. I've convinced him to wait until after the meeting with Faisal in a few hours."

"What about Colonel Macklin, Dad?"

"I have permission to use him but no one seems to know where he is. I'll call and apply some pressure. Have the embassy round him up." He headed for the study.

"You'll need to hurry. I'd like him along."

The senator nodded as he disappeared through the door.

"It's dangerous, for both of you," Mike said, looking after her dad.

Jerry didn't answer and kept his eyes focused on the plate of food before him, his fork playing with the eggs.

"Where are the kids?" he asked.

"Where else?" Mike glanced out of the window at the pool. "That's funny, the boys are gone, only Issa is there. They must be upstairs."

Jerry stood and started for the door. "Let's check." They could see Issa sitting on the grass with her back to them, looking down at something.

As they approached she didn't look up, and she seemed to be crying.

"Issa?" Mike said, going quickly and kneeling in front of her. "Where is Rashid?"

Issa's head hung to her chest and Mike couldn't see her eyes. She touched her chin, pulling upward, finding tears rolling down Issa's cheeks.

"Issa! What's wrong? Where is Rashid?"

Issa threw her small form into Mike's arms.

"Gone! Mrs. Mike," she said as plainly as she could. "Gone!"

Rashid saw the guard and quickly pulled Raoul down. After the man with the automatic disappeared behind the house, they moved silently through the shadows toward the fence. Raoul, in a sudden rush of excitement mingled with the fear of getting caught, started forward, anxious to climb and be away. Rashid grabbed his sleeve, holding him back.

"Electric," he said firmly in quiet Arabic. Raoul looked up at the fence, his throat dry, unable to swallow.

Rashid pulled him along the fence line, looking for a low spot in the ground, or a limb hanging far enough over the top of the fence that they could maneuver across.

Rashid stopped. A short distance away lay a long log entwined in grass and overgrowth.

He pointed. "We take that and lean it up against a tree limb on the far side of the fence and above it. Then we can climb over."

Soon the boys found themselves over the fence, their quick feet moving them down a hill toward the road.

Nearing the pavement they walked more carefully, watchful for guards. A short distance away Rashid saw a red car of American make pulled off the road and in the trees, a man with a camera standing half-hidden at the top of a far hill. Rashid pulled Raoul into the bushes.

"A ride. He is probably taking pictures of Jerusalem. Use your talents, get us in the trunk, and we won't have to walk. It is a long way to the city."

Raoul smiled. The "talents" Rashid referred to was the taller boy's ability to pick locks. He was not a thief, but he did use this gift and his tiny, self-made tool when needing a place to sleep out of the cold and wind some nights.

They sneaked through the heavy brush, wending their way carefully to the car trunk. Raoul quickly opened it and they bustled inside, shutting it softly over their heads.

Raoul had seen the blanket and expected a soft padding. The hard object pressing into the flesh of his backside told him how wrong he was. He reached around, trying to remove it, startled at what he found.

"Rashid!" he said in a loud whisper. "A gun!"

"Shh." Rashid could hear the opening of a door. He put his mouth near his friend's ear and spoke in a careful whisper. "When he stops in the city we will throw open the trunk and escape into the crowds."

Raoul took a breath, trying to relax.

The motion of the car on the winding road created a sick feeling in Rashid's stomach. He was in danger of losing his breakfast when the road straightened and gave him some relief from the nausea, but the lack of air inside the dark enclosure was nearly unbearable.

Suddenly the car came to a stop. Raoul went to open the trunk but Rashid stopped him. He could hear voices. One spoke English with an Arabic accent. The other was a foreigner, like the German tourists to whom Rashid often sold items.

"Are they where we were told?" the Arab asked.

"Yes, I could see them in the backyard," the foreigner said. "The place is heavily guarded."

"Pike said it would be. Any other visitors?"

"A man in casual clothes. Probably Israeli secret service. He came and left.

"Look, Muzra, the place is impregnable. We'll never get in."

"We're not going in. Pike says they'll be coming out. We just have to be ready."

Rashid's eyes were open wide. Muzra! No wonder the voice sounded familiar. Rashid had worked for the east Jerusalem Arab in his olive wood shop.

"What happened to the plan to have Daniels kill Hoshen and the others at the temple mount?" the foreigner asked.

"The others disappeared," Muzra answered. "This plan will work even better. Make arrangements for more men and anything else needed, Zalinka. You will be directly responsible for the assault on Daniels. The meeting place is the

Christian basilica on Mount Dothan. Everyone who is with him is to be killed, especially Minister Hoshen and Moham-mad Faisal. Do you understand?"

"How do we know they will all be at the basilica?" Zalinka asked.

"Sabrila has a source inside the Israeli government," Muzra said. "She says it is most dependable and that these orders are directly from him."

"You know Mohammad Faisal by sight?" he added.

"We have worked together. I know him. What about pay-ment?"

"You must leave Israel as soon as this is finished," said Muzra. "Here are the passports you asked for, and the tick-ets. The rest of the money will be deposited in your Cayman Island account when word comes of your success."

"What's Pike doing while I'm at Dothan?" Zalinka asked.

"He and the woman have other duties. A man that has seen too much."

Rashid smelled the pungent odor of Muzra's Turkish cig-arettes, a smell he had learned to hate.

"You will go in early and get in position to use your skills?"

"That, my Arab friend, is none of your business," Zalinka said. "Did you bring the weapon?"

"In the trunk."

Rashid froze, his hand clutching the cold steel underneath him, Raoul's hand gripping his wrist. They heard the key slip into the lock, hopeful that the latch was permanently jammed. Rashid closed his eyes, asking Allah for invisibility, then felt the rush of hot midday air blow across his sweating brow.

CHAPTER 26

3:20 P.M., Hadassah Hospital, Jerusalem

Ruth sat in the plastic-covered chair, the constant thump and beat of Ativa's life-support systems filling the otherwise quiet room.

He looked pale, bloodstained bandages across his chest accentuating the lack of the fluid in his veins, while the yellow-orange antiseptic that doctors use like water added a sickly taint.

Ruth hated hospitals. They smelled of sickness and the inevitable death it caused. They reminded her too much of the past.

Ativa moved slightly—a twitch in his hand, a flutter in his eyelid. Would she ever look into those steel-gray eyes again? Feel that rough but tender thumb as it rubbed the back of her hand, giving her much-needed comfort?

She stood and walked to the window. She felt guilty about walking out on Tom. Should have left him a note explaining what had happened and where she had gone, leaving him at the hospital the previous day. How she had been so despondent that she had tried swimming to Italy, or into oblivion, whichever came first.

She folded her arms tightly across her chest, a cold chill raising goose bumps. She had been out of control, and it scared her. Without Tom . . . she shuddered . . . she wouldn't have come back, another suicidal statistic in a country where such things were on a disastrous climb.

But she hadn't left a note. She had awakened with a start, Papa Ativa filling her mind. Dressing hurriedly, she felt she must come to the hospital, quickly. She just hadn't taken the time . . .

Chaim moaned. Ruth went to his side, his unconscious body wracked by pain. Her eyes went to each of the monitors. She knew nothing about them, and except for a quicker beep for a few seconds, then a return to normal, she saw no difference.

The nurse came in, saw Ruth, and hesitated.

"I . . . I'm sorry. I didn't know . . . No one is supposed to be here." She hurried to the monitor, looking efficient as she checked each instrument, apparently a bit nervous—at being watched, Ruth supposed.

She was a pretty Israeli. Black hair, olive skin, dark eyes—she almost looked Arabic. The usual white uniform, insignia on the sleeve, name tag over the left breast. "Happerstein." Eastern European.

She smiled nervously in Ruth's direction, hesitated a little, then left the room. Ruth returned to the window, watching the city in the distance, wondering if Macklin had discovered yet that she was gone. She smiled a little. He was deep in sleep when she slipped by him, the blanket held tight at his chest, a light snore coming through a half-open mouth.

The quick movement outside caught her eye. A nurse in a hurry. Ruth's eyes focused. Happerstein. Must have just been getting off duty. Then she saw the car, half a hundred feet away, a man standing, leaning against it. A Mercedes, a blond, English-looking . . .

Pike! Her eyes grew wide. She spun around and looked at Ativa, then the machines. One seemed different, slower, the line on the monitor . . .

She lunged for the door! "Doctor!" she screamed. Ativa's assigned guard was lying asleep, lifeless, in a chair . . . "Help!" A nurse came quickly from behind a desk, running, then a doctor. They dashed into Ativa's room. "Check everything! Someone was just here, dressed like a nurse . . . an assassin! Check everything!" She ran from the room and down the hall, the hot anger and hatred welling up inside her. She knew the stairs and dashed down them two at a time. She must stop them! She must get them!

She burst from the side door and into the parking lot. The blue Mercedes was just exiting into the street. She sprinted to her own car, grateful that she hadn't set the alarm this time, hadn't even locked it. In seconds she was screeching through the lot and bumping into the street, with traffic flashing, spinning around her, dodging to miss the sudden appearance of her white Mercedes.

She saw Pike's car turning a corner and floored the pedal, swerving to miss a slow jaywalker. In seconds she was around the corner and in the straightaway. They were on to her, picking up speed, trying to elude her in traffic . . .

Her mind was filled with Chaim's helpless body on the hospital bed, the anger so hot in her chest that it nearly choked her. She reached for the jockey box, ignoring the police-band radio hidden there, her fingers wrapping around the American-made .45-caliber nickel-plated Colt. Chaim's present to his son on the day he had graduated from basic training. And now hers.

She spun the wheel to make the corner, the car's wheels sliding toward the curb, banging against it and knocking her back into traffic. Pike was good. He had done this before. But so had she!

She floored it again, closing ground. Her Mercedes had

the bigger motor, it was clear. She'd catch them! She released the safety on the .45, then rolled down the window while dodging half a dozen cars. Only fifty feet separated them now, only . . . She fired the gun and saw the back windshield of the blue Mercedes disintegrate, the car swerving from left to right and back again as Pike tried to regain control. But he couldn't, and Ruth watched, her eyes riveted on the Mercedes as it hit the curb and became airborne, flipping . . .

Ruth slammed on her own brakes and jerked the wheel as she saw the flash of white out of the corner of her eye. Too late. The third vehicle had swerved to miss Pike but lost control, hitting the back end of Ruth's Mercedes, slamming it into a rotation. She helplessly watched the front do what seemed to her mind to be a slow-motion ninety degree, then a full circle. The car hit something. She felt it fly in the air, turn in slow motion, then come crashing down on its top, sliding down the street.

The impact jolted her in her seatbelt. The gun, knocked from her hand, exploded near her ear, sending hot pain through her neck. Window glass shattered toward her and she instinctively put up her arms to ward it off. Sparks flew in all directions and she felt the hot embers burning the flesh on the back of her hands.

The last jolt came as the car rammed into the side of a building, knocking in a wall, and bringing it down on top of the vehicle in a series of thumping crashes. Crashes Ruth never heard.

3:30 P.M., East Jerusalem, the Old City, Arab section

Rashid felt cold, even though sweat trickled down his neck and sides. The uninsulated storage room was hot, even in the late afternoon sun. And with no window for fresh air, Rashid was dripping wet with the perspiration.

"Raoul, what are you doing?" Rashid asked in quiet Arabic.

"Still trying to free my hands."

Rashid knew where they were. He had recognized the place the minute his blindfold had been removed. Muzra's olive wood shop. The fat little shopkeeper and his friend had bound them, then wrapped them in blankets. They hauled them inside and dumped them on the storage room floor, locking the door as they left. Rashid remembered Muzra's last words: "I will take care of them tonight. Outside the city." The words gave him a chill.

"We must get free, Raoul. They intend to kill us and hurt Mr. Jerry!"

"I know, but the ropes are so tight!"

"We must work together. Can you turn your hands so that I can try the ropes with my teeth?" Rashid asked.

Raoul wiggled and turned until his hands were in position. Rashid used his lips, finding the rope, then the knot. Baring his teeth, he grabbed at the knotted strands, working, pulling them free. After a few moments he rolled onto his back, catching his breath.

"You are not giving up? I think they are looser, Rashid. Really, it's working!"

Rashid inhaled, rose to his knees, and bent his head to the task. Moments passed as he ripped at the strands, his teeth hurting and his gums and lips starting to bleed. Finally, the rope gave way and slid free. In less than a minute Raoul had untied his own legs, then Rashid's. As he worked on the smaller boy's wrists, he spoke.

"How can we escape? What must we do?"

"This is Muzra's shop, the olive wood vendor. I worked for him. If he is here, he will be in the shop up front, helping customers . . ." Rashid heard the footsteps in the hall, then a key in the door. He shoved Raoul to one side, and as the door swung open, Rashid lowered his head and tackled the fat shopkeeper, knocking him against the wall. In a flash he was up and moving through the hall.

"Come on, Raoul!" he yelled as the older boy stood staring at the stunned shopkeeper. "*Run!*"

Raoul's new Nikes caught wings, and the two boys were through the shop and at the door before they heard Muzra's cries for help.

"Stop them! Thieves!" Muzra yelled in loud Arabic.

The boys bolted into the street as Muzra's assistant grabbed for them. Their new Nikes slammed against the cobblestone, moving them quickly away into the sparse, early-morning crowd.

"Come back!" the assistant shouted, leaping after them. "Thief! Come back! Stop them! Thief!" he yelled as he ran after the boys, his sandaled feet slapping against the stones.

Rashid saw the eyes turning toward them, then bodies

responding to the shopkeeper's pleas. "Duck, Raoul!" he yelled as one man tried to grab the taller boy by the neck. Raoul eluded the grasp and sprang past the man, jumping onto a small cart.

"Rashid, get on!" he yelled, pushing the cart down the cobblestone street, picking up speed. Rashid knocked an arm aside, ducked another, and flung himself atop two sacks of beans stretched across the four-wheeled cart. The bump-bump of the cart's wheels jarred his teeth as they ran over uneven stones, picking up more and more speed.

Raoul had driven such carts many times, earning small amounts of money for survival by bringing goods to the shops along the Old City's narrow streets, where vehicles weren't allowed. It was easy going into the city, because the streets sloped ever downward, as they did now, creating a quick trip for cart drivers and packages alike. Many a time Raoul had used all of his strength to keep the cart from running down pedestrians as the heavy dolly plummeted down the stepped streets. Not this time.

Raoul and Rashid ducked as adults tried grabbing them. One burly Arab, thinking himself stronger than the speeding cart, tried to stop them by jumping in front of it, using his weight as a brace against the vehicle's momentum. He was knocked aside like a paper doll, screaming with pain, cursing the backs of the two boys as they disappeared around a bend farther down the street. Raoul knew the way and quickly had them out of Muzra's reach. As the street began to flatten, they jumped from the cart and dashed into Al Wad road, running south toward the temple mount.

Raoul's longer legs moved him ahead of Rashid, forcing Rashid to yell. "We must find the house and Mr. Daniels, Raoul. We must stop what they intend to do to Mr. Jerry!"

Raoul didn't seem to hear, his body coming to an abrupt halt in the narrow street. Rashid's Nikes gripped the stone street as he came abreast of his friend. He looked behind them, afraid he might see a dozen others closing in, ready to wring their necks. But the crowd merely mulled about, seemingly uncaring of the two boys. Rashid breathlessly glanced at his friend, then at the spot on which Raoul's eyes were fixed. It was dusty red and beat up, the small seat in shreds. Its three tires, bald and bulging in spots, looked ready to explode. A three-wheeled monstrosity older than Rashid and ready for the junk heap.

"Allah has provided for our speedy return," Raoul said. "Allah always provides for the needy."

Rashid gulped, shaking his head. Allah's blessing seemed to be a two-edged sword.

4:00 P.M., Hadassah Hospital, Jerusalem

It was dark, but she could hear voices in the distance talking about her, calling her name. She saw the light, dim at first. It grew larger and brighter, blinding her.

"Take it easy, Colonel Levona. You're in the hospital emergency room."

Her eyes focused on the ceiling's fluorescent lights, then on the curtains and a young doctor's face, light instrument in hand, held over one eye.

"Ruth." She felt the squeeze on her hand.

"Tom? What . . ."

"You made a convertible out of the Mercedes." She tried to sit up; he gently pushed her back. "Relax. You're okay, at least as near as we can tell. A few stitches here and there . . ." He smiled.

"Chaim . . . Pike and that woman . . ."

"The general is still alive, thanks to your quick action. The phony nurse plugged the oxygen line and shut off a couple of the support systems. Hard to tell unless you knew the machinery. They got it on quick enough. No damage. The Mercedes you chased crashed. Pike is dead. The woman escaped in the crowd. There is a bulletin out on her."

"We're going to keep you here," the doctor said. "For observation. You have a concussion and possible internal damage, bruised liver, maybe the pancreas, as well."

"I can't—"

"Yes, you can," Tom said forcefully.

"A few hours, Colonel. At the most, overnight," the doctor said as he put his instrument away. "I'll send a nurse in to get those wounds ready for a few stitches. She'll arrange for a hospital gown." He turned to Macklin. "She'll need clean clothes . . ."

"I'll take care of it," Macklin smiled.

"Oh, and how will you do that?" Ruth asked.

"I have the keys to your apartment. Actually, when you

214

left this morning, you forgot to lock it. Foolish of you. Strangers like me take advantage of pretty ladies like you."

"Sorry I didn't leave a note. I had this feeling . . ."

"It paid off. You saved his life, at least gave him a chance at one."

He walked to the window. "I've never felt so panicked in all my life as I have during the last twenty-four hours. It's all your fault. Are you going to keep this up?"

She laughed lightly, then grew serious. "A lot has gone wrong in my life, Tom. You happened to come along when it all came to a head."

"I love you, Ruth. I'll stand by you in whatever it is you're fighting, but I can't watch you self-destruct."

"I'm . . . okay . . . I—"

"No, you're not, Ruth," Macklin said as he turned to face her. "You're a ticking time bomb ready to blow up. You nearly killed a dozen people in that crazy stunt this afternoon. Nearly killed yourself! You're not thinking, Ruth. You're out of control."

"No, I'm not. I had to go after them. INFERNO . . . !"

Macklin pressed his hand against the back of her neck where a bandage covered a wound. "That was your worst wound, Ruth. The .45 went off during the accident. You nearly blew your own head off. You should have stayed with Ativa. But even if you did have to go after them, you could have gotten help, used that radio. We both know it. Instead, you try to play John Wayne and blow them away while dodging cars at seventy miles an hour. *That* is out of control."

For a fleeting second Macklin thought he got through. Then he saw her jaw set, the eyes focus on a spot beyond him, hard and cold. As she began to speak through tight lips, the nurse opened the door. Ruth looked away from him and concentrated on being cooperative. He took the hint and slipped from the room. A message had come from Gad; a phone number he was supposed to call when he got a chance. He walked to a pay phone and dialed. Maybe Ruth just needed time.

The voice sounded familiar. "Mike, is that you?"

"Colonel! I'm so glad . . ." Her voice was anxious. "Jerry has been trying . . . He's gone. Can you come? Right away?"

"What is it, Mike? What's going on?"

"They . . . he and Dad . . . They went to meet with Mohammad Faisal."

CHAPTER 27

5:35 P.M., Near Mount Dothan, northern Israel, the West Bank

The black limo climbed the switchback road easily, its big, 520-cubic-inch powerhouse engine never missing a beat. It carried a lot of weight with armor plating, thick bulletproof windows, and special tires that gave new meaning to the term steel-belted radials.

When Macklin hadn't been found, Jerry called Hoshen and made arrangements for a few necessary items, including the thick-skinned limo and semiautomatic weapons for each of its occupants.

Their "team" amounted to four: Jerry, the senator, Hoshen, and one man from among the "bodyguards" patrolling the safe house grounds. Benjamin Nitani wasn't given warning of his new duties. Hoshen simply had told him to bring his weapon and get in the car. He was to drive.

On the first part of the journey they discussed Mohammad Faisal. They finally convinced Hoshen that the former terrorist was friend and not foe by showing the minister the envelope and telling him about the senator's subtle intelligence "inquiries" about the individuals named. As near as the senator could tell, Mohammad had saved nearly a hundred people from sure death at the hands of the PLO.

The next half of the ride was spent explaining to the minister what they knew about Jerisha Duquesne and what she might be up to.

"Then she's behind the factory," Hoshen had said matter-of-factly. "Wherever it is."

"Possibly that's what Mohammad has to tell us," Jerry said.

"Umm. Well, what have we to lose?" Hoshen said wryly. "We certainly won't be any more in the dark after we meet with him than we are now." Jerry could see that Hoshen was hoping for a miracle. Something that would save him from drowning in political seas made rough by a lost factory, a general turned collaborator, and an American working for the CIA.

Jerry's brow wrinkled as he thought about leaving Mike in a tizzy. The boys had left without a note, a word, anything! He was angry at first, then realized that these were kids—street kids at that—who came and went as they pleased. It was apparent that swimming had gotten old, but Jerry had thought Rashid would never desert Issa. Never!

Where had those two little whelps gone? When he got his hands on them . . .

Would he ever get the chance? He shoved the thought aside. They'd find both of them! No matter how long it took!

During the drive they passed new Israeli settlements and several inhabitated by Palestinians. Even though Jerry had seen it before, the contrast was shocking. Probably because of all that he'd learned over the past few days. So many differences—laws, standards of living, religion, traditions. He shook his head. A country trying to find its real identity, torn between two very different and yet very similar peoples.

As they neared the top of the mountain switchbacks Hoshen pulled away a false panel under his seat and withdrew weapons. Some Uzis with several clips apiece and American-made .45's. He handed each person his share. "No sense being lambs at the slaughterhouse until we find out if the butchers are working today," he smiled. Jerry didn't care for the analogy, but he couldn't argue the point.

They entered the first gate and drove between trees planted in an area known as the Franciscan Ground. The second gate was open and led into a courtyard. On their left was a small building near what was known as the Cave of Endor, the traditional place where Saul had visited the witch during Old Testament times.

Nitani slowed the car, driving with one hand and holding the Uzi with the other. The small Church of St. Simeon was now on their left, the Basilica of St. James directly ahead.

Jerry remembered the beautiful yet simple interior of the basilica and its wonderful acoustics. On the day he and his now-deceased first wife, Liz, had visited, a group of pilgrims from New York sang hymns, the voices resonating off the walls and sounding like angels from heaven. How he wished he was just another tourist.

The tension in the car was thick, each person wondering if they were walking into a trap, yet excited, hope—or fear—pushing adrenaline into their bloodstreams.

Jerry took a deep breath, releasing the grip on his own

gun. Calm must rule. They must not give Faisal reason to fear. Both sides were extremely nervous, afraid the other might be setting them up. He must be the first to show total trust. Years of tradition and prejudice made it nearly impossible for everyone else. And if he didn't appear calm, the others might bolt.

He shoved away his fear of being caught in the middle by focusing on the basilica again.

The two towers on the left and right of the central chapel housed the bell towers. The main church had what seemed to be a peaked roof with a cross in the front center, three arched windows directly underneath on the top floor. A similar archway was over the main entrance.

The driver stopped the car and turned off the ignition.

Jeremiah saw the men standing half in and half out of the basilica doorway. The blue and white checked kafeyeh was wrapped across the face of one, but Jerry knew it was Mohammad. To his side stood Doctor Jamel and Saad Khourani, all carrying automatic weapons. The tension in the car thickened.

The senator leaned forward and spoke in Jerry's ear. "No offense, Jeremiah, but we're sitting ducks."

Jerry smiled, then looked through the window at Mohammad, who was holding the Kalishnikov by both hands. It was then that he noticed a fourth person standing at Mohammad's left, menacing, ready for battle. Faisal's right-hand man.

Jerry could see what they all saw—extreme vulnerability. He looked up at the bell towers again. A sniper could pick them off like geese on a pond.

But he also felt strongly that their worst enemy wasn't each other but was the unseen mistrust that had everyone pressing fingers against triggers. In his next action he must defuse that deadlier weapon.

He inhaled, exhaled, then laid his gun on the seat and opened the door, stepping into the dusty courtyard. Without hesitating he walked toward the basilica.

Faisal handed his rifle to Khourani and moved toward Jerry, extending his hand in friendship and allowing Jerry's heart to slip out of his throat and back to his chest where it belonged. Jamel and Khourani leaned their weapons against the wall and followed Mohammad. Jerry's feeling of euphoria dispelled when he noticed that the fourth man remained armed and ready while watching them and the car beyond.

The senator opened the door, his gun left on the seat. But Hoshen hesitated, rubbing his hand nervously against the cold metal, struggling to put aside years of fear. Finally, he dropped it and slid out of the seat, joining the others. The driver followed.

Mohammad removed the kafeyeh from his face. "Mr. Daniels." He made a slight bow with his head. "You honor me with your trust, but I give you a suggestion. We both have mutual enemies. We shall go inside, then to the patio beyond. Have the driver retrieve your weapons and bring them into the church."

Jerry was impressed. He nodded to Hoshen, who instructed the driver.

Introductions were made, each shaking hands as they moved toward the brass-covered oak doors.

As he let the others go through the door, Jerry turned around and took one last look at the area. He saw nothing wrong, but he sensed . . . what . . .?

He let his eyes drift again, searching shadows, his ears attuned to hear the click of metal against stone, soft shoes on dusty ground or hard rock. Nothing.

He moved inside the church and started toward the small group. He saw Mohammad's soldier come through a side door and lock it. The one man not introduced. From the look of him, Jerry wasn't sure he ever wanted to know the man. Even though he was now unarmed, he looked menacing. His cold eyes, firm jaw, and nearly shaved head gave him the appearance of a short-haired terrier about to rip something or someone apart, just for fun. It made Jerry shudder.

"He is Nabril Al Razd," Mohammad said.

"You read minds?" Jerry smiled.

"Faces. It is my business, the way I stay alive."

Now Jerry knew why he feared the man. Al Razd had been one of the PLO's best assassins before disappearing a few years ago. He was wanted by every Arab country Jerry knew of. He kept order in the PLO's own backyard.

"You are the one who stopped Fillmore Duquesne," Mohammad said.

Jerry glanced at the senator. "I had a lot of help. How did you know?"

"Again, Mr. Daniels, it is my business to know these

things. Just as I know that you have not finished off what you think he began. Just as I know," he looked at Minister Hoshen, "that the minister was to be a dead man, along with Mr. Khourani and yourself.

"How . . . ?" Hoshen started to ask, but Mohammad raised a hand.

"First things first, Minister. The priests of this church prefer that we meet outside this holy building. They have given us permission to use the rear patio. It is cool, partially shaded now, and seating has been provided. Is that acceptable?"

Al Razd and Hoshen's driver took up positions at opposite ends of the patio. Their vigilance gave Jerry a greater comfort level, but he still felt uneasy, as if they were being watched.

After they were seated, Faisal began the conversation. Jerry listened while keeping his eyes roaming over the terrain, his ears pinned on the breeze and the message it might carry. He noticed the shadow of the basilica creeping almost imperceptibly across the patio's stone floor. In an hour it would cover more than just where they sat.

"I did not ask you here to force concessions out of you for the information I hold, but I must ask one favor. Now that my position on the West Bank has been betrayed, I can no longer protect people like Mr. Khourani. I wish the American government to take this responsibility."

The senator responded. "Why not Israel? It seems to me—"

Mohammad smiled. "Protection from a government you are trying to change can be intimidating, Senator."

Hoshen's face was red. Jerry couldn't tell whether it was from anger or embarrassment.

"Very well," the senator said. "We will get them out of the country. Find—"

Mohammad held up his hand. "They must remain here, on the West Bank. The Israelis must be willing to allow you to protect them here."

Jerry looked at Hoshen, who was fidgeting, clearing his throat before speaking. "I can't promise. I may not be in office . . . "

"The information I give you, Minister, may elevate you to the prime minister's seat if you treat it properly. Will you give your word?"

Hoshen hesitated, then nodded slightly.

"I accept it as your bond," Mohammad said, leaning forward. "I swear to you, if you break your word to me, any of you, you will have to look over your shoulder for the rest of your lives."

Hoshen started to speak but held back. Jerry could see that the minister didn't like threat diplomacy. But then, Mohammad wasn't a diplomat. He was a terrorist. His threat could be considered as binding as any written document a diplomat had ever come up with.

"Then to business. All of us at this table are fighting a common enemy. Someone who wishes all here dead and buried.

"First, I was betrayed and nearly killed by my own kind. My enemies apparently found out what I was doing on the West Bank and knew that I would oppose any of their attempts to gain control there. I had to be eliminated so they could get to Mr. Khourani.

"Second, Minister, they intended to kill you and Mr. Khourani at the same time, blaming each for the death of the other." He smiled, looking at Jerry. "This was done for two reasons I can think of. One, to discredit West Bank leadership and rekindle heavy antagonism and distrust between Palestinian and Jew. Two, to create fertile ground for new leadership among my people.

"They selected you, Mr. Hoshen, because of your firm stand against giving up the West Bank. Perhaps they have other motives. My sources tell me that General Chaim Ativa was shot by our common enemy, as was Mr. Shomani. Possibly to cover whatever they are planning.

"Last, Mr. Daniels, we come to you. Our common enemy likes you least of all. You stepped on their toes very hard when you stopped something they called TERROR1. In fact, you nearly crushed them. Only one remained to rebuild and replan, continuing what she had begun before you came along."

"Jerisha Duquesne."

"TERROR1 was known to me when it was begun. I sat in several meetings between the Duquesnes and highly placed PLO officials. The intent of TERROR1 was to upset an enemy's economy, throw chaos into the American system so that you would stay home when a coalition, seemingly headed by Saddam Hussein, gained control of Arab leadership. The intent was to solidify the Arab world into one republic. There would have been great strength in such an organization, but I knew then, as I know now, it was nothing but a dream. The Arab world can never accomplish this. We are too busy fighting one another to ever really become united. I also believed that Jerisha Salamhani Duquesne had her own private agenda. Now I know it. Then, I had no power to control her greed for power. Now, I do, and I must. She intends to destroy even my people to accomplish her new order."

He leaned toward the minister. "Are you familiar with the house of Hassan?"

Hoshen nodded, waving his hand in dismissal. "A Palestinian family who feel they have the right to rule Palestine. Their leaders have long ago died, all of the heirs—"

"Yes, you found and killed them."

Hoshen's face was red again. This time Jerry could see that it was anger. "We didn't seek them out. Abu Hassan was a terrorist who had killed many of our people. He lived by violence. He died by it!" Hoshen said this through his teeth.

Mohammad gave a patient smile. "You thought he was the last. There are two others. One was killed in 1965 while trying to smuggle guns to Palestinian Liberation Army leaders in the Sinai. The other is Jerisha Duquesne."

"Then TERROR1 was an attempt to return her to the throne, is that what you're saying?" the senator asked.

"Yes, and she continues with her obsession."

"So my kidnapping was only part of a larger plan?" Jerry said.

"As with TERROR1, Jerisha knows that she must bring about political chaos to discredit the United States, if only for a short time. Just long enough for her to create a power vacuum in which she will act as savior. If she can make the world believe that you and Israel are planning some heinous plot against the Arab nations, she sows seeds of doubt and anger. She is prepared to reap the harvest through an act of war."

"The factory. She is responsible—" Hoshen caught himself.

"Yes, Minister, she is," Faisal said. "I saw her there two nights ago."

"You went to Syria?" Jerry asked.

"I go there all the time. As well as to other Arab countries. I have friends in Damascus who believe as I do, and who, as I, are tired of the violence. They secretly work for the overthrow of dictators like King Hussein of Jordan, and the governments of Iraq and Iran. We want peace to come to our lands." He turned to Hoshen. "Your General Ativa was working with us. I pray to Allah that he will survive his wounds to work for peace again."

"But how can Jerisha justify an attack?" the senator asked. "Even if she has nuclear warheads and first-strike capability, she knows Israel will retaliate."

"I cannot answer that, but I'm sure she has thought it through. Possibly we should travel to Syria and ask her." He smiled. "For now, I think it best that we unite our efforts and stop her. The warheads are finished; most of them chemical, at least one nuclear. They have the new version of the SCUD missile. There are several launchers at the factory site, but most of the warheads are carted and ready for shipment. My guess is that she has the other missiles secreted in bunkers in most nations bordering Israel."

"You have seen—"

Jerry grabbed the minister's arm. "A chopper!"

Everyone looked at him surprised. "I know the sound, gentlemen. I used to jockey one. We're too vulnerable here. Let's—"

Jerry's blood pushed through his system with the rush of adrenaline as Al Razd bolted toward them, yelling something in Arabic. Jerry glanced at the senator, who was already out of his chair and headed for the doorway.

"Get inside! *Now!*" Jerry yelled at Hoshen. The minister knocked his chair over and darted after the senator.

The driver yelled. "Cars coming through the gate. Ten men!" He bolted for the back door, hard on the heels of the senator and Hoshen. Jerry only hoped they'd get there in time to bolt the doors and hold off the enemy. If not, they'd be overrun in minutes.

He grabbed Mohammad by the arm. "You gentlemen bring any extra firepower?"

Faisal smiled. "Like you, we came prepared for interruptions." Nabril had retrieved two semiautomatic rifles from a nearby hiding place and now tossed one to Faisal.

Jeremiah saw the shadow of the basilica suddenly change, then heard the sound of the enemy chopper as it hovered just above the three-story building. Then sudden regret of leaving his gun at the door seared his brain like a hot iron as he dived under the heavy oak table, bullets from the chopper's gunner splattering into the patio where he had been standing.

Mohammad flipped the safety catch on the Kalishnikov as a bullet struck him in the fleshy part of his upper arm. He felt the pain, but the adrenaline already had the gun moving upward, the bullets on their way, ricocheting off the side of the chopper's bubble, forcing the gunner inside and stopping the barrage of enemy fire from the 30mm cannon. He and Nabril moved toward the door, Jerry scrambling to join them, his heart in his mouth.

The gunner returned to his door, swinging the cannon toward the three fleeing men and pulling the trigger. Faisal's gun barrel flew upward and began its song as they continued their dash for the door, red patio brick spewing into the air around them. Nabril stopped and aimed his rifle, giving Jerry time to cross the forty feet of patio that separated him from cover. As he reached the back entrance he turned to see the chopper sweeping away, diving for the edge of the hill like a rabbit looking for a hiding place.

Jerry rushed through the door and Al Razd slammed and bolted it. Jerry dashed to the front of the church, grabbing the Uzi and shoving the .45 and extra clips into his pockets. Hoshen was slamming the front door as a series of bullets ripped into the brass-covered oak.

"Two cars, ten players already in position, all with automatics," the driver said as he peered through a small corner of missing stained glass.

Hoshen opened the door a crack and shoved the Uzi out, pulling the trigger. The light bark of the fast-repeating automatic was answered with a searing barrage of bullets that sent splinters of the wooden door into the basilica.

Hoshen gripped the wall with his body, satisfied that the enemy meant business. A look of disbelief and fear was etched in the dimples of his cheeks.

"Got any ideas who might have told this bunch of blood-thirsty terrorist types where we were going to be?" Jerry asked Hoshen.

The automatic fire slammed into the front door and both men jumped for cover.

"One," Hoshen said, "Get us out of here, then I'll skin him alive! You can boil his remains in oil and feed them to the birds!"

"They're fanning out," Nitani said. "Trying to get behind us."

"Any other doors to this place, Mr. Khourani?" Jerry asked.

"One, besides the back door. Over there." He pointed to the far side of the basilica.

Jerry gave orders, hoping nobody minded, putting the members of the small group in strategic positions that would prevent anyone from getting inside. "I don't suppose we have a phone in this place somewhere."

Khourani shook his head. "In the friar house near the gate."

Another round of bullets hit the brass door, and Jerry suddenly found himself very angry at the enemy's total disregard for something as sacred as the ancient church. At the same time he was grateful that it was a door and not one of his group.

"What about the roof?" Jerry asked.

"If the chopper gets someone up there, in the bell towers . . . " Khourani's voice trailed off.

Jerry waved for Nabril to join him. He needed his talents, and it was apparent that Al Razd didn't want him dead or he would have let the chopper gunman finish him.

"They cannot get in from the bell towers." Nabril said, stopping Jerry in his tracks.

"What?"

"I checked them before you came. Both towers were empty. I nailed the doors shut. However, there may be exits on to the roof."

Jerry eyed Nabril. "Too steep . . .

"It only appears that way from the front. The two sides of the basilica each have their own peaked roof, with a lower roof in the middle, nearly flat. Plenty of hiding places."

"All right. Let's check it."

They were up the stairs in ten three-step leaps, each with his gun ready.

At the top Jerry kept himself positioned behind a column. His eye scanned the upper balcony for doors, nooks, and crannies. There were several, and all needed checking as they moved toward the one he thought probably led to the roof. He signaled to Nabril, was understood, and the Arab moved quickly to the first door. As he checked the doorknob, his back against the wall, Jerry caught movement at the far end, behind the marble banister. He grabbed Nabril's shirt

Saint James Basilica

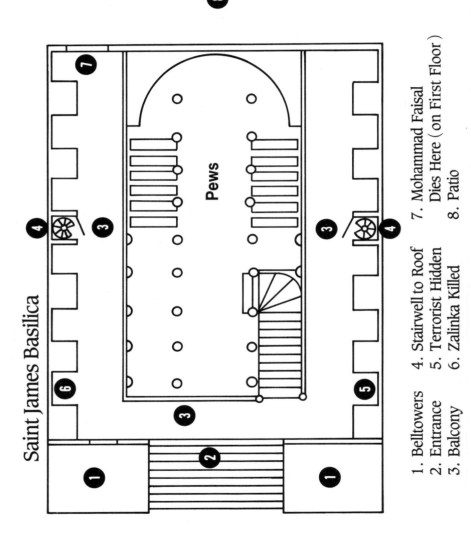

1. Belltowers
2. Entrance
3. Balcony
4. Stairwell to Roof
5. Terrorist Hidden
6. Zalinka Killed
7. Mohammad Faisal
   Dies Here (on First Floor)
8. Patio

Pews

and jerked him to the floor as a half dozen bullets lodged themselves in the door frame where the Arab had been standing.

"I think they found a way in," Jerry said as they slid to better cover. "How you wanna do this?" he asked Nabril as they stood behind opposite columns and peered toward the enemy's hiding place.

Nabril's answer was a smile, then he bolted from behind the column and ran the distance to where the banister turned sharply left. He threw himself to the marble floor, sliding across its slick surface, while keeping his gun aimed at the spot where he thought the enemy was hiding. He pulled the trigger and sent a hail of bullets, pinning the man in a tight corner.

"Don't shoot," the man said in a thick foreign accent, throwing his weapon to the marble floor. "I'm coming out!" Nabril kept his gun aimed at the spot as the man put one leg out, then forced the rest of his body to join it. "I—"

The arm was fast as the man jerked a silenced Makarov from behind his leg—but it wasn't fast enough. By the time he had it positioned, he was another unfortunate statistic of people killed through stupidity.

Jerry ran past Nabril to the attic access door from which the terrorist had come, slamming it shut and bolting it, then putting his back against the wall, catching his breath. "You in a hurry to meet Allah?" he asked Nabril.

The Arab only shrugged.

"Everything all right, Jerry?" the senator yelled.

"Yeah. You?" Jerry yelled back.

"Okay. Either of you hurt?"

Jeremiah looked the Arab over as he joined him. Only a burn on his arm from sliding across the floor. "A few scratches. What's the enemy's count out front?"

"Eight, now. Hoshen still remembers how to use a gun."

Jerry changed his position and found that he could see a large section of one side of the roof as well as the patio where they had had the meeting. Three men were moving across it and toward the back door.

"Faisal, you've got company," he yelled.

Gunfire punctuated the sentence, and Jerry heard Faisal return it. He couldn't see the outcome, and more gunfire at the front of the building gave him the impression that things were turning bad. He ran to the top of the stairs where he could see the senator, whose face was dripping wet, hair clinging to skin. He and the others were firing their weapons through broken windows and a crack in the door.

"They're getting mean out there," Hoshen yelled during a break in the firing. "Any chance you two could get on the roof, get these boys off our backs?"

"Maybe . . . I—" Jerry saw Doctor Jamel bolt for the back door.

"Faisal's hit!" Jamel yelled.

"No! Stay down, Doc!" Jerry hollered, taking the steps three at a time. When he reached the bottom, Jamel already had a hold of Faisal's collar and was pulling him out of the way, his gun aimed at the slightly open door. Their opponent was careless, sticking his gun through a crack. Jerry watched Jamel shoot through the lower portion of it, then heard the gunner hit the ground, his weapon clattering across the bricks of the patio. This was followed by a noise like that of an animal scurrying for cover.

"How is he?" Hoshen asked from where he stood near the front door, back flat against the wall.

"Not good. Chest wound." Jamel ripped a piece of Mohammad's shirt away to find a gaping hole. Pressing his hand against Faisal's neck, he tried to find a pulse. It was weak. "We've got to get him out of here! He's barely alive!"

Jamel looked at Jerry, desperate for an answer.

"Take care of him. We'll try to get above them."

"The chopper's back," said the senator. "Might be putting people on the roof. Be careful, Jerry."

Jerry nodded, then bolted up the steps and ran toward the access. He found it open and Nabril nowhere in sight.

Jeremiah warily approached the door, slipped through, and found himself in a narrow space with a staircase circling toward the roof. Taking the steps carefully, his gun poised, he moved upward. Near the top he felt a breeze, then saw light cascading brightly through a turret-like trapdoor that exited directly onto the sloped roof.

He tried picturing in his mind what he would see. The roof was comprised of two long sections facing east and west, with a connecting roof in between. The hole he was about to expose himself through was on the down slope of the southern section, near the middle. If he was lucky, the enemy would be on the far side of the northern section. If not, Jerry would be a clear target.

He heard shots. Cautiously sticking his head through the opening, he peered out across the tiled slope of the roof to find Nabril lying flat near the exit and the roof's peak, firing at something on the far section. Jerry's luck was—

Out of the corner of his good eye he saw movement! He ducked inside as a bullet lodged itself in the edge of the exit casing approximately where his head had been. *Two* terrorists! As he wiped the sweat from his brow with his shirtsleeve Jerry wondered whether there were more.

"Nabril. Second man is to your left!"

He heard the single shot from a high-powered rifle, and then the clatter of Nabril's Kalishnikov. Jerry stuck his gun through the trapdoor, firing in the direction he thought the shot had come from, then turned to see Nabril sliding down the roof, headed for the edge and a four-story fall to stones below. Jeremiah lunged after him, grabbing a hand while hanging onto the lip of the exit, giving the Arab a chance to get a foothold. Jerry saw the blood on Nabril's shirt but didn't think it was serious. He let go when Nabril nodded, then swung his rifle back toward the spot from where the enemy had fired.

He kept his head down. This one was a real, honest-to-goodness sniper with a high-powered rifle. Jerry couldn't help but wonder how long he had been on the roof. If he had been there during their little meeting, why hadn't he fired? Then he remembered the shadow. They would have seen him in the shadow. He hadn't taken the chance, but had called in reinforcements.

Both he and Nabril were shielded from the sniper by the access, and the other man by the peak of the roof, out of harm's way for the moment, but they were pinned down.

A bullet warmed the hair on the crown of his head. He ducked while realizing that he hadn't gotten down far enough. He hugged the tile roof, his heart in his throat. Too close.

Nabril removed a pistol from under his jacket, then pointed at a chimney a few feet away. Jerry nodded, put his gun over the top of the access, and fired in the direction of the sniper, giving Nabril a chance to move to cover on the far side of the small smokestack. It worked.

Jerry took a deep breath. Both of them were shielded now, and Nabril had a good view of the entire roof. Jerry had the only rifle, Nabril's Kalishnikov being somewhere four stories below.

"Nabril. Where is the one with the automatic?" he asked through clenched teeth.

"Moving left to right. Far roof. If you fire at your two o'clock position on my say, right at the roof's peak, you may have a chance to nail him." Nabril said this in perfect English.

Jerry took a deep breath, waiting. He didn't want to kill anyone. Why was this happening? How could he be here? Now? The world falling apart around him. He didn't have a choice. They would kill him. Kill all of his group.

"*Now!*"

Jerry raised his body just enough to see over the peak and fired, his weapon on full automatic. He saw the black form lurch backwards. At the same time he felt a searing pain in his hand. He hunkered down, glancing at the spot of pain to find that he had been grazed in the fleshy part of his palm. He took out his handkerchief and wrapped it around the wound. It wasn't serious, but he wondered why the sniper had missed.

"That one is dead," Nabril said.

"Where is the other one?"

Nabril's silence seemed forever. "I think he is gone."

"Gone? Gone where?" Jerry said.

"The chopper. It is coming back!" Nabril was running across the twenty feet of roof toward the exit when the chopper swung above the trees and zoomed in for the kill. The gunner was aiming the .30-caliber weapon and pulling the trigger as Jerry raised his rifle. He was squeezing the trigger when the chopper disappeared in a flash of light and explosion that nearly threw them both off the roof. Jerry felt the flames sear his eyebrows as he saw the dark black monster fly at better than 180 miles per hour toward them. He was stunned by the sight of the .50-caliber machine gun spewing forth vengeance into the courtyard. The calvary had come. Why and who ordered it didn't matter. Then he remembered the sniper.

"Come on!" he yelled at Nabril. Jerry was through the access and down the stairs in five seconds. If the sniper got to the balcony above the others . . .

Bursting through the door and into the basilica, he ran around the balcony toward the other section of the building underneath the killer's portion of roof, Nabril five paces behind. He saw the door already opened and realized his mistake. He went to the floor as the bullet dug into his back, knocking him against the far wall, his Uzi flying from his hand and sailing through a window. In the back of his mind he heard the popping sound of a small weapon, then the clatter of a rifle on the marble floor.

Jerry couldn't figure out why he was still able to move, but he rolled over, his shoulder wrenching in pain. Nabril stood there, the .22-caliber pistol in hand, staring at the body that was lying twenty feet away. He walked to the downed assailant, knelt, and checked a pulse. Jerry struggled to his knees, his head spinning, barely able to hear Nabril's next words.

"Rani Zalinka. Czechish gun for hire. He is the one who tried to buy my betrayal."

Gunfire erupted from the air and sprayed the courtyard. Hoshen ran for the door and opened it a crack. He found the terrorists in disarray, running while firing in the air just above them. He could hear the loud response of several 30mm cannons coming from a spot in the air he couldn't see. Then he saw the belly of a chopper with Israeli markings. It was the LION. Two more men were lying wounded on the dirt outside, others throwing their weapons aside, putting their hands on their heads.

Hoshen saw a foolish one run for a car, only to be stopped by the LION's cannon in midstride. No one else followed.

He moved cautiously into the courtyard, watching for any stragglers as the big chopper thundered overhead, hovering, looking. Most of the attackers had come to a complete standstill, their eyes riveted on the monster that was hanging in the air above them.

Hoshen saw a movement out of the corner of his eye and ducked back in the doorway, the bullets splattering and shaving pieces of rock from the corner he had just moved around.

He reeled and shoved the automatic in that direction and pulled the trigger, nailing the terrorist in the legs as he tried to move to better cover, his gun clattering across the rocks and into the bushes several yards away.

Hoshen went back to the door of the basilica and opened it wide. "It's . . . it's over," he said. "The . . . the LION." He felt the warmth of his blood on the front of his shirt, touched it, wondering if the wound was serious, as everything went brown, blurry, then black. He slid to the floor unconscious.

———————

Jerry held his shoulder with one hand, a handkerchief pressed against the wound, his head spinning. With the other hand he held Faisal's head, cradling it in his lap, trying to give him comfort as the doctor desperately sought to stop the flow of pulsating blood in his chest. Jamel had tears in his eyes and was shaking his head back and forth.

Jerry had come to hope, if only for those few fleeting moments on the patio, that peace really could be achieved: Arab and Israeli fighting a common enemy, working together for a better land, a better life for all. Now the dream was vanishing as fast as it had come.

Faisal's eyes opened and his lips formed a slight smile, the blood dripping out of one corner of his mouth. Then his eyes closed against the pain. He tried to speak, but Jerry couldn't hear. Jerry leaned down, gritting his teeth against the pain of his own wound, getting closer, hearing the breathless words. Jerry shook his head, smiling through his tears, as Mohammad's eyes became fixed on the ceiling above him.

———————

Macklin felt weak, his legs hardly functioning as he moved from the chopper to the door of the church, afraid of what he would find. Minister Hoshen was lying in the doorway, and Macklin directed two soldiers to his aid. He saw another man, exhausted and spent, his back propped against the basilica wall. He was okay.

The senator sat in a pew, his head resting on top of the seat in front of him, a spent Uzi at his feet. He looked up as Macklin approached, his eyes empty, glazed; then he laid his head back on the pew. Macklin signaled to another medic.

Where was Jeremiah? He saw a man he recognized as Nabril Al Razd sitting on the steps, gun across his knees, staring toward the back of the chapel. Macklin knew Nabril's reputation. He also knew he was Mohammad Faisal's right-hand man. Macklin could see several shadows: one lying still, his head in another's lap; one, prostrated on the floor, saying a prayer in Arabic. Tom's heart thumped against his chest. Where—and how—was Jeremiah?

They came into focus in the dim light. Jerry was hurt but alive. Macklin's chest breathed a sigh of relief that his whole body felt. He went to his friend's side and knelt. Jerry looked blankly into his eyes, a slight smile across his lips.

"Who will protect them now, Tom? Who?"

"You okay, Jerry?"

Jerry wiped away the tears, nodding. The grief was hot in Jerry's chest. Faisal had only wanted to save lives, both Jew and Arab. For it he had paid the ultimate price.

"Jerisha did this, Colonel."

Macklin nodded. "I know. Jerry . . . "

Jerry laughed lightly. "An Arab who saves Israel. A sworn enemy, a terrorist."

"I don't understand, Jerry? What . . . "

Jerry laid Mohammad's head gently on the stone floor. "His last words were the location of Jerisha's warhead factory. It has never been moved, Tom. Camouflaged, that's all. He was . . . he was there two nights ago. Nabril was with him. We can stop her now."

"How did this happen? How did they know about your meeting with Faisal?"

Jerry turned toward the door, his arm hanging at his side, blood dripping from his fingertips. He stumbled and nearly went down. Macklin grabbed him and lowered him to the floor, yelling for medics.

"Hoshen . . . Hoshen said he told someone. Find . . . find out from Hoshen. A traitor . . . " Jerry's eyes closed against the pain and exhaustion. The medic stooped over and started checking, then bandaging the wound. Macklin stood and glanced toward where Minister Hoshen was lying uncon-scious.

Hoshen knew who INFERNO was.

The senator dragged his feet toward Macklin. "Is Jerry all right?" he asked fearfully. Macklin glanced down at the medic.

"He's lost some blood, sir. We'll get him to a hospital. He'll be all right. Passed out from exhaustion."

"This was foolish!" the senator said stiffly. "So many lives . . ."

"Coming here will save thousands, Senator," Macklin said. "Thousands."

Two soldiers carried Mohammad's body toward them, his arms and legs dangling at obscene angles, clothes stained with his own blood, his unsupported head flopping loosely.

Macklin spoke as kindly as he could to them. "Put him down." They were taken aback, but did as they were instructed.

"Gentlemen, this man has given his life for Israel. Treat him with respect."

They laid him down on the marble, but before they could go for a stretcher Macklin stooped and picked up the lifeless body like a child's, holding him close in his arms as he moved toward the chopper, the senator by his side.

Few would know of Mohammad Faisal's sacrifice and of his victory. Thomas Macklin would see that the information he died to give them was acted upon.

He laid the body next to Hoshen, the medics working on the minister with nervous efficiency. Then he returned to help bring Jerry and the others. Ten minutes later the place was swarming with military brought in by trucks. Tom was the last to climb aboard the LION and give the order to head for the nearest hospital.

He looked down on the scene, shaking his head, an anguished prayer for mankind in his heart while his mind wondered if anyone but God could ever stop the killing.

CHAPTER 28

6:25 P.M., Hadassah Hospital, Jerusalem

Ruth ran quickly down the hall, her heart thumping. The nurse had come into her room in a rush. Ativa was conscious.

The doctor stood by the bed. "He's in and out. He may or may not understand what you're saying." He shrugged. "A couple of minutes, that's all you have. He is very, very weak. Don't endanger his life."

Ruth nodded understanding. She took Ativa's hand and bent over his face, kissing him on the cheek. He stirred.

"Papa?"

His eyes tried to open and he moaned lightly. "Ru . . . " His lips were dry, and the tube going down his throat made it difficult to talk. "Ruth?"

"Yes, Papa Ativa."

"Sho . . . "

"Shomani, Papa, Abdel Shomani?"

A slight nod. "Dead . . . Murdered . . . In . . . "

"INFERNO?"

Another nod.

"Who is INFERNO, Papa? Who?"

He seemed to fade away, sleeping, then came back again. "Dark . . . "

He was slipping into sleep again. She squeezed his hand. "Was it too dark, Papa? Is that what you mean?"

He rallied, hearing her question.

"Dark . . . Ara . . . Arabic . . . Can't be . . . "

"An Arab? Did you know him?"

A nod in the affirmative.

The doctor took her elbow; she pulled it away. "Please, Papa! I can't avenge you if you don't—"

Ativa's eyes opened wide, his face hardened. "No! Ruth . . . no!"

He started to cough, then moaned with the pain. The doctor pulled her away. "That's enough, Colonel!" They began helping him breathe freely again, then the doctor adjusted the IV, giving him more painkiller, more sleep.

Ruth went to the window, thinking, trying to piece it together. According to the IDF's report, the house was well-lit, it wasn't dark. He saw his assailant. He was Arabic. Nothing. Nothing substantial.

She turned and looked at her dearest friend, tears gathering in her eyes. "I'm sorry, Papa, it isn't enough. It just isn't enough."

She sat in the chair, placing her head in her hands. She was bone weary, exhausted to the core, but she'd wait. Wait to see if Ativa could give her what she needed.

She heard the door open and glanced up. Macklin stood there in bloodstained clothes.

"What . . . ?" She went quickly to him. "Are you all right?"

"Fine. How is the general?"

"He was conscious, just for a minute. He tried to tell me who INFERNO is."

"Sit down, Ruth. I have something I need to tell you."

In twenty minutes he had finished. "Hoshen's two flights up. Jerry is on this floor, just a few rooms down."

"And Faisal is dead," she added. "All because of INFERNO."

"And ANGEL. We must give the pretty lady her just reward, don't you think?"

She smiled, taking his hand and kissing it. "I'm sorry about the way I acted. I do love you, Tom."

"I know, and I love you. You remember that day you said you needed me to help you get through things?"

Ruth nodded. "It seems like so long ago. A bad dream."

"Are you ready to trust me, to let me help?"

She hesitated, wondering if she could ever quit hating. "I . . . I don't know, Tom. So many things . . . " She glanced over at Ativa as he adjusted his position and moaned a little, his words, "No, Ruth," haunting her.

"I can try."

"I know who INFERNO is."

She spun around. "You know? How?"

He explained. "Hoshen is conscious and under guard. He told David Stein about the meeting with Faisal. He trusted him."

"Black hair. Someone Ativa knew who looked Arabic. That was what he was trying to tell me."

"We must stop him," she said stiffly, moving toward the door.

"No," Macklin said, staying where he was. "Now comes the trust, Ruth." Tom smiled crookedly. "I don't want to stop him."

Mike took a deep breath, her hands trembling as she pushed on the door and quietly entered her husband's room.

The three children, eyes big and taking in everything around them, were close behind.

Jerry looked pale, his eyes closed, weak from losing too much blood. As Mike touched his shoulder his eyelids lifted and he forced a smile.

"I hate hospitals," he said.

Mike smiled. "It's a good thing we have good insurance. Between the two of us . . . " Tears sprang to her eyes and cascaded over her cheeks. She tried to laugh them away as she bent over and kissed his forehead, grateful, so very grateful he was still alive.

"Jeremiah, we leave this country. Tomorrow. We go back to Wyoming. We—"

He reached behind her head and pressed her face to his, kissing her tenderly. "Yeah, tomorrow. Maybe finding out we still had enemies wasn't such a good idea." He forced a grin, then noticed Issa staring at him around Mike's side, the boys standing nervously against the wall. Macklin had told Jerry about their return to the house. How their beat-up, three-wheeled motor scooter had given up the ghost some five miles away, and how they had run the rest of the way, arriving at the gate exhausted. How they had brought word of Jerisha's intent to ambush the men at Dothan.

Macklin had only just arrived himself at the safe house, but he was able to get Captain Ariel to pick him up and come to their rescue. The LION hadn't arrived any too soon.

Jerry shook the memory of Mohammad's death from his mind. He knew it would be some time before it would cease to haunt him. He patted the bed. "Climb up here, young lady," he said to Issa. "I have something I want to ask you."

Her eyes went to Rashid and he interpreted Jerry's words. She grinned and climbed up beside him.

"You have a very smart brother, and he has a very smart friend. Do you know they saved my neck?"

She seemed to understand a little and nodded.

Jerry forced his face to look serious. "They also scared us."

Her face lifted, a curious look in her eyes. "Scared?" she asked.

"Yes. We thought we had lost them. That they didn't like us anymore." He looked in the direction of the boys. "Come here, you two," he said firmly.

With big eyes and a brief glance toward each other they hesitantly moved to the other side of the bed.

"Don't *ever* do that again. Understood?"

Rashid gulped, then nodded firmly. Raoul followed suit.

"Good," Jerry grinned. "Because if you go to America with us, we can't have you running off. You'd really get lost."

The boys looked at each other blankly. Issa jerked on Rashid's sleeve and Rashid told her what Jerry had said. She grinned and clapped her hands.

Rashid spoke. "You . . . you wish us to go to America?"

"Yes, Rashid, all of you. We want you to live with us for at least six months. If you like it, we'll see what we can do to make it permanent."

Rashid translated quickly for Issa, his voice a high pitch of excitement. She bounced on the bed in response, causing a sharp pain in Jerry's shoulder. He grimaced, voicing his feeling. Issa practically stopped in midair. Mike lifted her from the bed as Jerry tried to smile at Issa, the concern for him evident on her face.

"It's . . . it's okay, little one. I'm fine . . . I just need a little rest."

As Mike ushered them toward the door, she eased their concern, asking them to wait while she tucked Jerry in. Then they would go to the house and pack their things. The excitement returned to their faces as they disappeared through the door.

Mike returned to his side.

"You're out of it now," she said.

"Yeah, you too. They have enough information to stop Jerisha. Hopefully, they can tree her as well. Have her thrown into some dark and dreary prison to spend the rest of her miserable days."

"You really want the children to come, don't you," she said.

"More than anything. I'm too old to have many more and see 'em raised." He smiled. "This way I catch up real quick."

She laughed lightly. "I'm good for at least three more." She leaned over and kissed him. "That is, if you're willing."

He smiled crookedly. "Always."

She sat in the chair beside his bed and held his hand as they talked quietly, making plans for their new family. A half hour later she still held Jerry's fingers as he dropped off to sleep. Then she let the tears flow. Tears of gratitude this time, thanking her Father in Heaven for intervening in their lives again. Then a prayer of desperation, that somehow, some way, Jerisha Duquesne would be trapped. And that they would at last be free of her.

7:10 P.M., *Road between Jerusalem and Tel Aviv*

The agent known as INFERNO hung up the car phone, the message from a trusted friend in Northern Command forcing sweat through the skin on his brow despite the air-conditioned comfort of the American-made Ford.

From his perspective, things had gone badly at Dothan. He needed the minister of defense out of the way in order to get what he needed to finally access the Sword of Megiddo. But Hoshen, although unconscious, had survived, and would soon reveal the one person to whom he had talked about the meeting at the basilica. David Stein.

He glanced at the mileage indicator. Now was no time to get picked up for speeding. He pulled his foot off the pedal and adjusted down ten miles an hour, checking his rearview mirror.

It wasn't just the operation at the basilica that had gone amiss. The entire plan—twenty-five years' worth of waiting for the right moment—was near failure. And it had all happened in a few short days.

He was to have been in position to assume Hoshen's duties when the minister was assassinated—ostensibly by West Bank leadership; then, because Sabrila had lost Khourani, by Daniels. Contrary to Sabrila's firm assertion, Faisal had lived and foiled that plan, but he had given them another chance by calling the meeting at Dothan. Stein had personally given Muzra the order to end things there, but that had been botched along with Sabrila's attempt to finish Ativa off at the hospital.

He shook his head in disgust. The woman had proven to be a total incompetent, adding stupidity to her list of sins by nearly getting caught. Only his diversion of the troops searching for her had given his niece a chance to get away. Finally she had done something right, made the necessary contacts, and was spirited from the country. And out of his hair.

Stein swore. He had done his part. *He* was in position. And *he* would finish it. Hoshen was out of the way, if only temporarily. He could not access the sword and still remain in place as previously planned, but he could get the sword. It would be dangerous, much more dangerous than originally planned, but he could do it. He *would* do it.

He pressed against the steering wheel, calming his shaking hands. He could only hope that Allah would give him enough time before Hoshen revealed his true identity.

He turned right off the main highway into Jerusalem. Seeing a phone booth, he lunged into a parking lot and walked briskly to the booth. In a moment he had dialed the emergency number, then waited while the call was routed through several European countries. He heard the ring, the answering machine answer, then the double click. He spoke the words.

"The INFERNO is out."

He then gave a coded set of numbers for the phone booth where he stood. He hung up the phone and waited. Two minutes later, it rang.

He lifted the receiver and spoke. "INFERNO. Things went badly at Dothan."

He laughed lightly. "No, the objectives were not accomplished, not exactly. Faisal is dead, Hoshen was wounded. Unfortunately for us, he survived. He's been taken to Hadassah Hospital. My last report says he is unconscious. Daniels escaped with a shoulder wound." He listened again.

"Faisal's death means nothing! Some of Sabrila's paid mercenaries were captured, most of them Arab. The Arab nations can make little of one Arab being killed by other Arabs, and the Israelis could make a great deal of it!" More listening.

"Hoshen's death would have accomplished much more. He should have been the priority! Now I have no choice but to leave." He took a deep breath.

"I cannot . . . I realize . . . Listen to me! I have spent years preparing for this. If your people had held up their end of things, I would have those access codes and still have my cover so I could leave here safely! It is your fault, not mine!" He held the phone away from his ear. She had never been an understanding woman. Never!

"All right! Yes, I plan to get it, but I must have a way out of here. Use your connections . . . "

"Yes, yes, I leaked it to the press already. A distorted version of what happened at Dothan, but it will confuse things for a while."

He ran his hand through his hair as ANGEL gave instructions. He repeated them. "El Al, Flight 411 to Rome. United to Athens. Tickets under the name of Benjamin Katz. I understand. You will have people waiting for me in Athens, a private plane."

"Where to? I need your biggest computer." Another pause. "Duma. Very well, I will meet you there."

He hung up the phone and climbed into his car. Hoshen's office was only five minutes away.

Ruth walked briskly from the prime minister's office and toward Tom. He could see that hurry and determination and stood, catching her arm as she rushed to the door.

"Come on. We've got to get to the car phone."

In seconds Levona had Gad on the line while moving the new car into traffic. The young lieutenant had turned up at the hospital as Macklin and Ruth were leaving and had joined them. Using her contacts within Jerusalem city police, Ruth had been able to have the entire on-duty force begin looking for David Stein. They had gotten lucky, and Gad had taken up the chase.

"Where is he?"

"Does he know you're following him?"

"Good. I want him stopped, do you hear me?" she said angrily. "The moment he comes out of that building I want him stopped!" She hung up the phone.

Macklin's mouth hung open. "I thought you were going to work with me on this," he said stiffly.

"The prime minister told me what the sword is, Tom, and I won't take any chances of losing it. None! Stein is accessing a weapon that will give him the power to annihilate this entire region, let alone Israel. Sorry, deal's off."

She picked up the phone and started dialing again.

Macklin grabbed her hand. "Whoa, slow down, Ruth. Give us a minute to think this through. Can he use the weapon while still in Israel?"

"Theoretically, no. We can stop him."

Macklin sat straight, fastening his seat belt as Ruth sped through a stop light. "Call Gad again, back him off. Let Stein think he is okay until we can decide what's best."

She glanced at him, taking a deep breath while easing her foot back. She picked up the phone and called Gad. When she was finished Tom asked her a question.

"All right, fill me in. What is the Sword of Megiddo?"

"It's an ultra-secret project we call Starburst. Israel has been working on it for nearly ten years. It is a laser optics weapon that can blow incoming missiles into small pieces while they are still miles from Israel. It can also be used to destroy ground-to-air missiles at great distances. There is nothing like it in the world, the closest thing being your Star Wars program."

"I've heard of the technology, but I didn't think anyone had such a weapon. No wonder Jerisha dubbed it the Sword of Megiddo. A weapon like that could cut through today's missile technology like a hot knife through butter."

She nodded while shifting down, making the corner. "The prime minister says we have the optics equipment set up on Mount Hermon to the north, Mount Nebo on the east, near the Dead sea, and Mount Tanir in the Sinai. A satellite system, secretly put into orbit three days ago, sits over Israel and is prepared to fire a laser ray at enemy missiles and airplanes. The whole system is run by a central computer and radar system. When its sophisticated radar locates a fired enemy missile, it automatically hones in on that target, adjusting the appropriate mirrors for the proper deflection of the laser beam, then fires the beam from the satellite, which also has been adjusted for the proper deflection angle. The beam hits the deflection mirror on the ground, which uses it to destroy the enemy target. Theoretically, in one minute it can destroy a hundred incoming targets and never miss. It is supposed to operate so fast that a hand-held TOW missile can be destroyed within feet of its original firing position."

"Supposed to operate?"

She took a breath. "It's never been completely tested. The scientists say there is still much to do. That is why the satellite was put up." She paused. "In the wrong hands . . . "

"Does Stein know that it still has kinks?"

"The minister doesn't think so. Stein isn't privy to information on Starburst's development. The people who *are* can be counted on one hand. This is the weapon Ativa told us about. Remember, even he didn't know what was happening with it." She took a breath. "However, Stein was involved in meetings where the capability of the weapon was discussed, and apparently he knows of the satellite's launch. He might assume it is ready, and that once he has access to the codes, he can use the weapon."

"Could he?"

"Yes, but it *is* untested. If it malfunctions, whatever it hits will be immediately annihilated."

"But how could they develop such a weapon without anyone's knowledge?" Macklin asked.

"You keep it compartmentalized. For example, the army is given orders to build a facility on Mount Hermon with fences, guardhouses, and towers for mirrors. They think they are building some sort of weather station or something. Then you have someone else working on the satellite components. It probably even looks like a normal satellite, except for the computer core, which is developed by someone else."

She slammed on the brakes and swerved, her vehicle narrowly missing a car that had the right of way. Macklin tightened his seat belt.

"Yesterday afternoon the codes that make the weapon operational were combined by the five major scientists heading different aspects of Starburst. Each put his in a computer, without knowledge of the others, then the computer combined them and will use them in its operation of the weapon. A back-up copy of those codes was stored on a disk in case anything should go amiss in the system. Minister of Defense Hoshen was given responsibility for the disk and has it locked in a heavily secured vault at General Command. If Stein manages to access those codes, he can both disarm and fire the weapon from any computer terminal in the world that has satellite telecommunications ability."

"What?"

"The satellite is the link to the system, and when a satellite hangs in the heavens above, it is easily accessible to anyone. However, if someone tried to use the system without proper codes, such as an enemy trying to break into the system so they could fire it, the satellite has a fail-safe procedure."

"Which means?" Macklin asked.

"It will call its mainframe computer, give the coordinates of where the enemy signal is being sent from, and order an immediate fire response."

"You mean it will shoot a laser missile at the installation trying to break into the system, blowing them into the next world." Macklin was thinking. "Couldn't we just change the codes in the mainframe so that when INFERNO used the system it would fire on *his* position?"

"That would be nice, but, no. It's not just the codes in the mainframe, it's the codes on board the satellite as well. Those must be changed over a two-day period with a very complicated telecommunications code. It was programmed that way so that if anyone tried to change the codes, say in an hour, or any other time other than what has been designated inside the satellite's computer, the system will read it as an unfriendly act and order a fire response."

"Boom! *We* get blown to pieces," Macklin said.

"If that traitor gets his hands . . . " Ruth couldn't finish.

"With Megiddo's Sword in their arsenal," Macklin said, "he and Jerisha could turn their new warheads on Israel anytime they please, knowing most of them would get through. If Israel fired missiles in retaliation, they could use the sword to swat them out of the air like flies."

"Then she will fire those missiles immediately," Ruth said, "because in two days we'll have the codes changed and the laser system beyond her control."

"Yes, she'll use the missiles, whether she has the sword or not, or whether it is completely functional. She can't turn back now. What a coup it would have been had INFERNO been able to pull this off without ever being discovered. Just walked away with them in a briefcase.

"One question, Ruth. Why did Stein have to get rid of Ativa? It seems to me that Hoshen would have been enough. As the assistant minister of defense, isn't Stein next in line? At least temporarily?"

Ruth shook her head as she shifted down, hard, and made a left turn. "Only for the political side of things. He would have kept the office running, signed paychecks, that sort of thing, but he wouldn't have been given access to the vault."

"Why not?"

"Security precaution. The department in which a death of one of its major players occurs immediately becomes subordinate to an outside authority. After a full investigation, the political machinery then appoints new leadership. This sometimes takes months, but keeps things clean internally." She honked her horn and slammed on the brakes, avoiding a donkey-drawn cart. "The Aman is the housekeeping department for defense. Ativa would have been responsible for Hoshen's position, its secrets, and the vault. Stein had to be head of Aman to get the sword once Hoshen died." She paused. "Stein knew he could never become minister of defense. He had to come up with this to achieve his purposes."

"Why couldn't he become minister? If he played the political game well . . . "

"Before a man is given such a position, numerous thorough background investigations are performed. The most dangerous for Stein would have been conducted by the Mossad. They might have delved deeply enough to discover his true identity. He couldn't take that chance."

"What identity?" Macklin asked, confused. "Isn't he just an Israeli gone bad?"

She pointed at her attaché case, keeping her eyes on the street and moving deftly through traffic. "A report from Mossad on Jerisha Duquesne. I ordered it after our meeting with General Ativa the other day."

He pulled out the papers.

"In it," she said, "is a discussion of her background. In 1965 Jerisha's brother, Mahmoud Salamhani, was supposedly killed in the Sinai while smuggling guns to the PLA. His plane crashed, the body burned beyond recognition, but there were several identifying items. The remains were buried in Egypt.

"You will note: In 1965, a month after Mahmoud's death, David Stein immigrated to Israel from Germany."

"But that doesn't mean—"

"The file includes a description of a wound Mahmoud received as a child. It seems he got his foot caught in the spokes of a motorcycle his sister was driving, nearly amputating it. The family lived in New York at the time and your fine American doctors saved it. He recuperated very well, even learned to walk without a limp, but it left a scar. David Stein carries that scar. I have seen it. Just above the ankle. A nasty-looking thing. Stein told me he got it from the Nazis and his history indicates the same, but I know different now. He is Mahmoud Salamhani, Jerisha's brother. He has been in Israel since 1965, working his way into high positions, biding his time, waiting for the right moment to move his family back into power. That time has come.

"Jeremiah Daniels's discovery of TERROR1 thwarted

them for a time, slowed down their plans. It was just as well, because at that same time there was a delay in the development of Starburst, which, coincidentally, was to be online for use at about the same time Hussein took Kuwait. A malfunction in a portion of the satellite's computer delayed it. All that has been happening is Jerisha and Mahmoud's continued attempt to accomplish the same goal: the destruction of Israel and their return to power on the bodies of her people."

Ruth picked up the phone and dialed Gad. Stein was still in Hoshen's office. She was about to tell him to move in when Macklin stopped her.

"Ruth, this is our chance to get INFERNO *and* ANGEL! Tell Gad to keep in touch, but listen to me a minute, will you?"

She hesitated, then spoke to Gad before putting the phone back in place. "Tom, we can't let those codes out of the country," she said firmly.

"Let's do a switch. Get the codes and still let him lead us to ANGEL."

"It is too late. He is probably inside that vault at this moment. We can't switch now."

"Yes, we can. At the airport, or on the plane."

"But who will make the switch? He knows everyone on the team."

"I have someone in mind, but you'll have to hold up the plane and make arrangements for a seat next to Stein, then set up a system for following him after he leaves the country. How will he carry the codes?"

"Probably in his briefcase. He is seldom without it."

"Make sure. When he comes out of Hoshen's office, have Gad see what he is carrying. If it is the briefcase, we'll need one exactly like it. One with a homing device in the lining. Can you do all that in the next hour?"

She smiled. "Yes. I know the briefcase. It was given to Stein by Ativa. A gift for twenty-five years of service in the Aman. I picked it out." She took a deep breath. "All right, you win."

She picked up the phone and dialed, giving the order to Gad. She also instructed Gad to follow Stein—carefully—discover his plan for leaving the country, and let them know. She gave him permission to use the team if necessary. Then she handed the phone to Macklin. "I'll have someone on that plane, Tom. If he still has those codes when he lands outside of Israel, they will not allow him off. If they have to kill him, they will. He will be armed."

"Armed? On a plane?"

"All Israeli Aman leaders can be armed on El Al planes."

Macklin hesitated. Then he dialed, wondering if he was more than a little crazy.

CHAPTER 29

11:00 P.M., Ben Gurion Airport

Mike sat apparently reading the newspaper, one eye on the door, the other on David Stein and the black leather briefcase he carried. Inside his briefcase was a small, black case exactly like the one Macklin had placed inside an identical briefcase sitting to the side of Mike's chair, underneath her dress coat.

She couldn't believe she was involved in this. Her husband was recuperating from a wound in a hospital only a few miles away, she had three children to take care of, packing to do, and she wasn't exactly at the top of David Stein's list of most-desirable women. In fact, if he knew who she was he'd probably rip her heart out without a second thought. She could only pray that he had never seen any picture of her and Jerry. But then, that was why she had changed her hairstyle and added more makeup than usual.

She sat back in the chair, breathing deeply while acting as if she were picking the lint off her skirt. She couldn't think about the dangers. Others were watching out for her welfare, and if Stein even acted as if he might pull his gun, he'd be standing at the judgment bar answering for his sins.

Mike liked that idea. After hearing what he was up to and what he had done, how he and his sister, one sweet little thing by the name of Jerisha Duquesne, were responsible for the deaths of so many, including her brother Dooley, she wasn't in any mood to let them get away. It was her chance to put an end to the fear they had fed into her life.

She moved to the bar of the VIP room and ordered a

lemonade. Sugar would help. She sipped while returning to her chair. The prey was nervously checking his watch, then the wall clock. The flight had been delayed. "Too much traffic stacked up over Ben Gurion," the PA system had announced. In reality, the airline had stalled, waiting for Mike to get to the airport.

Mike glanced at her ticket. Stein had seat A-3 in the first-class section of Flight 411 under the alias of Benjamin Katz. She had seat A-2. Name, Miriam Goodnough, a New York Jew visiting the Holy Land on business and pleasure. She stuffed the ticket inside her dress coat pocket.

She needed to switch cases. How? When? She hadn't decided yet.

If she could do it before they reached Rome, someone else would keep an eye on the traitor while sophisticated systems tracked the small homing device planted in the briefcase Mike would switch for Stein's. *If!*

She crunched the plastic cup with a loud snap, bringing unwanted attention in her direction. Mike smiled, then tossed the remains casually in the trash can.

Twenty more minutes of nervous thought passed before the call came for boarding. Mike took her briefcase, coat still over it, and moved toward the gate along with everyone else, her ticket between finger and thumb of the hand that held a copy of the *Jerusalem Post.*

She kept Stein several places ahead. Reaching the gate, the traitor put the briefcase down to search for his misplaced ticket. Mike wished she had been closer.

She felt the trickle of sweat roll down her side as she waited, then was checked and cleared for boarding. Mike walked down the ramp past smiling but busy stewardesses into first class. Stein had already placed his briefcase under the seat and was placing his coat on a hanger. He handed it to a stewardess to be placed in the accommodation closet.

"Hello," Mike said to Stein, forcing a smile. "I have the seat next to you. I'm Miriam Goodnough, from New York." She reached out with her hand. Stein took it and shook, but answered only with a guttural "Humph," before moving into the aisle, allowing Mike room to slip in. Enough of the beautiful-woman approach. The man was obviously preoccupied and not in the mood for flirting.

As regular passengers moved past them into coach, Stein put his head against the back of the chair and shut his eyes.

Mike could feel the tension. The man was a frightened rabbit, caught in the cabbage patch and afraid the farmer was coming with his hoe. She couldn't blame him. The farmer was coming.

Mike's briefcase was still lying under the coat on her lap and she wondered if now . . .

Stein moved, took a magazine from the holder on the back of the seat in front of him, and started to thumb through the pages. After a moment he stuck it back in the magazine pocket and reached for his briefcase, setting it on his lap and opening it. Mike faked closing her eyes, watching through a thin slit as the lid raised just enough so she could see inside.

She wanted to throw up! How could they have been so stupid? She couldn't just switch briefcases! There were half a dozen other items in Stein's. If she didn't switch those, too, the moment he opened the switched briefcase Stein would know that he'd been had! He'd never keep it after that! They'd lose the trail!

Inside, Mike panicked, wondering what to do. She had no choice but to switch the contents as well as the case. Her mind reeled! How could she do it?

The plane was soon in the air. A stewardess pulled Mike out of deep thought by asking her if she would like a drink. As Mike took the ginger ale from the pretty hand, their eyes met and she caught the stewardess's quick wink. Mike got the message.

After a moment Mike asked Stein to excuse her and went the few yards to the bathroom. When the stewardess saw her, she motioned toward the far corner of the adjoining galley.

"Mrs. Daniels," she said quietly, smiling. "A mutual friend of ours called and asked me to get on this flight. She said you would let me know what I should do."

"You're an answer to a prayer." She explained about the briefcase's contents and her need to switch everything. "Can you get him out of his chair for thirty seconds?" Mike asked.

"A little hot coffee across his lap will do it, don't you think?"

"Perfect." Mike hesitated. "Colonel Levona said she sent some others . . . to clean up if I fail . . . "

The stewardess smiled. "We will give your plan every chance of success."

Mike smiled.

"And don't worry. If he tries anything . . . Well, some

have tried with me and they ended up in the hospital." She grinned.

Mike started away, then turned back. "Do you have a name?" she whispered.

"Rachel," she responded.

Mike returned to the chair and waited. As Rachel got to their spot and began pouring coffee, another stewardess happened to back into the cart, and the hot liquid cascaded into David Stein's lap, creating an instant brown stain on his neatly pressed, light-gray suit.

The language he used would have made a cowboy blush, but in seconds flat he was out of the seat and headed for the bathroom. Mike fumbled with her coat, trying to get the briefcase free. A button caught on the latch. She yanked it, tearing the button off.

Mike hesitated, slowing her heartbeat, then grabbed Stein's case by the handle. But just then she heard Stein's voice down the aisle, cursing the stewardess, getting in his last licks before returning to his seat.

Letting go of the handle, Mike sat straight in the chair, quickly covering her own case and closing frightened eyes. She felt the movement of Stein dropping his frame into the seat next to her, mumbling under his breath.

Mike's breath wanted to come fast, and it was all she could do to keep it under control. So close and yet so far away.

Mike didn't remember her heart beating again until the pilot announced their descent to Rome Airport. She must do something, and fast!

Her mind tumbled over one idea after another, finally settling on what she considered to be her only real alternative.

She stood again, making some excuse to Stein. When she came into the galley, Ruth's friend sidled up close enough so only Mike could hear.

"You don't do this sort of thing for a living, do you?" she smiled, trying her best to get Mike to relax.

"You needn't worry about me threatening your promising future, I'll tell you that!" said Mike. She brushed her hair back from her eyes. "How can we catch this plane on fire without killing everyone?"

"What?"

"I need a diversion of major proportions, dear heart, and quick!"

Rachel laughed lightly. "Is this for my country?"

"Ye old star of David is in big trouble if that guy gets off this plane with that briefcase."

"He won't," Rachel said firmly.

Mike eyed her, deciding she meant it. "I don't know what Ruth has told you about all of this, Rachel, but Stein could lead us to a very big enemy of your country. Consider that before you get too anxious to use your gun on him."

Rachel hesitated. "All right, go back to your seat. You'll get your emergency."

Mike was sitting down with her seatbelt strapped. She felt the wheels hit the ground and simultaneously smelled the burning plastic. Smoke rose to the ceiling and filtered toward them. Rachel stepped confidently into the aisle as people began spreading the word.

"Please don't panic!" Rachel said calmly into the PA system. "It's all right! Only a small electrical fire in the kitchen. However, as a precaution, we wish to have you disembark using the safety chutes that will be unrolled at the doors. Please, calm down! Move in an orderly fashion . . . "

The plane came to a lurching halt and Mike prayed that no one would get hurt.

She glanced down the aisle. The stewardesses were moving everyone in good order. Stein's eyes looked worried, darting between the exit and the briefcase on the floor. There was sweat on his brow and Mike could see his confusion and near panic. Stein bent to pick up the case . . .

"Let me out of here!" Mike said violently, faking a choke. "I can't breathe! Let me out!"

She lurched into Stein's side, knocking him into the passengers filling the aisle. Chaos ensued, people shoving and pushing, falling over one another to the floor, Stein clearly on the bottom.

Rachel and another stewardess stepped toward Mike, using their bodies to block Stein's view while one pretended to help him and the others on the floor.

She could hear Stein screaming beneath the stack of three bodies. Others stumbled into the pack, creating additional confusion. Rachel reached down and removed the coat as Mike grabbed her case and sat it in the seat, using her body as a screen, flipping it open. Her hands were shaking violently as the stewardess pulled Stein's case free, handing it to her. She fumbled with the combination Ruth had given her, praying Stein hadn't changed it. She had it open in seconds, removing the contents as carefully as she could and placing them in the bugged case. Each paper seemed in proper order as she laid the small hand-held recorder next to the identical case full of phony codes. Mike shut it and shoved it under the seat, slapped her dress coat over Stein's briefcase, and collapsed in the chair as the traitor pushed and shoved his way free, yelling and screaming. The second stewardess grabbed Stein's arm firmly. "Sir, calm down. It's all right! Get your things and come with me."

Mike cowered in the corner, her coat-covered package held tightly as if she were in mortal fear, Rachel next to her, saying calm words that made Mike almost laugh.

Stein gave her a look of hatred, stooped, and pulled the bugged briefcase free, then was gone. As he disappeared through the door, Mike and Rachel laid their heads against the back of the chairs, laughing lightly at the release of pressure. Mike turned to Rachel. "You were wonderful!" she said. "Thanks."

"No. Israel thanks you, Mrs. Daniels. And her children thank you."

The children. Mike smiled. That was why she had done it. For the children.

And a little revenge.

She smiled, lying back in the chair, breathing deeply.

Now it was up to others.

Day Eight

CHAPTER 30

6:00 A.M., Jerusalem

Macklin heard the sound deep in his groggy gray matter, voices trying to pull him out of a comfortable sleep.

He was lying on the couch of the safe house, every bone and muscle revolting at being awakened. His mouth was dry and full of cotton, his eyelids plugged with the sticky sand of sleep. As he rubbed it free, his eyes focused on Ruth standing over him.

"Sorry, Tom, but—"

"And I always thought you were an angel. Go away!" he croaked, rolling over, closing his eyes.

Another voice shattered his attempt to slip back into euphoric slumber. "Morning, Colonel."

"Gad! When I open my eyes I'd better find you have disappeared like a bad dream." The room was silent.

Macklin moaned and turned on his back, his curiosity getting the best of him. "Any word of where the traitor ended up?"

"He is in an airport lounge in Athens," Ruth said from a chair a few feet away. "He is scheduled to leave by private plane within the hour."

"Hard to follow if it's a private jet," Macklin mumbled.

"The air force is working with us, along with two American spy planes over the area. They all have equipment for following the homing signal of the device placed in the phony case."

"Did the events at the basilica make the news again this morning?" Macklin asked as he sat up and placed his stockinged feet on the floor.

"Yes, but we'll have to live with it for a few more days until Stein is stopped."

"How is everyone? Jeremiah? Mike? Hoshen? Ativa?"

"Getting to be quite a list, isn't there?" Ruth smiled. A friend sent a private plane for the Danielses. They will be leaving today, for their own protection."

"Good."

Ruth filled him in on Mike's performance as seen through Rachel's eyes, then on Ativa's improving condition.

Macklin asked about Hoshen. "The minister in fine voice this morning?"

"He was a little upset about our treating the codes so lightly, but grateful they are back in the vault. He is . . . a . . . easier to get along with today. Trusted members of the Knesset have been informed of what has happened, and they are backing off on demanding his retirement. He will come out looking rather good when this is all over."

"Yeah! Don't most politicians? What about Khourani and the others? What's he doing for them?" Macklin asked as he put on his shoes.

"First, they are safe. Second, Minister Hoshen is trying to get them involved in peace talks. He might make something happen, although the prime minister is not very happy with him right now. Only time will tell."

"We can only hope," Macklin said. "Any of the prisoners from Dothan talk?"

"Two, and both are pointing fingers at the man Nabril killed—Zalinka," Gad said. "They say he's the one who hired them. We think the woman and the Englishman hired him."

"Are you rested enough?" Ruth asked.

"Two hours sleep? Bright-eyed and bushy-tailed," he said, yawning. "Can't you tell?"

She smiled. "We found out who the woman was. Jerisha's niece, Sabrila Hassan."

Tom whistled. "Nothing like keeping it in the family."

She grinned. "Mohammad was right about the factory."

"And Nabril has shared the details of their visit to Duma," Gad added. "He gave us some photographs."

Ruth flipped half a dozen onto his lap. Tom looked at each carefully.

Ruth pointed to a photo of the factory. "Notice the camouflage. That's why the satellite photos show the place deserted."

Macklin shuffled to the next one. "Wow! Caught them out in the open." The picture showed the back half of a tarp-covered truck disappearing through one end of the factory, several men standing close by.

"Notice also the number of guards along the fence in the next picture. It is still heavily guarded when they are moving men and materials. Nabril says we'll have to watch out for cameras. Badannah has enough to watch every square inch of soil." She handed him another picture.

"Jerisha," he said.

"That was only two days ago. She may still be in Duma."

"Do you think all of the missiles are still at the factory?" Macklin asked, handing the pictures to Gad.

"We don't know," Ruth answered. "But that truck is the portable SCUD launching vehicle your air force had a hard time knocking out against Iraq. They could have deployed some of them by now, but I don't think so."

"Why not?"

"Moving them before she had her Sword of Megiddo in hand would have left ANGEL very vulnerable. I don't think she wanted to take that chance. Second, gut feeling tells me she's not ready."

"I'll go with the gut feeling," he smiled. "It seems to prove right most of the time."

Macklin looked at each of the pictures again as Ruth continued. "Minister Hoshen wants us to go to Duma. We want the Germans, their files, their prototype, everything. We want them tried in public and their act condemned."

"Good. But you know what I want?" Macklin said. "I want to blow the bloomin' place into oblivion." He grinned.

Gad and Ruth laughed. "We happen to have a team ready who agrees without reservation."

"Did you get your hands on the right kind of explosives? There will be chemicals in there."

"Yes, we have them ready. Everything is ready."

Macklin nodded. "They won't be expecting us, will they. With the traitor gone, no more leaks." He thought a moment. "Does the prime minister know?"

"No, nor does your president at this point. Manlik Hoshen is in charge. I have full authority again. We get everything we need, no hesitation. As you may guess, he wants Stein back very badly. If the traitor happens to be handy . . . "

"Ummm. My government looking for me?" Tom asked.

"Frantically."

"Then we'd better get this done quick."

"Will you use the same plan, Colonel?" Gad asked. "The one you prepared earlier for this factory?"

Macklin thought a moment. "A few alterations are in order, I think, but the men and materiel are about the same. Nothing that will slow us down.

"Where's Nabril?"

Ruth looked at him curiously, her head cocked.

"Nabril deserves a shot at the people who killed Moham-mad. And don't forget, he *is* Arab and has been near the premises of this place within the last few days."

"I'll ask him," Gad said. "If you will excuse me, I will join you later at the safe house."

They nodded as he closed the door behind him.

Tom wiggled his fingers at Ruth to join him on the couch. She smiled and moved to his lap, putting her arms around his neck. They kissed tenderly.

"I had a dream about that."

"I haven't had time," she responded. "I love you, and thank you for everything. You have put your life on the line for Israel enough to receive her highest medal of valor."

"No thanks. Too heavy to pack around. Another dozen kisses maybe?"

"Maybe. After you get rid of your halitosis," she grinned.

He grew serious. "You'll stay home this time?"

Her face clouded for a brief moment. "I'm in control again, Tom. Ativa . . . well, things have changed for me the past few days. I looked at what I was becoming and it frightened me. I've lost a lot. The light in me went out and was replaced with a violent sort of darkness I can't explain. When you came into my life the light flickered again. The darkness tried to put it out. You're winning." She kissed him.

He forgot to ask the question again.

5:00 A.M., *Jackson Hole, Wyoming*

There wasn't a moon, and the black cap, shirt, pants, and shoes kept Alex Manners and three others, one his girlfriend, well hidden in the trees.

He had planned an accident, an explosive device under the propane tank at the side of the main house, but found it impossible to get close enough. The place was jumping with a party most of the night, the ranch hands and their girls using the backyard for a barbecue. By the time that had settled down, it was nearly midnight.

They had waited and watched. Manners considered himself a patient man. But it was an hour prior to first light before he felt that it was safe enough. Then, with his last look through an infrared scope, he had seen Bob Freeman and his wife saddle horses and head into the hills toward Crystal Creek Canyon, a child riding with each parent. At first Manners was scratching his head, cautious. Then he remembered the monthly camping trips into the hills to check cattle. Bob Freeman and his wife always took the young ones along, a family affair. It would do.

Manners's group had followed, keeping their distance, biding their time. The farther away from civilization he let the Freemans get, the less chance of their deaths being discovered.

The horizon was turning a light blue when Manners watched Bob Freeman lead his little group into the cliff's opening. By sunrise he had reconnoitered and returned to give his people their instructions.

"It's a box canyon, but we can get above them from this side. Be like shooting chickens in a henhouse." He laughed. "Dirk, I want you and Wilf to go over that ridge to the east. One of you work your way around behind them. The other stay up there so they can't climb the wall and get out." He laughed again. "The rest of us will go in through the canyon and stir 'em up. The ones we don't get, you can pick off."

Everyone mounted up, the cool morning air sharpening their adrenaline-aided senses.

The three waited while Dirk and Wilf worked their way carefully up the ridge and disappeared. They waited another ten minutes for them to get in position.

"All right," Manners said, pulling his 30/30 from its sheath. "Let's do it."

Alex felt like the old-time cowboys he had seen on the silver screen. Three horses riding into a box canyon, rifles ready. The waiting lamb ready for the slaughter.

The horses entered the water, splashing, making noise. No matter, Freeman had no way of escape.

He saw the movement above his head and glanced up, then felt something pulled tight around his shoulders. It squeezed his body hard and began lifting him from the horse.

"Hey! What the . . . "

The woman dangled next to him, and Sid Barnes right next to her. The now riderless horses meandered into the canyon and began chewing tall, dew-moistened grass.

Manners kicked and tried to get free. Fifteen minutes later, exhausted, he quit. He saw two men approaching through waist-high grass, their hands on their heads. One looked to have blood rolling down his forehead. That was Wilf. Dirk had a gun shoved in his back. On the other end of it was a big man Manners had never seen before.

"Gentlemen, lady," someone said from above. Manners forced his head upward, staring at the cliff top silhouetted by a rising sun. His eyes ached for relief as he strained to see who stood there. "We were kinda hopin' you folks were comin' for breakfast, but when you took those guns out, and these two stumbled over the ridge into my friend's hands . . . Well, we could see you weren't going to be friendly."

The big man shoved Wilf and Dirk forward, then positioned himself so his gun was on everyone. "I'm disappointed, Bob," Trayco said. "Your ropes ended up a little low. Let the albino down and let's get it around his neck."

Manners began to sweat as he felt himself being lowered through the air, then into waist-high water. He thought about the gun in his belt, but the water passed over it, making him wonder if it would operate properly.

"Okay, Manners. That is your name, isn't it? Alex Manners? Put that noose around your neck."

Manners hesitated, afraid. How did they know who he was? What was going on?

"You deaf?" Trayco said tightly. "Put it on!" He cocked the rifle, ejecting one shell for another as a sign of his intent. Manners edged out of the rope and placed it around his neck.

"Good. Now, there is one way to keep us from stringing you up, and you know what it is. Spill your guts, boy, or meet your Maker!"

"We were just huntin', that's all. We—"

The rope tightened, shutting off the last few words.

"You're gonna look awful funny when you're ninety percent neck. Answer the question without any of the baloney," Bob said from his perch above them.

Manners's eyes jumped with fear, but the rope loosened and he began talking. "A woman paid me. Fifty thousand up front, the rest when we finished."

"Name?"

"She never gave it to me. Pike knew her."

"Pike's dead. You're the caboose, boy. The train you were runnin' with has been derailed."

———————

The five assassins were bound and flung over saddles, their horse reins tied together and hooked to a rope behind Trayco's mount.

"It was a good plan, Kenny, but they could've shot us before we ever got free of the house."

"Manners had you in his sights, but his hand never touched the safety. If he had, I'd have shot him through it."

"How far away were you?"

258

"Twenty feet, maybe less. They weren't expecting to be the hunted. Never knew I was there."

"Stinger still loves his work."

Trayco smiled. "Some things you never forget."

"Beautiful morning, isn't it," Charla said, pulling her horse next to her husband.

"One of the best," Bob said.

Trayco looked at his watch. "Still dark in Israel. I hope Macklin is having as good a day as we are."

He nudged his horse in the flanks, feeling a sudden urge to get off the mountain and to a phone. Jeremiah would be wondering.

CHAPTER 31

10:00 P.M., Duma, Syria

Colonel Badannah opened the message and read it, his wet body dripping beneath a terry-cloth robe. He went back into the bathroom to grab a towel. Rubbing his black and gray hair dry, he moved to the phone and picked up the receiver, dialing a coded number written on the paper. It was a local call.

He spoke in Arabic. "Badannah."

He listened to the question.

"As per your instruction, Ahmoud, only five missiles will be armed here, the rest of the warheads will be sent to the missile sites, attached, then armed."

He listened again.

"Tonight? But that is two days sooner . . . Yes, I understand. No, there is no reason why it can't be done. The warheads we will deliver by truck are already loaded. They can be taken to the airport and sent by transport helicopters, arriving on-site and ready for firing one hour before sunup. The five missiles we have here can be transported via their launching trucks.

"I will need to open the envelope and get the coordinates for delivery."

He listened to Ahmoud's voice again. The voice had an edge on it, as if hurried. Possibly the fear of voice interception. Badannah's back straightened.

"They are coming here? I assure you that I do not need anyone—" He pulled the phone away from his ear, Ahmoud's voice reverberating angrily throughout the room.

"All right! I understand. Yes, the computer facility has only the best. Yes, it is satellite telecommunications ready.

"No, I do not question—" The line disconnected.

He hung up the phone and went back into the bedroom, glad to be rid of the angry voice at the other end of the line. Kneeling down in a corner near a bookcase full of cheap reading, he flipped back the rug, removed several boards, and turned the dial on his personal safe.

The lid opened toward him. He reached inside and removed the letter-sized sealed envelope. Running his rather long fingernail along the seal, he quickly opened it, anxious about what it contained.

He held the enclosed map in one hand, reading the letter while going to a chair in front of a desk crammed into one corner of the room. He blinked several times, reluctantly picking up reading glasses and placing them on the bridge of his nose.

The orders were fewer than three paragraphs long but contained names and coordinates.

He unfolded the map, laid it flat on the desk, took out several instruments and rulers, and began marking. When he was finished there were twenty-five marks. The first five were located at the northern end of the Golan Heights, just a few miles inside the border separating Lebanon and Syria. The five armed missiles with chemical warheads sitting at the factory would be sent to those. Another five locations were in the corner of that country from which Hussein had recently fired SCUDs at Israel with dubious accuracy. The new ones were much more efficient.

Five more were at locations along the Jordanian-Israeli border, three in Saudi Arabia, two in Lebanon, the rest in the Egyptian territory of the Sinai.

He returned to the letter. All sites were specially prepared bunkers containing missiles ready for launching. Badannah now was assured that ANGEL was getting military help from within each government. There was no other way for preparing such sophisticated bunkers.

He took a deep breath. With the weapons dispersed in this manner, ANGEL could wipe out eighty percent of Israel's population in less than five minutes.

He refolded the map, wiping his now-sweating brow with the back of his robe sleeve. He placed the map, then the letter, back inside the envelope, went to the closet, and placed them inside the coat pocket of the uniform he would wear the next day.

Slipping a small flask from the right-hand, outside pocket of the same coat, he took a deep swallow to calm his nerves.

He was arming twenty-four chemically lethal missiles, each of which could kill one-fourth of the population of Damascus, and he was placing them in the hands of madmen!

He took another swig from the flask, dulling what little conscience he had left, then picked up the phone and dialed Sergeant Khalis's number. At the last second he hung up. He would give the orders himself. Call the drivers, make the arrangements, then go to the factory. Khalis had acted strangely the last few days—aloof, almost belligerent. He could not be trusted with such an important task.

He began making the calls, comfortable in the knowledge that all was well.

10:00 P.M., Over Dumayr Airfield, Syria

As the big transport circled, Macklin looked at his watch. They had left Dan, Israel, nearly three hours ago.

In order to make things look right, Ruth had worked out a flight plan that took them into Turkey, where they landed, refueled, then took off again, going farther north. When the transport lifted off the next time, it had changed its markings and was flying south, reporting on radar and radio as a Russian transport carrying military supplies to Syria.

An hour earlier, Kalitnick, the pilot and a friend of Mori's, had communicated with the Syrian air defense system near the northern border. Their plane had been told to wait while air traffic control sought clearance from Damascus, creating fifteen tense minutes during which Macklin felt as if he aged a good ten years while wondering whether permission or missile-loaded fighters would be the eventual response.

Permission was granted, and Macklin found himself giving thanks for Mohammad Faisal and Nabril Al Razd and their connections inside the Syrian military. A General Labib Assad had put himself on duty at Syrian General Command and had covered their tracks.

Macklin felt the tires skid against the airport pavement. "All right, be alert!" he ordered. Each man was equipped with a small headset for communication and responded immediately by moving to his assigned position. Irbev, Akitsa, (whom Macklin had nicknamed Kit), and Mori loaded into the interior of the refurbished Bradley along with Macklin. The three of them were of lighter complexion, and they and Macklin had dyed their hair and darkened their skin with makeup, hoping that in the dark they could pass for Arabs. Gad and Mizrah could pass for Arabs anywhere in the world. They and Nabril were dressed in Syrian officers' uniforms, carrying phony documents attached to a clipboard. As soon as the big rear door of the transport opened, they would be on stage, convincing airport military authorities that they were under orders to deliver the fast-track vehicle to Badannah's headquarters before sunup.

As the door of the transport began a slow lift upward, Macklin stuck his head out of the top hatch of the vehicle and Irbev slid into the driver's seat. Each prepared himself for combat in a different way. Mori rapped his knuckles on the side of the door, twice then three times, again and again. Mizrah kissed his Kalishnikov for good luck. Irbev mumbled, going over his assignment one last time. Nabril was dangerously silent—his dark eyes a reflection of hate that made Macklin grateful he was not an enemy. Macklin prayed, tapping the survival manual in his shirt pocket.

"Here we go, gentlemen," Macklin said. He felt the adrenaline flow as he cocked the turret's 25mm gun. One never knew when one might need it, did one?

10:20 p.m., Northern Israel Command

Levona saw the dot leave the screen and knew that the transport had landed. She went to her quarters, pulled on fatigues, and packed her flight bag. This time she attached a holstered .45 to her belt and flung her Uzi strap over one shoulder before placing the combat helmet on her brown hair. Macklin had given her a wary look as he climbed in the jeep to be taken to the transport. She had only smiled and waved, giving him the impression that she would be a good little girl and stay seated in Northern Command's war room.

She didn't like deceiving him, or anyone, but she *had* to be in Syria. She knew Stein and Jerisha were in Duma; she wanted to personally see that they paid for their crimes against Israel. It was her duty. Then there was Badannah.

The uncontrolled hate for Badannah no longer existed. Only a cold, empty determination remained. But she never could be whole again as long as Fami Badannah haunted her dreams as her father's killer, the terrorist who had started the domino effect that took away her childhood and her family. Ruth was no longer out for revenge because of hate; she simply wanted to be free, cleansed of deep-seated nightmares that had controlled her dreams. In her mind, absolution lay in Badannah's death.

The LION waited in the staging area at one end of the hangar. She looked at her watch—10:30 P.M. on the dot. An hour and a half until they would fly into Syria for pickup.

She slapped the clip into her Uzi and injected the first bullet into the chamber, then flipped on the safety. This time she would be prepared to do more than rescue helpless children.

11:30 P.M., Duma, Syria

The trip from Dumayr to Duma had been uneventful, with little to no traffic on the highway. There was a checkpoint at the outskirts of the city, but Nabril had handled the half-sleepy guards beautifully. Earlier, as they were leaving the airport, Macklin watched Kalitnick fly off in the Russian transport. It struck home that the rest of them had only one way to return to Israel. It lay through a factory in Duma.

Macklin sat half out of the vehicle's top hatch watching carefully, making sure they made all the right turns. They were less than two blocks from the apartment complex when he spoke softly into his mike "Ready. Target is just ahead, on the left." He watched the darkened buildings slip by, his eyes looking for the markings he had memorized. "There it is! Gentlemen, let's do it! By the numbers."

The Bradley came to a halt next to its look-alike vehicle in a small cul-de-sac. The door dropped and Kit nonchalantly took up a position next to the other vehicle, surveying the area carefully before signaling to the others. Mizrah joined him, shoving a small amount of C-12 explosive under the Syrian vehicle's hood, preparing it for blowing the latch with a sound no louder than the snap of the fingers. Mori and Irbev moved into the shadows of the street, watching for unexpected visitors. Macklin slipped through the darkness to the complex entrance, Gad and Nabril on his heels. The front door was open and the hallway empty. The informant's description was, so far, exact.

They moved down the hall to the third door on the left. Macklin quietly tried the knob. Locked. Gad shoved the small wad of explosive in the hole and ignited it. They averted their eyes from the bright flash as it burned through the metal in less than five seconds. Macklin pushed lightly. The door squeaked on old hinges. He felt more than saw the movement in the room and swiftly went inside and grabbed at the spot, filling his hands with damp flesh, and knocking the man to the floor. In his effort to fight Macklin, Khalis knocked over a lamp, but Nabril caught it before it hit the floor, placing it back in an upright position.

Macklin pummeled the man in the back of the neck and felt the body go limp. Gad was already gathering a uniform and other clothing, shoving the man's personal possessions into pockets, while Nabril picked up the prey and headed back toward the vehicle. After Gad followed, Macklin pulled the door shut, putting a sticky substance on the jamb to hold it closed. He quickly took a can of spray paint from his pocket and sprayed the burn marks around the key hole and latch, making them look like nothing more than scuffs. Without a sound he slipped from the hallway and into the open air, where the others were quickly loading into the vehicle.

Mizrah had blown the hood latch and disabled the other vehicle's motor. If the driver came and tried to move it . . . too bad.

Macklin looked at his watch as the vehicle pulled back into the street—11:35. It had taken five minutes. They were right on schedule.

11:30 P.M., Duma, Syria

Colonel Badannah had sobered himself with another shower, this time a cold one, and dressed. It was time to go to the factory and see to the deployment of ANGEL's toys.

He closed and locked his apartment door, then joined his driver in the front yard. He checked his watch—11:40 P.M. Good. By now, the scientists would be in their quarters asleep, and, by his order, all personnel at their stations or in bed, out of the way. The truck drivers would arrive at 12:30 A.M.

He sat in the limousine's comfortable leather seat and signaled his driver. A moment later they passed the apartment complex. Khalis's armored vehicle was still sitting in the cul-de-sac. He wondered if he should stop and roust the boy out, then decided against it. He might ask questions. He had done that often lately—too often.

He unrolled last night's newspaper, turned on an overhead reading lamp, and perfunctorily scanned the pages. One stop on the way.

Macklin saw the factory and tapped Irbev on the shoulder.

"Pull over." He still wasn't through talking to the now fully dressed, young, and extremely anxious Syrian sergeant. Macklin told Nabril to translate.

"I don't know if you're aware of what is really going on in your factory. It doesn't matter. We're here to stop it. Your cousin gave us the information about you and the layout of your apartment, but made us promise to offer you freedom in Israel. The offer is good, or you can stay behind, alive—if you cooperate. Your choice."

The sergeant hesitated, thinking. Nabril translated his hurried Arabic. "Is my cousin all right?"

Macklin took a picture from his pocket. It showed the Syrian informant with his family in front of the Dome of the Rock Mosque on temple mount. They looked happy. "This will answer your question."

Khalis took the picture and held it under Nabril's flashlight. He seemed surprised and glanced quickly at Nabril, who was speaking, then nodded.

"What did you say?" Macklin asked.

"I told him who I was. I said you were an honorable man and could be trusted. He says he will cooperate, but only because he knows Badannah is doing a very evil thing."

"Tell him about General Labib Assad. Then tell him who Badannah's bosses really are."

Nabril spoke in Arabic, surprising the young sergeant again, his head nodding with understanding and relief. Nabril turned to Macklin. "He says Labib Assad is a good Syrian; Badannah is a devil. If Labib comes to get Badannah, he will stay and help."

The informant had been right. This young man was not one who relished making chemical and nuclear weapons, but that didn't mean he would betray his country.

"Ask him about the bunkers and the men there. Will they be any threat to us?"

Nabril got an answer. "No, they are a long distance from the main building. Unless the alarm sounds, they will not even know we are here."

"How many men inside now?"

"He says twenty, most of them at the doors toward the far end. Ten on the roof."

Macklin was surprised. "Only ten?"

Nabril translated again. "He says Badannah cut the number back tonight. He wants most of the troops available at the front gate."

"Umm, apparently the colonel is expecting company and needs the men for show."

Macklin turned to Khalis and spoke while Nabril translated again. "We already had pictures of your vehicle, thanks to one of our agents."

"The one who took my cousin out?" Nabril translated.

"Yes. He died saving your cousin and his family."

Macklin pointed at the front passenger's seat. "I have been told that's where you sit in the mornings, getting fresh air."

The sergeant looked at him mystified as Nabril translated.

"I want you to sit in your usual place. Nabril will drive. You must get us through the gate without your men knowing who we are."

Khalis nodded understanding. Macklin motioned and Nabril took the driver's seat from Irbev as Khalis moved to the passenger's side. They pulled away from the side of the road and Macklin checked the time again—11:50. Two minutes lost. Acceptable.

Nabril greeted the gate guards lightheartedly in perfect Arabic with a Syrian dialect, making excuses about why he was driving in place of the regular man. New to the unit, but being related to the sergeant, he had gotten a soft job. They all laughed. The sergeant sat with his hands in his lap, joining in with a comment, acting natural. A minute later they were through the gate and headed up the slope toward the factory itself.

"Okay, Sergeant," Macklin said. "Back here." Nabril continued to translate while driving them to a small door in the factory wall, explaining that Khalis would go with them in order to convince his men that everything was all right. Khalis nodded.

"Everyone knows what to do." Macklin straightened his uniform and took a deep breath.

The vehicle halted a few feet from the door. Macklin knew that soldiers would be positioned inside, but with Khalis's cooperation, they shouldn't be a problem. He looked at his watch. Forty-five minutes until Labib and his troops arrived to round up whatever was left. If things worked out, Khalis would order most of the men away from the factory before they blew it. If the plan didn't work out . . .

"The scientists have an apartment at the far end. Kit, let's you, Sergeant Khalis, Nabril, and I pay them a visit, shall we?"

The others were already walking nonchalantly into the building, watching, ready, as Macklin pushed the remote button, closing the vehicle doors, locking it up from possible nosy intruders.

As he entered the building he heard voices speaking Arabic. He glanced about him, his eyes taking in every movement and position. No one was close enough to question their identities. Khalis yelled a greeting at the men on the catwalk high above the factory floor, and waved at their response. They went about their duties confident that all was well.

Macklin first heard the loud thump, then watched as the huge doors at the end opened. Khalis seemed surprised and said something to Nabril.

"He says they must be taking the missile trucks out soon. There is no other reason for opening the bay doors."

Macklin nodded, concentrating on the building. It was huge; the area in front of them was filled with piles of boxes stamped in German, Russian, and English, along with the expected Arabic. Some were marked "Chemicals," with specific names and warnings listed beneath. Others were stamped with "Explosives" in different languages. Beyond them was a large prefabricated building that Macklin knew served as the Germans' laboratory and work area. Inside, they would find what they were after.

At the north end stood five missile launching trucks covered with tarps, under which they knew lay SCUDs, probably with warheads intact. Another truck stood near the center of the building, loaded with containers. The warheads.

"Gentlemen, I think we best get a move on. The sergeant says they aren't opening that door for fresh air. The trucks should be dealt with first, then the laboratory. Gad, start at the other end and work your way back to the container truck. My guess is that those are warheads ready to be shipped out of here to other missile sites."

He, the sergeant, Nabril, and Kit turned and walked left, trying to blend in, keeping their movements casual. Macklin's brain had registered half a dozen guards standing about talking, but once they saw Khalis they paid little attention. The lights were dim and would make Macklin's men less noticeable, their faces harder to distinguish.

Acting as unobtrusive as possible, they walked the short distance between a line of crates stacked two high, approaching the solid steel door that marked the entrance to the prefabricated quarters and laboratory.

While Macklin and Nabril took a military stance and watched for onlookers, Kit used a small set of tools to pick the lock on the doors. He was so fast that the sergeant asked if he had a key.

They found themselves in a hall. The apartment door was on the left and was also quickly breached. The two Germans were still sleeping in their beds when a syringe was stuck in the fat one, putting him in an even deeper sleep. Macklin roughly woke the tall, thin one and stuck his 9mm Makarov up the man's nose.

"Good morning for dying, isn't it," he said in good German. The sleepy blue eyes suddenly grew large as silver dollars. "We're here to get everything you have on the development of warheads for the SCUD missile. Your paperwork, drawings, and the prototype you developed."

The German gulped, his Adam's apple bobbing in his skinny throat. Macklin pushed a little harder on the gun and pulled back the hammer. He had no time to fool around. "Where are they?"

The German pointed toward a set of file cabinets and a large drawing table. Macklin could see a stack of schematic drawings atop it and pointed. Kit began shoving them in a canvas bag while Nabril pillaged the cabinets, throwing everything in the bag after the drawings.

"The prototype?"

The German let his hand do the talking and pointed over the edge of his bed toward the floor. Macklin glanced, finding nothing but tile floor.

"A hidden safe?"

The man nodded.

"Open it. And I warn you, if any alarms go off I will pull this trigger and you will never see the motherland again! Do you understand?"

The German's nose was long and soft and hung over the end of the gun at a grotesque angle, making Macklin want to laugh. The man nodded as his thin fingers felt under the edge of the heater and pushed a switch. A large two-by-two-foot section of the tile slid back, revealing a safe with two dials.

"Any alarms if you open it?" Macklin asked in German.

The German slowly nodded.

"How are they shut off?" Macklin pulled the gun back enough so the German could talk plainly.

"In my lab jacket. A . . . a remote . . . keyboard. If . . . if I punch in the right numbers . . . it disarms the alarm in the main building."

Macklin pressed on the gun again. "You had better remember those numbers. Kit, get the jacket. But be careful. This guy might be lying."

In seconds, Kit was back with the remote. The German, sweating now, thought for a few seconds, then carefully hit each button. He had decided his life wasn't worth setting off the alarm.

When the safe was open, Macklin stuck the skinny German with another syringe and put him to sleep. Then, while

Khalis watched the main building through a corner of closed shades, and Kit and Nabril finished cleaning out the files, Macklin lifted the lid to the safe and began emptying it of papers and several stacks of American hundred-dollar bills, throwing them toward the sack.

"Bingo," he said as he came to the prototype. He lifted it carefully from its resting place and handed it to Kit. Nabril had gone into the laboratory with Khalis and returned with a sealed box. Plutonium. Not a good thing to leave lying around when you intend to blow a place up. They'd take it with them.

"All right. Let's take these two sleeping beauties and be on our way," Macklin spoke into the mike. "Any problems in the main building?" Each of his men reported nothing unusual. "Gad, you and Mori about done?"

"Two more trucks, sir. Guards near them. Avoiding them is slowing us down."

"You have five minutes, that's all." Then, "Let's move it, Kit, Nabril." He motioned; the sergeant opened the door.

"Mizrah, we're coming out. You and Irbev ready?"

"Yessir." Macklin pictured it in his mind. Mizrah and Irbev had worked their way onto the catwalk two stories up, using the indelicate butt of their rifles as sleeping pills and replacing the two guards found there. They now had a secured view of both the inside and outside of the building. Each had a high-powered Remington 40XB rifle and a 12x Redfield telescopic sight with night vision capability, just in case.

"Hold it, sir." Irbev's voice. "A car at the gate. Mercedes limousine."

Badannah! Macklin wanted to swear.

Colonel Badannah was just finishing reading his paper when the driver pulled the limousine to the gate, soldiers appearing quickly from hiding and unlocking it. He shoved the last large bite of pastry into his mouth and licked his sticky fingers. Next to alcohol, pastry was Badannah's great weakness. Each day, no matter the hour, he stopped at the residence of a local baker to select several delectable items for his breakfast. This morning had been no exception. He looked at his watch—12:15.

His driver pointed in the direction of the road they had just traveled. Another set of headlights was beaming through the darkness. His guests had arrived.

The driver pulled further into the compound and Badannah got out, giving orders for the night watch to call his men out and keep them on guard. With the missiles leaving, it made little difference if they were discovered now.

As the man stepped from the car, Badannah made note of his coffee-stained business suit and the tightly held briefcase. The visitor gave a brief nod in Badannah's direction, then went directly to Badannah's limousine. The Syrian colonel followed, joining INFERNO as the driver put the limousine in gear.

As the car moved toward the factory, Badannah noticed the armored vehicle parked in front of the small side door. So Khalis had arrived early. Must have passed them while he was selecting his pastry. But he did not remember. Surely . . .

"Balul," he said, tapping the driver on the shoulder. Go to Sergeant Khalis's vehicle."

"Is there a problem, Colonel?" the Israeli said in fluent Arabic.

Badannah shook his head firmly. "Khalis is responsible for security. I just want to check with him and make sure we have our men in place. For your protection." He forced a smile, hiding the turmoil that was making his stomach churn, and wishing he had skipped his pastry.

———

"Another limousine!" Irbev said, then paused. "Stein!"

The traitor was early, Macklin thought. He must have come directly from the airport. Macklin hadn't planned on that, figuring Stein would join Jerisha first.

"He's with Badannah," Irbev said. "The car is moving this way."

Macklin looked at his watch. Thirty minutes before the first of the cavalry arrived. Twenty until the explosives ignited. Fifteen until he and his team must be gone.

"Mori, you and Gad done?"

"All except the warhead truck. We can't get to it."

Macklin thought for a minute. "Join us down here. It'll never survive the blast. Irbev, Mizrah, you hold position, keep us informed." He motioned for Khalis to open the outer door as Gad and Mori knocked, then they all retreated into the Germans' apartment.

Macklin went to a far door and peered inside, eyeing the computer room and lab. Then he remembered the codes. The Sword of Megiddo.

"They're coming to use the computer. We'll take them, then. Gad, you and Mori hide in the laboratory. Move in on my signal."

The men moved to position. "Nabril, tell Khalis to go in the bedroom and keep an eye on the Germans until we call for him." The Syrian nodded at the translation and moved through the door and into the room where the two scientists were sleeping like babies.

"Everyone!" he said into the mike. "Silenced weapons. No gun play unless they leave us no choice."

"Hold it, sir!" Irbev practically shouted. "Another limo!"

"Can you tell how many?"

"They are joining Badannah's group just outside the building. A woman . . . "

Jerisha! The ANGEL had come!

Badannah watched as the woman he knew as Sabrila stepped from the newly arrived limousine. Ibrahim got out next, then Ahmoud, and finally a heavily veiled woman. The Israeli joined them. The veiled woman looked at him carefully, his hands held tightly in hers. She dropped her veil, revealing a mature but beautiful face. She kissed him tenderly on each cheek before pulling him close.

"Allah is merciful. You are free, my brother!" she said. "Free! And the years of patient waiting now pay a hundredfold for the House of Hassan. Soon we will rule again!"

Stein thought to make a comment on how close it had been, how near failure, but he bit his tongue. It was finished; they had succeeded. Nothing else mattered now. "Yes, Jerisha. Very soon. Come, Badannah was about to show me into the computer facility."

Badannah still had confusion registering across his face when they reached where he stood. Ibrahim spoke.

"Colonel, may I introduce you to ANGEL."

Badannah's amazed look brought light laughter to everyone's faces. "You . . . ?"

She smiled. "Your service is nearly finished, Fami. The warheads are ready?"

"Yes, of course! Inside, but—"

"See that they leave as soon as we are finished. They must be in place on time. We will be going directly to Dumayr Airport from here." She walked toward the door, an arm around Sabrila and Stein, Ibrahim and Ahmoud a few steps behind.

Badannah was stunned. A woman! A woman to lead a new Arab world? He shook his head in disbelief. Allah would never allow it! Never!

The team listened as, from his window high above the factory floor, Irbev described the arrival of Badannah and his guests, then their approach and entrance. They spent only a moment as Badannah explained various facets of the huge building, then pointed toward the prefab.

Irbev spoke. "Two—well armed. Ibrahim Ibn Allah and one called Ahmoud Hassan. Deadly, very deadly."

Macklin checked his watch again. Ten minutes before Ruth would be close enough to assist them. He prayed silently as he heard the group enter the outer hall then go into the computer room by way of its main entrance. He joined Nabril at the door that entered the same room directly from the Germans' apartment. He listened, wishing he had learned more of the Arabic language.

He noticed Nabril's agitation, the hate for those who killed Mohammad pushing through the normally calm, emotionless surface.

Stein spoke in agitated Arabic, and Macklin heard Jerisha's voice, harsh. Nabril translated with a wicked smile.

"She is not happy. The codes aren't working." They continued listening. The discussion on the other side of the door was getting heated.

Nabril tensed. "Stein is coming in here for one of the Germans. He thinks it must be a computer error."

Macklin raised his gun, and as Stein came through the door, he whipped it across his neck and shoulder, stunning the traitor, whose legs melted like butter. As he fell, he reached, grabbing Macklin's shirt, preventing Tom from getting past him and into the room.

"Go!" Tom yelled in his mike. By the time he had shoved Stein aside, Gad and Mori were taking fire from Ahmoud and Ibrahim on the other side of the lab, the two women disappearing through the hallway door. Badannah tried to follow, and Macklin fired, sending the fat Syrian scurrying for cover behind a table.

"Mizrah! Irbev! The women are coming out! Don't kill them! I want 'em alive! Try to keep 'em in the building!" He leaped through the living area, grasping the doorknob and flinging the door open, then slamming himself against a wall as two small-caliber bullets lodged themselves in the door frame. Jerisha was armed.

Jerisha knew she had missed the pursuer as she ran into the main building. She heard the thud and plink of bullets around her and dived for cover near Sabrila.

"They are pinning us down! You must go that way." She pointed at the steps leading to the roof. "Get help! Hurry! If they get free of this building, everything is lost! Everything!" The hate welled inside her and spilled over into her angry voice.

Sabrila ran, dodging bullets. Jerisha jumped from her position, her quickness and athletic ability moving her impressively through the maze of crates and equipment. She heard the dull thud of bullets and felt the sting of concrete in her ankle, but kept running. She saw several Syrian soldiers running for cover, one dropping in his tracks as he lifted his rifle toward the ceiling and tried to fire. The snipers were on the catwalk.

She saw the truck and ducked around the left side. In a second she had the door open and was in the driver's seat. A hole appeared in the windshield, then another. The first bullet lodged in the seat. The second grazed her arm, then hit the metal of the floor. She turned the key and fired the motor. She knew the big doors at the other end were open, and were her only way of escape. If she could get the truck turned, the snipers would not be able to shoot her and she could get help. Then she would mount an assault of her own. Whoever they were, they would die!

As she slammed the vehicle in reverse, hitting crates and boxes and knocking a path open, she saw a man running toward her. She threw the machine into first gear and rammed on the gas. The big truck leaped forward and she yanked on the steering wheel, swerving, hitting a fifty-gallon barrel and knocking it into the man, bowling him over and slamming him against crates as she sped by.

Bullets riddled the windshield, shattering it into her lap and cutting her arms and legs. She didn't feel the pain, the adrenaline rush masking it. She saw the flash of black to her right and raised her gun, ready to fire at the assailant as he showed himself at the passenger door. She let go of the trigger as Sabrila's face appeared. The girl opened the door and managed to get quickly inside. Jerisha shifted to second, then third; the big truck was a speeding target honing in on the huge opening, and victory. A hundred yards to freedom.

———————

Macklin saw the bull of a truck spear the barrel into Nabril, then hurtle toward the exit. He could hear rifle fire in the lab and around him, and he was torn. Go after her, or . . . He raised his rifle and fired rapidly, trying to puncture a rear tire, throw the truck off course. He watched, helpless, as Jerisha flew through the opening into the night. Now all he could do was get his men away, and he must do it quickly. He knew the men on the catwalk would prevent anyone from coming through the doors from the outside, but they couldn't hold them off forever.

He ran back to the lab door just as Gad burst through it, dragging an unarmed Ibrahim. Mori followed, Ahmoud in tow, his left arm bleeding onto the floor, his eyes full of anger and hate.

"You okay, Mori?" Macklin asked.

"He got lucky. Bullet in the bicep. I'll be fine!" He shoved Ahmoud forward, using his rifle barrel as a prod. From the look on Mori's face, the Arab was lucky to be alive.

"You will never get free of here! Never!" Ahmoud spat in Macklin's direction. Mori shoved again, knocking Ahmoud into some crates head first. Macklin grabbed the Israeli's rifle as he was about to bring it down on the Arab's forehead.

"Take it easy, Mori. If he tries to escape, kill him. But don't butcher him for a word! That puts us—"

Mori waved. "Yeah, okay. I'm seeing red, that's all. I'll . . . I'll be okay."

Macklin looked at his watch. "Let's get outa here! Abort!" he yelled into the mike. "Everyone meet one hundred feet inside the far doors. Repeat, rendezvous one hundred feet inside bay doors!"

He went back into the apartment and flung a German over his shoulder, grabbing the bag of papers as Nabril joined him.

"Get the prototype and that other money monger, and let's get outa here!" He ran down the hall as best he could and into the main building, Nabril on his heels.

Badannah saw them leave and quickly scurried out from under the table. The Germans had a rifle in the bedroom. If he could get it . . .

He ran across the room and knocked open the door. As he blindly searched for a light switch he felt someone grab his arm, then shove him forward toward the bed, where he ingloriously tripped and fell half on and half off the coil mattress.

The light came on and Khalis stood there. Badannah jumped to his feet, yelling.

"What? What do you do, Sergeant! Can't you see who I am?" He headed for the closet, where he knew the gun was, but Khalis, even though thirty pounds lighter, jumped in his path.

Badannah tried shoving him aside, an unbelieving look

troubling his face. "Get out of my way, you fool! The Israelis escape! We must stop them!"

Khalis was not big, but he had a powerful chest and a firm grip. He used his hand to bruise Badannah's arm as he forced him back. "You, Colonel, are a traitor to this country, and to all of humankind! You will go nowhere!" He shoved him down. "Soon our own soldiers will arrive under General Labib Assad! He will stand you up against what is left of this building—he paused, smiling—"and I will gladly give the order to shoot you."

———————

Levona looked at the terrain speeding no less than fifty feet below them and couldn't help but think about the similar flight in the same direction only days earlier. Their mission now was the same as then: extraction of their people from a hostile environment.

The rear of the chopper was empty except for her and the 30mm cannons sticking menacingly through the side doors. They would need all the room they could get if they were to get everyone out.

She looked at her watch—12:29. One minute and they would be on top of the rendezvous. She looked through the door to the east. Still dark, but a few city lights were visible on the horizon.

"Shevil! Shevil! Come and get us! North end of factory! Inside bay doors one hundred feet! Any minute to fireworks!"

She heard the words and came to sudden alert. They were in trouble. Operation Path was a go! The old retrieval point out of the picture. The pilot adjusted to the west. Quickly the buildings of Duma were below them. She looked at her watch. If Gad had set the explosives, they had ten minutes to reach the factory and extract the men before it became a pile of rubble!

"Shevil! One minute to your position!" Captain Ariel said. "Any enemy fire?" he asked over the mike.

Irbev's voice responded. "A lot of confused guards. They're firing at the truck Jerisha took out of here a few seconds ago. She swerved left and went through the fence. Headed north on Dumayr highway. She's got the warheads!"

Macklin listened to Irbev's report as he ran back inside the apartment and gathered up Stein's still-unconscious body. At first he wondered if he had pummeled him too hard, but knew better as the man groaned with pain. As he went to leave again he heard a sound from the bedroom and remembered Khalis. He walked the few steps and looked in. Khalis smiled, a rifle in his hands pointed menacingly at Badannah. The young sergeant waved him on. Macklin knew Badannah was in for big-time trouble.

"Five minutes!" he said, trying to make Khalis understand. "Five minutes!" he motioned with his free hands. "Boom!"

Khalis nodded, understanding crossing his young face. Macklin gave a hesitant thumbs up, received the return smile and thumb with thanks, and ran from the building toward the rendezvous as quickly as his legs could carry him.

Ruth felt the LION turn sharply to the left and buckled up in the gunner's safety harness, then scrambled to the side door as the chopper swooped low over homes and buildings. Within seconds they were twenty feet off the turf, flying across the open ground of the factory compound at better than a 120 miles an hour, the bay doors a huge mouth about to swallow them.

She heard the bullets hitting the underbelly and quickly grabbed the gun, firing toward the ground, pinning soldiers down as the chopper flew by.

As they entered the lighted building she saw the team ready to load, and the "I knew it" smile on Macklin's face when he saw her. She reached down and took the bag of paper, then the prototype, then the box of plutonium, as the men loaded and buckled up.

Then she saw Badannah.

He had his hands on his head and was being shoved from the building by a Syrian soldier. She saw several other soldiers appear from behind boxes and crates and head for the side door at a run, apparently at the sergeant's orders.

Ruth grabbed Irbev's Redfield rifle and quickly placed the cross hairs on Badannah's forehead.

"His fate will be worse at the hands of his own kind, Ruth," she heard Macklin say in her headphones. "Let it go."

She hesitated, then flipped the safety into firing position, adjusted the cross hairs and began squeezing the trigger.

Then she dropped the rifle to her side. "Go! Captain, get us out of here!"

The LION danced, swinging its tail around, its nose pointed at the exit. Suddenly a man came around the corner directly below and in front of them, a thin deadly object lying across his shoulder.

"Exocet," Ariel said calmly. He pulled back on the throttle, waiting twenty-five feet below the roof. Macklin took a deep breath, watching from the open door. He felt something in the belly of the LION as the man fired the exocet, and watched as a rapid-fire sequence of .50-caliber shells honed in on the missile, blowing it apart in midair. The shock wave nearly drove the chopper through the roof, the blades coming dangerously close to the ceiling beams. The computer corrected and Ariel held the sleek machine steady and gave full throttle.

"Get down!" he yelled into the mike. "Heavy small arms fire coming up!"

"Just get us out of here, Captain!" Gad returned. "Those charges I set will blow this place sky high any second!"

The LION lurched forward, ejecting itself from the building. Ariel yanked back on the handle, sending the bird straight in the air as the five trucks exploded in unison, filling the sky with hot fire and debris. The flames reached for the chopper like clutching fingers, grabbing and tearing at the air in an attempt to fling it to the ground.

Macklin had been thrown to the floor and was hanging on for dear life as Ariel jammed the stick right, throwing Tom's unharnessed body out of the door, leaving him dangling by his fingernails. Gad flipped off his safety belt and lurched for him, his strong arm grasping Macklin's, the colonel's body whipping in the wind and crashing into the chopper's short missile wing. He felt the pain and a wave of nausea, his muscles suddenly weak, his grasp loosening.

He felt another grip on his collar, then the weight of his body being dragged over the edge of the doorway and onto the floor. He opened his eyes to find Gad lying on the floor beside him, their heads nearly touching, both gasping for air. The Israeli lieutenant smiled a knowing smile. "Buckle up," he said, breathing hard. "The life you save may be your own."

Jerisha was sweating, her sandaled foot pressed to the floor, forcing every ounce of power from the huge motor. She looked at the rearview mirror again, watching as the huge ball of flames turned the factory to rubble. There was nothing left now but escape.

When they had exited the factory and rushed toward the guardhouse, the Syrian soldiers had become confused, firing on them. It had been only the miracle of Allah that had kept them from being killed by her own people.

The anger was hot in her chest. Everything had been destroyed! Years of work, millions of dollars! Her entire plan for returning and redeeming Palestine from the decadent Israelis had come to nothing! Her father's dying wish to have his son and daughter carry out his dream had kept them focused, determined. Now it was burning in the rubble of the Duma factory. All of it fire and smoke in her rearview mirror! Her brother dead.

No! All was not lost. She had at least twenty warheads with her. Properly armed . . .

Sabrila saw it first. A chopper nearly on top of them, then swooping onto the road ahead, trying to force Jerisha to stop.

"Ram them!" Sabrila yelled. "Don't stop! They will kill us!"

Jerisha already understood the options, but knew another choice. Her mind, used to constant pressure of life-threatening decisions, remained calm. She jerked the truck left and into the sand, avoiding the collision. Then she jerked right, the truck nearly tipping over as it jumped back onto the highway.

She looked in the mirror, a wry grin on her face. The chopper was in the air, bearing down on them, preparing to fire. She must survive. She grabbed the latch on the door, jerking it upward as flames shot from the wing of the chopper. The Stinger would take five seconds. Jerisha launched herself through the door.

The chopper landed twenty minutes later in northern Israel. Macklin watched Ruth's eyes as they sat on the floor across from one another, the chopper blades winding down, then stopping. The team disgorged themselves from the monster's belly.

He frowned, giving her a hard look. "What am I going to do with you?" he asked.

"Marry me, make me your property. Then you can tell me what to do."

"Yeah, I'll bet. When?"

She shrugged.

He slid over in front of her, taking the helmet off her head, then removing the earphones. Her hair was damp with sweat, but felt good against his hands. He lifted her head and kissed her gently. "In your uncle's backyard, under the canopy."

She smiled. "With plenty of food for the guests. My uncle will be elated. His only remaining responsibility is finally getting me married."

They kissed again until someone behind them cleared his throat.

"Excuse me, sirs," Gad said. "Any more orders?" Nabril stood at his shoulder.

Two military police jeeps skidded to a halt outside the door. Stein and the two Germans were loaded into one and taken away. At best, nothing but a life of prison awaited them. At worst, they'd be shot. In this case, Macklin didn't know which would be worse. He'd bet that even incarcerated Jewish criminals loved their country and hated her enemies.

Macklin pulled himself away from Ruth's arms long enough to reach for the prototype, handing it and the sacks of papers to Gad and Nabril. "You have enough explosives left to rid the world of this stuff, don't you?"

Gad smiled, nodding affirmatively.

"Do it some place where we don't have a mess to clean up, will you?" The two men jumped from the chopper and commandeered the second jeep, speeding away into the dark night.

"Hoshen won't be pleased," Ruth said.

"Give him Stein. That'll make him happy." Macklin

grinned. They started walking toward the main building, dressing rooms, hot showers, beds, and sleep. Macklin needed it. Lots of it.

"Jerisha was foolish," Ruth went on.

"Hate does that."

"I know," Ruth responded, remembering how close she had come to being like Jerisha. Letting hate rule her life. "I love you, Thomas Macklin."

They stopped in the dark as Macklin heard the explosion set by Gad and Nabril. It was over.

He pulled Ruth close, relishing the moment of peace below a star-riddled sky. He had found someone to live for. Now all he wanted was time. Time to love Ruth Levona.

CHAPTER 32—ONE MONTH LATER

Aman Headquarters, Tel Aviv

Tom was helping Ruth clean out her desk. She was moving into Stein's office in the adjoining building. Hoshen had offered her Ativa's old job, but she refused, insisting that he would return.

And he might. He was sitting up now, communicating. His wounds had healed for the most part, leaving him only a gimp leg and a small speech impediment that slurred his language; a sign of the lack of blood and oxygen to the brain when his heart had stopped beating. The doctors said both the affected areas would become perfect again.

Tom looked at his new wife. The wedding had been a good one; a cross between Jewish and Christian, mostly Jewish. David Levona had showered them with gifts, and Jerry had handed him the keys to a new apartment. Down payment paid in full.

He was glad Jerry and Mike had returned for the wedding, children in tow. They made things complete. He and Ruth would be visiting the Danielses' Wyoming home in the spring. He was looking forward to it.

The first peace talks had been held. Though they were

considered to be a success in some quarters, Tom saw them as a disappointment. Khourani's people had been forced to compromise, but at least they had a place, thanks to Hoshen. And Mohammad Faisal.

The man was buried on the West Bank. Near Nabulus. His wife and children had been at the funeral. A shock to Ruth and Tom. Mohammad's sacrifice had been even greater than they had imagined.

The commotion in the outer office brought Tom out of his reverie. Ruth's secretary burst through the door, babbling something about Hoshen. Ruth ran out and down the hall, Macklin on her heels.

Hoshen's aide stood outside the door, pale, rigid. Merriame stood inside and to their right, a cocked Uzi in her hand, the barrel pointed at Hoshen's chest.

"Stay back," she said. "I want only to kill him."

She was frightened, angry, bitter. All of these emotions were firmly etched in her face. Her hair was a mess, her frame twenty pounds lighter than the last time Macklin had seen her; the day they brought Imad back from Sahles Sahra.

"It was his fault! He ordered Eytan back to Syria! Eytan didn't want . . . He knew . . ." The tears came, her arm went slightly limp with the memory. Then she stiffened again.

Ruth slipped through the door and took a step toward her friend.

"Shuli, please, put the gun down," she said softly. "This won't bring Eytan back. It won't help."

Hoshen looked as if he was about to have a coronary, his life flashing before him, again. Macklin wondered if the man would stay in politics if he got free of this one. He looked as if he'd had about enough.

"No! Stay back, Ruth! He must pay! He killed Eytan . . ."

Ruth took another step. Macklin's heart stopped. "Don't push it, hon. She's shaking. That gun could go off—"

"I mean it, Ruth! I'll kill you first!"

Ruth stepped back. "All right, but listen to me. Eytan's mission saved Israel. We destroyed those missiles. Without his informant, we wouldn't have done it. He died for Israel, Shuli, not for Minister Hoshen, and not because of him. The people who killed Eytan are in prison or dead. Killing Hoshen will accomplish nothing. Nothing, Shuli. Nothing but more hardship for your parents. They have only you left to watch marry, have their grandchildren. Only you, Shuli. Don't deprive them of that."

The arm lowered a little. The face—the tired, beleaguered, hate-filled face—drooped.

"I . . . hate . . . it . . . Israel . . . enemies . . ."

"I understand. I know what you feel, Shuli. I can help you. Please believe me. I can help you." Ruth walked to her side and took the gun as Shuli's hand dropped down. Hoshen took a breath, gulping air into his pressed white shirt. Then he went pale, his eyes rolling into the top of his head, and he fainted, sliding awkwardly under the desk, his Italian leather shoes sticking out at the front.

His aide went to his rescue. Macklin helped Ruth take Merriame back to her office. He poured ice water while Ruth patted Shuli's hand, kneeling, taking off her shoes before lifting her legs onto the couch.

"A mirror. Like looking in a mirror. I've been where she is, Tom. I really do know what she feels. A lot of my people feel it. The hate will destroy us long before the Arabs do."

Tom sat in the chair and pulled her into his lap. They'd wait for Merriame to rest. They'd do what they could to help her. The president had been quick to respond in the affirmative to his request for assignment at the embassy until retirement. After that he'd still stay in Israel. He and Ruth would spend their lives helping Israel rid herself of the hate.

CHAPTER 33—MONTHS LATER

9:00 P.M., Jackson Hole, Wyoming

Jerry sat in front of the fireplace, his damp, stockinged feet close to the heat, sending up whiffs of faintly odored steam.

Mike was upstairs. Issa had to have a story every night, but now she was reading it to Mike. Her English was improving quickly.

The boys had proven determined, willing, and able to learn. Rashid was more disciplined than Raoul, but both had quick minds and an insatiable thirst for knowledge. It hadn't taken long for tutors to become obsolete.

Jerry loved the evenings. Theirs was a studious household, the children constantly excited and questioning while still full of fun and laughter. Assimilation was a challenge. The children's minds were like computer banks, receiving tons of information and experiences but needing help pulling it all together, discarding the unnecessary and useless. He was proud of how well they were doing.

Religion for them wasn't yet settled, although the kids enjoyed church very much. Rashid was actually a year younger than Raoul, who had just reached his thirteenth birthday. But Raoul trusted Rashid more than Jerry had ever witnessed in two young people, and he was waiting for Rashid's verdict.

Jerry loved the talks, the questions. Rashid needed answers, and both Jerry and Mike were amazed at the depth of his understanding. He knew Rashid was reading the Book of Mormon to Raoul, in English, but Jerry was still unsure of how it would all turn out.

There had been a few challenges in the valleys of Wyoming. Prejudice was alive and well, and kids could be cruel.

Mike had defused the first signs of anti-Arabism toward the kids when a knock-down, drag-out fight between Raoul and a kid at school took place. Raoul bloodied the would-be cowboy, but Mike fumed over the treatment Raoul had received. After she calmed down she called in an old favor from the editor of the local newspaper. The next edition carried a story about who the children were, what they believed, and how they felt about their country and the United States. After people read it, really knowing the facts, things had improved, leaving the three children on solid enough ground to make friends. Raoul had even tried out for the junior high wrestling team and was their best man at a 102 pounds.

Mike was showing beautifully. They had been tempted twice to have an ultrasound and find out just what kind of little monster they should expect, but had resisted, waiting for that moment when the new personality was presented to them in the flesh. The doctor was pleased with Mike's progress and had prophesied the middle of March. Mike didn't think so. Her mother had always given birth at least two weeks early. By her clock the baby's room could be occupied anytime after February first.

Mike came down the railed stairway to the large open living area with its beamed ceiling and sat her smocked frame next to Jerry, putting her head on his shoulder.

"Tired?" he asked.

"Yup, but pleasantly so. Did you go through your usual ritual with the boys?"

"To the last detail."

"Your confidence makes them proud."

He chuckled. "They saved my neck a couple of times. Who better to trust. As far away from civilization as we are, we have to rely on each other. There isn't anyone else."

"We could live in town for a while," she said half-heartedly.

"We already discussed that. We can't let this wreck our lives now anymore than we could have a year ago. It may never happen."

"Your great-great-grandfather's .50-caliber Hawken is a very imposing weapon. Are you sure . . ."

"Sure. The gun is loud, and deadly if need be. The bow quiet. Anyhow, it's fun to show them a little bit of American history. I've told them Finan's story a thousand times. They never get bored while they're holding those weapons."

She slugged him gently. "Shooting that arrow into the log wall gave them the wrong idea. I've noticed half a dozen similar marks mysteriously appear near the same location."

He chuckled. "It's amazing that that old bow still works, and is deadly accurate."

She looked out of the window. "Snow."

"That's news?"

"Pretty, always pretty."

They sat quiet, the crackle of the fireplace mesmerizing their thought processes.

The house around them sat on twenty acres in the mouth of the canyon that led to the property Jerry's grandfather, Finan Daniels, had been given so many years earlier. Jerry and the government had reached a compromise on the land, and the twenty acres had been deeded to him as only part of a land swap. The rest he had yet to decide about.

The house was a four-thousand-square-foot, precut and milled log cabin, three stories high. In the basement was the two-car garage and storage for snowmobiles and tools. The ground floor contained a spacious living room with rock fireplace, a large family kitchen, a formal dining room, a den and hobby room, along with a guest bathroom. All of the bedrooms and the playroom were on the top floor.

The house had a few other additions that most owners neither needed nor spent money for. Jerry had added them on their return from Israel, and, although expensive, they were needed for peace of mind. The average person who visited their home would never know what those changes were. They were hidden, a necessity against a forced need Mike and Jeremiah knew would come.

"Are you ready for bed?" Jerry asked, kissing her gently on the cheek.

"If you'll help me get out of this couch."

He stood and pulled her up. She started up the steps while he poked the last of the fire's coals. Then he joined her.

17 December 1991, Jackson Hole, Wyoming

Jerry was mentally jerked away from his magazine by the noise, but couldn't place it. A light clink of metal against what? Stone?

He stood, a sudden anxious feeling in his stomach. He had waited for months. Was this it? He looked at Mike and saw the fear. "Remember, Mike, we're prepared. Push the button."

Mike reached under the table and hit a button that set off a quiet alarm in the children's rooms just as she and Jerry heard steps on the outside stairway.

The dark forms of six heavily clad figures burst through the front door, snapping the locks as if they didn't exist. They fanned out, three quickly going upstairs and slamming their way into the bedrooms while three others aimed their weapons at Jerry and Mike. Jerry calmly laid his *Newsweek* on the end table, glad that he hadn't started a fire that night.

"Gone!" one yelled from the upper balcony.

The woman ripped off her stocking mask. "What?" She started upstairs. "Check again!" She yelled at the two now standing in the living area. "Check the basement."

Mike stood next to Jerry, grabbing his arm and nearly shutting off the blood. He patted her hand. "It'll be all right. The kids are safe now. We have to do our part."

One of the intruders came back to the banister. "Gone!" he shrugged.

The woman assailant glared at Jeremiah. "Where are the children?"

"At the senator's," Jerry said. "If we had known you were coming, Jerisha, we would have insisted that they stay here tonight. They've never met a woman quite like you."

She removed a pistol from a pocket, pointing it in Jerry's direction. "You knew I would come," she said through clenched teeth. "I warned you. Blood for blood."

She gave additional orders, and her men spread out and searched the house. Jerry glanced at his watch. His stomach churned; now that Jerisha had come he was wondering if he had been smart in refusing to live in town. But he knew it didn't matter to the woman where he lived, and innocent people might have been hurt there. No, this was between his family and Jerisha. Hopefully, their preparation would pay off.

Another part of him celebrated the end of waiting. It had been four months since receiving Jerisha's cryptic message. The first week he spent with a gun in one hand and the message in the other, waiting, afraid for his family. After six and a half days of his torturing himself and his family, Mike had convinced him that waiting in such a manner was exactly what the woman wanted, forcing him into untold mental suffering. To beat her, they must overcome their fear.

The next morning he had met with the contractor, who then undertook the physical changes and preparations on the house. The following weeks the family spent in planning different methods for different seasons, all based on beating Jerisha Duquesne at her own game.

Jerisha's men returned, taking up their positions again. Jerry smiled inwardly. So far, so good.

Jerisha held Jerry responsible for her husband's and her brother's capture (he had checked with the newly married Macklins about that one), and blamed him for the fact that her family was denied their rightful place as leaders of Palestine.

Mike sidled closer, the chill air coming through the open door making goose bumps on her skin. She was shaking. Jerry pulled her tight, rubbing her arm gently. She settled down.

"These last four months I have given you enough time to think, Mr. Daniels. Has it been time well spent?"

"I have several hobbies that keep me busy, Jerisha. Thinking about you isn't one of them. Sorry."

She unzipped her coat and pulled out several papers, throwing them toward him. He picked them up.

"The *Jerusalem Post*," he said. "Nice paper. I read it a couple of times while on vacation in Israel."

"Front page," she said harshly.

Jerry glanced at it. "Ah, yes, David Stein. The traitor caught in Syria. They say he was part of a group with plans to use chemical warheads on his own country. Caught him red-handed." He glanced at the picture, then at Jerisha. "Mahmoud Salamhani. Striking resemblance. Related?"

Her face held its emotionless stance. Jerry went on.

"Didn't Chaim Ativa come out of a coma and finger Stein for an attempt on his life? Say, Jerisha, weren't you two taught how to do anything good when you were young?"

"Mahmoud was an agent in Israel longer than any other," Jerisha said harshly. "He would have freed our people if you—"

"Come on, Jerisha. At least be honest! All you wanted to do was rule your people, not free them. And you were planning on killing most of them to get the throne! Don't plead holy causes, for pete's sake! You're the worst kind of terrorist, the Gadianton kind. All you want is power over people, to rule with blood and horror on this earth! You've been stopped, now you're still bent on revenge!"

Mike was positioned now, tense but ready. He was close enough. He hoped the children were prepared. He felt the ache in his stomach, the fear that somehow something might go wrong. The enemy might get off a lucky shot, but if they didn't move soon the shots would not need to be lucky. They would be placed at point-blank range.

"Face it, Ms. Salamhani. Those years were a total failure. Your whole project was a failure."

"You forget those we killed. Enemies to our cause."

Jerry felt his gut tighten. Robert Doolittle, Mohammad Faisal, the oil well workers, others. Murdered by this woman's greed for power. His palms began to itch for the feel of her throat. He calmed himself. He must worry about his family now. He couldn't let Jerisha push his hate button.

"As much as it would have pleased me, Jerisha, I didn't blow up the factory," he said.

"You were responsible. It was you who stopped TERROR1 —you who forced our hand in Israel. You—"

Jerry shrugged. "People who fail always need someone to blame. I guess I'm as good for that as the next guy. Anything else you want to place on the shoulders of this sacrificial lamb before you attempt to slaughter it?" Jerry asked stiffly.

She didn't reply.

"One last question, then. Stein was to bring you the Israeli codes to this weapon you called the Sword of Megiddo. Why that name?" He was buying a few more minutes of time.

She was in a talkative mood. "You are familiar with the legend?"

He nodded.

"The Arab world needs a new champion. One who holds in his hands a weapon that can cut asunder all our enemies. All, Mr. Daniels, including your United States.

"The missiles at Duma were to be secretly taken into each of the Arab nations surrounding Israel. They would have been fired on Tel Aviv and Jerusalem, along with twenty other locations in the country, mostly military. In order to assure chaos in which we could assume leadership, the Israelis must return that fire, hitting the population centers of the Arab countries. Armageddon would be ensured. Of course, by use of the sword I could have protected myself and my friends." Even her smile lacked life.

"And Palestine laid waste," he said. "How many people, your own people included, were you willing to kill for your power, Jerisha? One million, two, four. How many?"

"All of them, if need be. We would rebuild on their ultimate sacrifice."

Jerry had thought Fillmore Duquesne embodied wickedness. Now he understood how the man had become so evil. "You're the author of TERROR1, aren't you?" Jerry said.

She smiled.

"Two attempts, two failures," Jerry said snidely. "Poor average, I'd say. If you were a baseball player, you'd be fired."

Her face flashed red, then she calmed herself with a reminder that Jerry's life was in her hands. She would make it a slow death.

Jerry chuckled. He needed to push her button one more time. "You're a fool. You did nothing right, Jerisha, and you were discovered at almost every turn."

"Mistakes are common to large-scale operations. My people did quite well under the circumstances, but fate was against us."

"Allah was against you, not fate."

She showed no emotion.

"Well, ANGEL, Armageddon might come, but it won't be because of some self-appointed butcher like you. You were stopped, Jerisha, because your plan was flawed from the beginning. It was motivated by hate, greed, and power lust. You haven't got a good motive in your whole body."

Jerry saw her hand tighten on the pistol. He knew it was now or never. He could only pray that the children were ready. Cooly he took Mike's hand while placing his other in his pants pocket, pushing the tiny remote button. He had a dozen of these hidden around the house, all easily accessible day and night, each giving access to several exits created just for Jerisha's arrival.

The lights went off as the sound of Finan's big gun fired in the dark and the whoosh of an arrow traversed the room. As he and Mike darted out of the way and to the paneled wall, he heard a man scream. Probably prompted by the arrow. He pushed on the wall and it gave way. They had practiced enough in the darkness that he knew where the lever was and grabbed hold, pulling. In a flash of time the panel closed and the floor dropped away, elevator style, into the basement, a process punctuated by gunfire and shattering glass in the room above. Jerry pointed the remote switch and pushed. He heard the locks on the door at the top of the stairs jump into place. He pointed again and the garage door quickly and quietly ascended.

Issa waited in winter attire holding Mike's coat. His expectant wife grabbed her boots as Jerry shoved his arm through the sleeves of his parka and put his night goggles in place, then pulled on his snowmobile boots. The boys appeared out of another hidden elevator wearing large smiles and ready for winter travel.

Rashid jumped on one snowmobile, Issa right behind him, grabbing tightly around his waist. Raoul was already pushing on the automatic start of his Polaris Indy Classic as Jerry and Mike jumped aboard the big, powerful 650. In an instant the three machines were blasting across the snow, leaving the house behind. As they reached the road they did a sharp left into a path already mapped out in their minds. They traveled without lights, the night goggles giving them the advantage.

Jerry glanced over his shoulder and saw the enemy

rushing down the stairs. He knew they must have machines close by and would soon be after them.

The uninvited guests were in for a few surprises.

Raoul's Indy was ahead, the boy's keen talent and quickness moving him expertly around drifts and trees. Rashid and Issa saw the fork in the path and knew exactly which way to go, speeding ahead as Jerry stopped the 650. Mike pulled hard on a wire dangling from an overhead limb, causing a white rope to jump into the air at chest height across the path. Jerry throttled the machine and they raced across the open meadow after the kids.

Jerry had taken out the taillights on purpose. When they put on the brakes, no light gave them away, and in the wooded trail, at the speeds they were moving, they used the brakes often.

They came to a stop in some trees at the top of the knoll and shut off their machines, using the night-vision goggles to watch their back trail.

Seconds later Jerry saw the first machine, then another, their lights flashing along the trail. At the rate they traversed the ground, Jerry knew that Jerisha's bunch had the best in machines, probably the newest models. He saw two men race into the lead, both hitting the rope at the same time. Jerry didn't see what happened to the men but watched the machines crash into the trees, one exploding into a small fireball.

That, he thought, should make Jerisha slow down some.

He pushed the button on the 650 and motioned the kids ahead. They spun through the snow and down the far side of the knoll into the cottonwood and pine trees, weaving their way carefully until they hit another meadow. The boys slowed almost to a standstill as they searched for the red marker. Rashid found it, eased his Phazer onto the boards placed there, and traversed the hidden ditch. Raoul was next, then Jerry and Mike. After they had crossed, Jerry got off his machine and carefully reached under the white, snow-covered tarp and dislodged the heavier planks, letting them fall into the three-by-six-foot pit below. Their trail still looked normal, and he jumped aboard just as he saw the first of the pursuing snowmobiles enter the trees, working its way through.

He gave the 650 full throttle, catching the kids on the far side of the meadow. They stopped, watching the string of lights weaving down the far hill, the first hitting the edge of the meadow just before the others, his lights on their trail. Jerry could hear him give the machine full throttle and knew he must have been going sixty when he hit the ditch.

Three down, three left.

They moved down a ravine, separating into three trails, Rashid and Issa working their way up another hill without trouble. Raoul deftly moved through and to the end of the narrow, tree-infested space, where he also began a climb. Jerry and Mike turned right, going through trees, then working their way back to the left, scooting across a narrow bridge and along the river's far side. After nearly a mile, they crossed another bridge, arriving at a predetermined rendezvous just after the kids.

"Everyone okay?" Jerry asked, grinning. They all returned the smile. "All right, this is the last of it. Ready?" They nodded, then Raoul and Rashid throttled their machines, disappearing into the trees and climbing the far hill. Jerry looked for signs of company, but still couldn't see lights. As the children disappeared over the ridge he shut off the 650, listening for sounds of their pursuers. He could hear them in the distance, their machines working to climb a hill.

As he pushed the automatic start and followed the kids' trail up the mountain, he was glad it was finally coming to an end. In deciding to face Jerisha, he had discussed it with Mike, then the children. All of them wanted Jerisha Duquesne alive, paying for the damage she had done, the suffering and death she had caused. It had been a daring plan, a chance that his family might get hurt. But they might anyway. Jerisha could have shown up at anytime, taken one of the children—tortured them, killed them. Or Mike. They had decided that sticking together and preparing was the only way to win.

Jerry and Mike careened down the far hill and raced over the old logging road toward their last trap. It was ingenious, really, and Rashid's idea. Timing was important, and it would pain Jerry some, but not nearly as bad as it would their pursuers. The children were nearly out of sight as he came around the last bend and into the meadow, their dark shadows disappearing toward the snow cave and a battery-operated cellular phone. Jerry raced to some rocks and Mike jumped off the snowmobile, digging in the snow at the base of a large boulder. She removed a plastic pouch containing her 30–06 and unwrapped it. In a few seconds she had ejected a shell into the chamber, then tested the infrared scope. She wouldn't use it unless Jerry's plan failed.

As she settled herself in the snow behind the boulder she gave Jerry a pained smile and waved him on. He swung the machine quickly around, went back a hundred yards to where he had a clear view of his back trail, and anxiously waited.

It wasn't long.

The lights sped down the hillside. He looked at the mound 300 yards down the meadow, then back at the oncoming enemy. They would try running him down, then shoot him when close enough. He unfolded the thick shield from its compact position and snapped it in place behind him. The bullet-proof Kevlar should protect him from anything less than a .30-caliber shell—unless they got within a hundred feet. At least, that was his hope, but he felt comfort from the bullet-proof vest Mike had sewn into the back of the coat he wore.

Jerry waited, his hands nervously gripping and releasing the handlebar covers of the 650. His breath was coming quick now, his body oblivious to the cold air stiffening his nose and lips.

He measured the distance, watching the spot he knew they must reach before he started his move. Five seconds passed, the lights flashing closer. He revved the throttle, flipped on his own light, and swung the machine down the meadow as they reached the spot he was waiting for. The 650 bit into the snow and thrust him ahead, reaching 60 miles an hour in less than one hundred feet. He crouched low in the seat, keeping his eye on the place he knew he must hit. He heard the whack sound of bullets hitting the shield and back of the machine.

Seventy. The machine was a blaze of black body flashing across the white surface, the terrorists following like crazed wolves after prey.

A hundred yards to go. Seventy-five. Then fifty. Twenty-five!

He felt the nose of the machine hit the edge of the ramp, lifting toward the sky. He gave full throttle, the 650 shooting for the stars like a rocket launch at Cape Canaveral. He slid back on the seat and lay flat, closing his eyes, prepared for the impact. He had practiced only once, the hard jolt of the landing nearly separating his spine from the rest of his body.

But they had added another five feet of snow to the small island, and this time . . .

The 650 hit the snow and sank nearly out of sight, knocking his two front teeth into the soft flesh of his lower lip.

He rolled off the machine and waited, knowing there was a slim chance that one of his pursuers would be directly in his tracks and traveling at exactly the right speed to land on top of him.

With his good eye he saw the lead machine hit the top of the ramp and fly through the air, unseating its shocked rider and sending him plummeting into the cold water of the river below. Another followed, hitting the brakes at the last second. He was hit by the third, both riders and machines a jumble of bodies and metal rotating in disarray, skipping onto the icy water, then sinking out of sight.

A moment later their heads bobbed to the top as they splashed to recover before their heavy parkas pulled them downstream or underwater.

Cursing in any language can be recognized by the passion of the expletives. Jerry could imagine what they were saying as they struggled for survival in the frigid waters.

He heard the sirens and saw lights flashing through the trees as two four-wheel drive vehicles plunged along the plowed access road. As the officers shined spots on the river, Jerry saw the first of the assassins pull himself to shore a hundred yards downstream, half frozen from the dunking. Farther down, another struggled free of the parka and grabbed hold of the third member of their group. He could tell it was Jerisha as the two collapsed on the cold snow, drenched in the bright light of the sheriff's spotlight.

As Jerry crossed the narrow bridge from the island to the bank, his glove pressed against his torn lip, he was joined by Rashid and Issa, then Raoul, who had gone for Mike. They watched as the sheriff's deputies rounded up the three terrorists, their Arabic denunciations loud even against the muffling snow.

The sheriff joined them and looked through squinty eyes at the black shape buried in the snow of the small island.

"Lucky shot?" he asked.

Jerry only smiled. "Those are three of the guests I told you might drop in for a chat. You'll find three others up near my place. Attempted murder ought to stick real good, but they're wanted for worse in the Middle East. Don't let anyone near them." He removed a slip of paper from his wallet and handed it to the sheriff. "That's the number of a man in Las Vegas. Call him and he'll take them off your hands, return them to their country.

"Trayco?" the sheriff asked.

"Remember, Sheriff, they'll kill at the bat of an eyelash. Especially the woman. Especially!"

The sheriff nodded, went to say something, then smiled and walked away, shaking his head and chuckling.

Mike put her arm around her husband's waist, pointing with her gloved hand. "Raoul, Rashid, think you can drive the 650 on across? Then we'll go to the Bucklers' for the night." The boys dismounted, worked their way across the narrow bridge and began to free the big machine, laughing and talking about what they had seen. Mike dabbed at Jerry's cut lip with a hanky. It had nearly stopped bleeding.

"We gonna keep this bunch together?" Jerry asked Issa.

She smiled and nodded, speaking in broken English. "You be in trouble without us."

"Yeah, wouldn't I. Come on. Let's go find a fire." He sat on Raoul's machine while Mike boarded Rashid's. Issa snuggled her way in front of him and put her gloved hands on the handlebars.

"Okay, Dad," she said, smiling. "Move it!"

Two months later, 10 February 1992, Mike gave birth to a five-pound-one-ounce slightly premature baby girl. Issa held her new little sister for the first time while her family decided on a name for the dark-haired, dark-eyed infant. Her name would be Shai—Hebrew for *The Gift.*

About the Author

Robert Marcum was born in Teton Valley, Idaho. When he was ten, the family moved to Moreland, Idaho, where he was reared, graduating from Snake River High School in 1964. He served as a full-time LDS missionary in the East Central States Mission from 1965 to 1967. He attended Brigham Young University, receiving a bachelor's degree in history from that institution, and later attended Idaho State University, where he received a master's degree in education.

The author has served in the Church Educational System for nineteen years and is currently a professor of religion at Ricks College. He also worked for two years with an international brokerage firm in Las Vegas, Nevada.

Robert Marcum has written several articles for the *New Era* and for various professional publications. He is the author of one previous book, *Dominions of the Gadiantons*.

He is married to the former Janene Andreasen of Grace, Idaho. They are the parents of one daughter and seven sons. The family resides in Rexburg, Idaho.